CONVERSATIONS WITH AMBEDKAR

10 AMBEDKAR MEMORIAL LECTURES

CONVERSATIONS WITH AMBEDKAR

10 AMBEDKAR MEMORIAL LECTURES

Edited by
VALERIAN RODRIGUES

Tulika Books

Ambedkar University Delhi

Published by

Tulika Books
44 (first floor), Shahpur Jat, New Delhi 110 049, India
tulikabooks.in

in association with

Ambedkar University Delhi
Lothian Road, Kashmere Gate, Delhi 110 006, India
aud.ac.in

First edition (hardback) 2019

ISBN: 978-81-937329-5-3

Printed at Chaman Offset, Delhi 110 002

Contents

Foreword

I have been waiting all these years with much anticipation to write this foreword. I had always dreamt of the Ambedkar Memorial Lecture (AML) series completing its first 10 years and a volume being brought out. I must confess that this was more by way of meeting a challenge and proving a point than pursuing any personal aspiration. The challenge in question had been thrown at us by Professor Bhikhu Parekh in the summer of 2009 while delivering the first AML. He had said right in his opening remarks: 'Infant mortality among our institutions is fairly high and I like to hope that the Ambedkar Memorial Lecture will prove an exception.' Sitting on the dais and listening to him say this, I realised how important it was for a young university to ensure that whatever it did, it did consistently and in a sustained manner, because every small but significant step it took was the starting of a new tradition. An activity becomes an institutional tradition only when most members of the community that populates the institution begin to own it as their own and carry it with them over time as something from which they continue to derive meaning and significance. The irony was that when the first AML was organised in May 2009, Ambedkar University Delhi (AUD) had only one member on its core faculty and twelve students, besides the Vice Chancellor and his team of two! So, when new faculty came in, we had to take care that they were socialised appropriately into the 'traditions' of the infant university! It took enormous effort on the part of our team to ensure that the string of AML lectures was never broken during its first 10 years. On the one occasion when the fifth AML by Professor Upendra Baxi, scheduled for 14 April 2013, had to be deferred because of his ill health, we feared that the string might be broken. But, thanks to Professor Baxi's remarkable resilience and his insistence on honouring the commitment he had made to us, and the organising team's tenacity and perseverance, we could organise his lecture in March 2014, a month ahead of the sixth AML.

Those of us in the founding team of AUD had always thought that it was our university's good fortune to be named after Babasaheb Ambedkar. There was such a great wealth of ideas reflected in Dr Ambedkar's life and work from which to distil an institutional vision for the young university. For that matter, any public university of the 21st century, located in a society that is ridden with inequalities and struggles to transform itself through a democratic polity, might draw inspiration from Ambedkar's life and work. While we were setting up the university, we were guided by the principles of equality, social justice and constitutional morality that were cardinal in Ambedkar's work. We were also quite drawn towards his 'attitude', an irreverence that we saw in his disposition while critically engaging with dominant ideas of his time. We were particular that the institutional culture of AUD, the seeds of which we were sowing at that time, should be characterised by these very principles and attitude (no wonder the annual cultural festival of AUD came to be known as 'Aud@City'!). The three key phrases that we kept in mind while setting up the university were 'collegiality', 'nurturance of creativity' and 'engaged scholarship', all of which became crystallised through our attempt to comprehend Dr Ambedkar's life and work.

Institutions are dynamic entities, and their essential character is likely to evolve and transform with time and with changes in the composition of the institutional community. Sustained adherence to the core values by members of the institutional community needs painstaking efforts to remind them constantly about the circumstances that were associated with the founding of the institution. For a young university, therefore, it was important to invent and institutionalise rituals involving collective introspection, reflection and reavowal of the core principles and institutional vision. I was therefore very particular that we had to have an important public event on the university's annual calendar where we renewed our commitment publicly to the ideals that we had internalised and had instituted as our guiding principles, drawing inspiration from Dr Ambedkar. This was the genesis of the AML series.

We had also been considering AUD as a university of the city of Delhi. It was important for us in those initial years to make AUD's presence recognised and acknowledged among the citizens of Delhi, given that few knew we existed. We therefore decided that the annual Ambedkar Memorial Lecture should be delivered to an audience drawn from the general public and not merely the university community, and therefore should be organised in a prominent public space in Delhi. In that sense, the AML series also became AUD's way to pay tribute to the city of Delhi, where we were located and with which we believed we had a critical organic link.

That we must get 'an eminent scholar or public personality from among the best minds across the world' to deliver the lecture every year was the basic consensus with which we began. But, we did have considerable debate over the following: Must we insist that the lectures in this series be on or about Ambedkar—should these lectures be based on the study of Ambedkar's life and his contribution to the world of knowledge and praxis? Alternatively, should these lectures be products of serious exploration of various aspects of our world and our times viewed and made sense of through the lens of Ambedkar scholarship? We concluded that the second alternative was a more inclusive one, which subsumed in some sense the first alternative. The announcement for the AML series said that the lectures would be on 'areas of knowledge and human experience such as democracy, constitutional law, equity, social justice, social transformation, social action and engaged spiritualities'.

We took care that the personalities invited to deliver these lectures were drawn from various areas of knowledge and practice. To deliver the first 10 lectures, we had a political philosopher, a social anthropologist, an economist, a political psychologist, a scholar of law and jurisprudence, a practitioner of public policy and governance, a social activist, a historian, a political scientist, and a literary theorist. Some of them talked directly to Ambedkar scholarship, but others used Ambedkar as a springboard for explorations on themes and problematics that interested them.

In the fifth AML, Professor Upendra Baxi had called upon AUD to promote what he called the Critical Ambedkar Studies Movement (CASM). Right from the beginning, we at AUD had been very particular about considering Ambedkar as one of the tallest personalities of India of the 20th century, whose thoughts and ideas had influenced immensely the shaping of the post-colonial Indian state and society, not just as someone who led the drafting of the Constitution of India, but more as a powerful thought leader who contributed intellectually and in terms of political energy to the cause of transformation of a semi-feudal society into a modern and just one. We did not want Ambedkar to be treated as a cult figure who could not be critiqued without risk of being charged with heresy. We believed that Ambedkar should be subjected to the same level of rigour of critical appraisal that he himself had adopted while critiquing other important thinkers and leaders of his time. The choice of personalities whom we had invited to be speakers for the AML series was based on the credibility each of them held in their respective fields, and was clearly not based on whether they subscribed to Ambedkar's views. We definitely did not want ideologues. We wanted to listen to credible voices from different areas of scholarship and practice who could engage actively with Ambedkar's world view, ideas and humanism. And this we thought was critical to the furtherance of CASM. We understood CASM in this context as something that AUD needed to take forward with rigour and seriousness.

When AUD managed to create a corpus of funds for the purpose of establishing and supporting a chair, the first idea that came up was that of setting up an Ambedkar Chair, primarily to take the idea of CASM forward. Fortunately for AUD, we could persuade Professor Valerian Rodrigues to join us as the first Ambedkar Chair Professor. While briefing Professor Rodrigues about AUD's expectations from the first Ambedkar Chair Professor, one task on the list that I had set out in front of him was the compilation of the first 10 Ambedkar Memorial Lectures into a single volume held together through a long introductory essay. I must admit that I had flagged this idea to Professor Rodrigues with considerable hesitation, for I knew that this was not an easy task. The lectures were from diverse areas and addressed disparate sets of issues. These were primarily stand-alone pieces of intellectual exploration and did not fit into a common a priori framework; neither did they address a shared set of issues or questions. Only someone with deep insight into Ambedkar scholarship and a passionate commitment could undertake the task of stringing these lectures together with the aid of a long introductory essay that would lend coherence to the whole collection of lectures, and at the same time make this a step in the direction of CASM. I was very clear that this was the task that Professor Rodrigues could do very well. However, I would have reconciled myself to it, albeit sadly, had Professor Rodrigues declined to take up this task. But he gave this matter the most serious thought and eventually agreed to do it, for which I felt most grateful.

I feel a sense of deep satisfaction seeing the full manuscript of this volume in front of me. Professor Rodrigues's long scholarly introduction goes well beyond its specific objective of introducing this collection of lectures. It is in a way an introduction to CASM itself. In his essay, Professor Rodrigues paints analytically the broad canvas of Ambedkar scholarship— the wide perspective within which to view the context, the foundation and the edifice of Ambedkar's work. This he does with remarkable competence and authenticity. He then locates the 10 lectures within this canvas. This clearly may not have been an easy or straightforward task. He draws from each of these lectures the essence that 'demonstrate[s] the ground they share in common with the scholarly concerns that take off from Ambedkar and the themes that his intellectual scholarship has provided to a collective academic endeavour centred around India today' (p. 37). With the introductory essay holding these 10 lectures together with ease, the volume does not in any manner appear like a set of disparate pieces of scholarship sitting uneasily next to each other. The volume has truly become a collection of intellectual explorations and expositions that are complementary to one another and that constitute in a syncretic manner an important initiative in the project of CASM.

It is truly heartening that the present volume is being published under the joint auspices of Ambedkar University Delhi and Tulika Books. I feel proud of the manner in which AUD has taken this initiative forward.

This has become not so much a foreword to this volume, but an attempt to describe the context and genesis of the AML series as an institution and the spectacular manner in which its armature has unfolded over the past 10 years. Over the years, the organising committees of the AML series have with much imagination started the practice of curating a whole bouquet of cultural programmes, discussions, exhibitions, and so on around the main event. The AML has thus become an integral part of AUD's annual calendar, and undoubtedly the most important public event that the university hosts. I hope that the unbroken string of AML lectures in the first decade of the series' life will go a long way in ensuring its continuity and sustenance as an institution.

As for CASM, I hope this volume will prove to be the first in a series of major initiatives that AUD will take, located as it is in the larger ecosystem of critical scholarly interest in Ambedkar, not merely as a subject of study, but increasingly using Ambedkar scholarship as a major repository of perspectives, frameworks and tools with which to make sense of and intervene in the emerging complex social and political realities of our times.

Delhi, 27 July 2018   SHYAM B. MENON

Preface and Acknowledgements

I thank Ambedkar University Delhi (AUD) for giving me the opportunity to edit this volume containing 10 lectures by some of the most outstanding scholars and public personalities of our times. These public lectures were delivered every year from 2009 to 2018 on 14 April, the birth anniversary of Ambedkar (except on two occasions due to exceptional circumstances), as part of the Dr B.R. Ambedkar Memorial Lecture Series instituted by AUD. The lectures are an engagement with and a celebration of the memory of Dr Bhimrao Ramji Ambedkar, whose name the university bears. At the same time, each lecture reflects the speaker's specific concerns within his/her own domain. This volume collects all the 10 lectures in the series so far, accompanied by an introduction.

The volume seeks to retain the informal tone of the lectures as originally addressed to a live audience. This includes occasional allusions to public perceptions of the university, or to the events of the day, although some of these events have had subsequent trajectories of their own. In some cases, short notes have been provided on such events and issues for the benefit of readers who might be unfamiliar with the context. Glosses are also provided for non-English terms, although in many instances a gloss does not adequately capture all the nuances of a term as reflected in a speech.

All the lectures included here have been reviewed by the speakers, and in the process some have referred to subsequent writings and publications. Such references have been retained as reflecting the conversational stance of this volume.

While a volume of this kind involves many people, particularly given the significance the Ambedkar Memorial Lecture (AML) series holds in AUD's academic calendar, I have to limit myself to recalling a few names immediately involved in the making of this volume: Professor Shyam Menon, Vice Chancellor of AUD throughout the course of these 10 lectures, has entrusted his own labour of love to my hands. Professor Salil Misra, Pro-Vice Chancellor of AUD, has evinced a close interest in the completion of this volume. The publication of this volume was both proposed and planned by Professor Radharani Chakravarty, Professor of Comparative Literature and Translation Studies, who also heads the Publication Division of AUD. Veeksha Vagmita, a PhD scholar in English at AUD, has been an ideal research assistant, bringing in much needed competences and skills to annotate the text. Shaunna Rodrigues, who reviewed the text initially, saw this volume as filling the gaps in existing Ambedkar scholarship and reaching out to a wider audience. Aruna Ramachandran has given the finishing touches to this volume with a sharp eye for inconsistencies and missing details, and has helped to make the text more lucid. Above all, I thank all the speakers whose lectures appear in this volume. All of them, eminent in their respective domains, set aside time to respond to the queries that I sent them, keeping in view the deadlines that I set.

New Delhi, July 2018   VALERIAN RODRIGUES

INTRODUCTION
Ambedkar as a Scholar and Ambedkar Scholarship Today

Valerian Rodrigues

The founding vision of Ambedkar University Delhi, an initiative of the Government of the National Capital Territory of Delhi,[1] emphasises the blending of social justice with excellence for furthering the ideal of equality, among other pursuits. For this, the university has actively sought guidance from B. R. Ambedkar and made his concerns integral to its institutional layout, curricular content and research engagement. One of the activities it has pursued is organising an Ambedkar Memorial Lecture every year on 14 April, the birthday of Ambedkar, by inviting an outstanding academic/public figure of our times, with credible and sustained impact on public life, to speak to the university community and the public at large in Delhi. The tenth lecture in this series was delivered on 14 April 2018. The university felt that the issues and concerns raised in these lectures, and their engagement with Ambedkar's oeuvre, are of critical importance to our public life, and need to be disseminated to the wider public, inviting them to join the exciting journey of a young university.

With his name on its mast, Ambedkar looms large as the exemplar before the university, in the sense of being a template for its academic and institutional life. As an exemplar, he is our current dispensation and not merely a historical figure: we need to reckon with the great body of scholarship that his writings and public interventions have spawned; and in the ongoing life of the university, it is important to critically engage with his ideas and concerns as well as with this body of scholarship. The 10 memorial lectures included here can be viewed as a critical engagement with the thought and concerns central to Ambedkar. We regard them as conversations that frame questions in a specific mode but speak to other unanticipated questions and concerns.

Ambedkar as an Academic Icon

Ambedkar was a quintessential university person, although his active public life sometimes camouflages this facet of his personality. Those who adulate him tend to focus largely on his formal degrees and academic laurels. While his formal academic endowments are important and impart much authority to his writings and actions, he was integral to an academic culture of great significance that has few parallels in the global South.

It is important to probe a little further into the academic culture that Ambedkar lived and breathed throughout his life and the kind of confidence it imparted to his personality, despite his 'untouchable' background and lifelong struggle against it. Ambedkar pursued his undergraduate studies (1907–12) at the Elphinstone College, Bombay, where the great debates on the priority of social reforms versus political reforms, gender rights versus swaraj, nationalism versus the caste divide, raged in the late 19th and early 20th centuries. He joined Columbia University, New York, in 1913, when he was just 22 years old. The university was then in the throes of a major revamping. Institutionally, it was trying to grapple with the idea of a United States of America caught in contradictions and social cleavages distinctly its own, as well as the intellectual and emotional resources it would take to weld the country into one. While many have seen in Fordism the specific response of the US to its social conditions,[2] little attention has been paid to the work of universities such as Columbia in responding to these conditions.[3] In the early 1900s, several of its faculty members worked actively to assemble the critical resources needed for a cohesive society. The interventions involved: (a) a conscious attempt to train their students as future leaders of American society; (b) institutionalisation of social science knowledge into clearly demarcated disciplinary arenas, which in turn would enable its dissemination to the wider society through appropriate tools and instrumentalities; (c) reaching out to the social expressions of the subaltern layers of society, such as the working-class, black and women's movements; (d) tapping into European intellectual and political resources to further these ends; and (e) extending professional guidance to the government and civic agencies.[4]

Some of the people that Ambedkar was closely associated with at Columbia University, and who were actively involved in redefining its role, are known for their activist academic orientation. Edwin Seligman, his PhD supervisor, did not just serve twice as the economic adviser to the president of the United States, but was also the founding president of the American Economic Association as well as the chief editor of the first edition of the *Encyclopaedia of the Social Sciences*. John Dewey, whom Ambedkar considered his 'teacher' and whose prodigious intellectual output he always kept as a reference point, was closely involved in working-class struggles, black protests and women's movements.[5] Dewey founded his own political party in the interwar period, which became an important reference point for Ambedkar when he himself launched the Independent Labour Party in 1937. The idea of the academic as a public figure who, alongside his scientific pursuits, plays a critical role in highlighting the concerns of the society as a whole, taking into account its cleavages and contradictions, was to have a lasting impact on Ambedkar.[6] The London School of Economics (LSE) – where he joined in 1917 and submitted his doctoral dissertation (for a Doctor of Science or DSc degree) in 1922 – was to reinforce this image of an activist academic. The LSE itself was founded, in marked contrast to the Oxbridge format, as an institution of higher learning where not only would the great concerns of society be studied but long-term solutions to social ailments would also be proposed through debate and discussion among peers and activists. Beatrice Webb and Sydney Webb, the founders of LSE, saw their two early empirical studies, *On Trade Unions* and *On Cooperatives*, as a template for the institution.[7] Ambedkar's intent to make study and reflection his lifelong pursuits may be glimpsed in his desire to pursue another PhD at Bonn under the well-known Indologist Hermann Georg Jacobi, cut short due to demands back home in Bombay. Much of his later writing on early India, and his familiarity with Sanskrit, can be traced back to this aborted attempt.

Ambedkar's massive scholarly output and his professional life as a lawyer and educationist went alongside an active engagement with social concerns as well as an intense political engagement with the questions of the day. This made him think on his feet rather than pursue an intellectual life disconnected from the context in which he found himself. Some of the important elements of this context were: the contempt and lowliness in which the quotidian existence of an Untouchable is caught in India and which stamps every moment of his/her life;[8] the marginality of working-class existence in suburban Bombay;[9] the legacy of the intense devotionalism of his (Ambedkar's) family; the penury of his life, particularly till the mid-1930s;[10] the oppressive colonial rule, and the hopes and limits of the national movement;[11] the social and political assertions of Dalits and lower castes; and his own experience of the wider world. As a rule, Ambedkar avoided shrill ideological and political overtones and laid stress on problem solving, while drawing attention to the complexities of a concrete situation (see Teltumbde 2016). This approach, which reflected context-sensitivity and epistemological reflexivity, proved to be vital when he became actively involved in India's emerging public life, as he directed it against the colonial dispensation. In keeping with this approach, he addressed specific issues and concerns by studying the problem meticulously before attempting a resolution. He used this approach not merely in dealing with large issues, such as untouchability and constitutional questions, but also in his interventions in journalism, educational initiatives, etc. When he embraced Buddhism, he studied it closely, attuned himself to it, and carefully mapped out every step of his journey towards it.[12] The moral concerns in which his transformative politics is caught and the avowal of a rigorous epistemological reflexivity can be regarded as the hallmarks of his lifelong engagement.

Ambedkar brought much methodological rigour to his academic endeavours. All his major works revolve around a central problem. He also carefully framed his perspective on an issue and sorted out the sources and data for its investigation. Given this, he did not let himself be faulted either on the substantive aspect of a study or on procedural grounds.[13] His ethnographic work, particularly on the prevalence of untouchability and its measurement, would be deployed by him to demonstrate the flaws of the empirical method as well as its strengths. Many of his studies provide copious references to documents, manuscripts and archival work. He also cited such works in a 'scientific' way in his research writings. He used different methods of study, depending on the subject matter, after making a case for their appropriateness and refuting adversarial stances. Irrespective of the method he pursued, or sometimes methods in conjunction, he would assert the necessity of weighing the countervailing evidence before taking a stand on the issue under investigation.

His two important election studies, after the 1937 and 1946 elections, employ electoral data extensively to debunk the Congress's claim that it enjoyed overwhelming support from the Scheduled Castes across the country. In many of his studies he adopts an argumentative format rather than a descriptive one, and it is important to keep the structure of the argument in view while taking a stance on specific details. For instance, there is a lot of historical data in the book *Thoughts on Pakistan*,[14] but this data revolves around a central argument, namely that nationalism is a feeling of fellowship that marks out a people from the rest and calls for the founding of a distinct political community. While race, language, culture, religion, etc., are useful for forging such a fellowship, the idea of nationalism itself is irreducible to them. Given this idea of nationalism, can Muslims and Hindus live together within the same fold? The book takes the stance that there is much that unites these communities, yet they are divided on several fronts – theological, historical, as well as over issues of belonging and identity. If Muslims and Hindus are willing and prepared to forget what divides them, then they can exist within the fold of a single nation.

However, if they assert their distinctiveness and name it 'nationalism', there is little possibility of keeping them in a common formation. Ambedkar deploys much historical and ethnological data to build this argument. One cannot randomly pick some data from his argument, which he develops methodologically and procedurally, and use it to support a substantively different argument.[15] The structure and texture of his argument have to be considered before deciding on whether the evidence deployed by him suits substantively different arguments. When the validity of his argument, or its implications, was questioned, as was the case with *Thoughts on Pakistan*, he would not shy away from an interlocutory engagement. He would reformulate his argument based on fresh evidence and studiously pursue its potential implications.[16]

A critical spirit that refuses to accept a position merely on grounds of authority, and which seeks to know the reasons for beliefs and actions, is central to Ambedkar. Such a spirit, he argued, is manifested in the kind of choices one makes and the consequences one anticipates. A servile disposition – submission without reason and adulation without scrutiny – is clearly opposed to the critical spirit. Such a spirit must manifest itself in specific modes of action in a concrete setting of social and cultural belonging. But, it can triumph only through an *interlocutory* engagement with all the contenders on the scene. In Ambedkar's view, possessing a critical spirit is an essential human attribute and the very ground of human worth. On this basis, he developed a theory of public action. He often described himself as an iconoclast and accused both Gandhi and Jinnah of giving in to public fanfare, thus encouraging submissiveness and docility rather than a critical spirit among their followers.

A moral impulse against the prevailing state of things and a deep bond with fellow sufferers sharing a common fate, that he later termed *maitree*, made Ambedkar's academic culture partisan. However, he thought that this partisanship expressed the common good from the standpoint of the marginalised. What seemed to others as advocacy of the cause of Untouchables, was to Ambedkar the cause of humanity as a whole. He argued that an emancipatory project that defends itself in the name of humanity has to accord priority to a social question where all modes of oppression are riveted. Pursuit of the common good in such contexts could only be by according priority to this question. He saw the struggle against untouchability as an expansive struggle that reached out to all the domains of oppression.[17] It invites everyone to join in this struggle on the touchstone of humanity. No one can be human, at least fully human, without rising in revolt against the practices of untouchability and kindred social realities. Ambedkar often employed terms such as 'energetic', 'forceful', 'positive', etc., to qualify the political action required to combat these practices. The moral impulse that imbues such action is not merely limited to the disposition of a person, but is manifest in active interventions in the form of social transformative action. Human action, even everyday action, should not merely become a set of habitual motions but needs to be charged, he argued, with the spirit of fellowship and social bonding with the oppressed.

Ambedkar felt that values such as liberty, equality and fraternity, irrespective of the context of their origin, and the social dominance to which they were made subservient, were inflected with a partisanship favouring the marginalised, particularly Untouchables. The latter therefore had to fight for this social capital in order to further their goal of social emancipation. Ambedkar clearly saw the Untouchables as the vanguard of social transformation rather than as recipients of social largesse based on a 'change of heart'.[18] This was his clarion call to Dalits in all his public addresses.

Ambedkar in Scholarly Writings and Cultural Representations

What kind of a reception has Ambedkar received in academic and cultural circles? It is, after all, these circles that have filtered Ambedkar's thought and linked it to the wider webs of thought and social practices. The modes of cultural representation play a similar role in this respect. Till the early 1990s, much of the writing on Ambedkar projected him as the leader of the Harijans/Untouchables/Dalits/Neo-Buddhists, distinguishing him from *national* leaders like Mahatma Gandhi and Jawaharlal Nehru, or *enclave* leaders such as Periyar Ramasamy Naicker who espoused Dravidian concerns; Jaipal Singh who deplored the Adivasi plight under the emerging Indian nationalism; and Chaudhary Charan Singh, who was apprehensive about the future of the agrarian classes under the pattern of development chosen by India. It was the Dalit movement across the country which kept Ambedkar's memory alive and turned to his writings as a form of collective self-reflection. The last 30 years, however, have seen an upsurge in interest in Ambedkar not just in India, but even abroad in many scholarly circles. Many factors have contributed to this development; these include shifts in academic trends and conceptual frames;[19] shared concerns, such as marginality, exclusion, powerlessness, and the denial of human dignity, across transnational networks and the felt need for proactive measures (Guru 2009; see also Natrajan and Greenough 2009); the discourse of postcoloniality and the search for self-definition in the global South (see Rathore 2017); the spread of the human rights agenda;[20] and the outreach of the Dalit movement itself.[21]

'Broken people' – refugees, forced migrants, the displaced,

the homeless, those despised by their cultures and kept outside the fold – and those who recognise the indispensability of communities for human flourishing, seem to find in Ambedkar their own voice. This growing popularity has set off alarm bells in certain Dalit circles, who feel that Ambedkar, the tallest representative of their cause, is being co-opted for furthering others' agendas.[22] With this new interest, what kind of representation and ideological leadership have been conferred on Ambedkar? While it is impossible to answer this question at any length, leave alone review the literature on this, it might be worthwhile to draw attention to some of the main lines of progression around which contemporary Ambedkar scholarship is poised.[23] The positioning and concerns of this scholarship in varied domains will help us connect and critically engage with the Ambedkar Memorial Lectures. The following pages provide a brief outline of the scholarly and representational output on Ambedkar as well as the issues of central concern in the last 30 years.

Studies on Ambedkar and His Thought

The publication of *Dr Babasaheb Ambedkar: Writings and Speeches* by the Government of Maharashtra has made Ambedkar's rich corpus of writings widely available, and at an affordable price, in spite of the bureaucratic hurdles in the marketing of these works.[24] These writings became the primary source for the popularisation of Ambedkar in English (see Kshirsagar 1992; Rodrigues 2002; Thorat and Kumar 2009; Jadhav 2013, among others). There have also been annotated critical editions of certain writings, such as *Annihilation of Caste* (Ambedkar 2014) and *The Buddha and His Dhamma* (Ambedkar 2011). The legacy of Ambedkar has drawn forth much scholarship in the last two decades, continuing the earlier trend but with greater methodological and conceptual clarity. Some of these studies have taken recourse to ethnographic and archival work, while others have highlighted Ambedkar's ideas on specific themes and concerns: studies by Jaffrelot (2005), Zelliot (2008), Jadhav (2014), and Teltumbde (2016) illustrate this. Many essays in a volume edited by Johannes Beltz and Surendra Jondhale (2004) also reflect this trend. Although a gross misreading and an affront to Dalit pride, Arun Shourie's (1997) indictment of Ambedkar can also be included in this slot. Much of Gopal Guru's work offers interpretative insights into the central concerns of Ambedkar (see Guru 2001, 2007, 2017), while Aishwarya Kumar (2010) sets up a critical engagement between Gandhi and Ambedkar, marking the latter's place within a body of modern European thought. Several scholars focus on specific issues of interest to them and present Ambedkar's views on these, or have teased out appropriate concepts and norms from his writings (see for instance Ganguly 2008; Omvedt 2008; Verma 1999, 2010; and Parekh 2015).

The greater focus on Ambedkar and his writings is evident from not just the scholarly output but also other modes of cultural representation. Several films and plays have been based on the life and thought of Ambedkar: Jabbar Patel's *Dr Babasaheb Ambedkar* (2000) in English; Shashikant Nalawade's *Yugpurush Dr Babasaheb Ambedkar* (1993) in Marathi; Sharan Kumar Kabbur's *Dr B. R. Ambedkar* (2005) in Kannada; and Subodh Nagdeve's *Bole India Jai Bhim* (2006) in Marathi, among others. Ambedkar also figures prominently in Shyam Benegal's *Samvidhaan*, a TV mini-series on the making of the Constitution of India.

The outpouring of literature in English, revisiting Ambedkar's legacy, pales in comparison to the works focused on Ambedkar in regional languages in India. While the trend can be observed in all the major languages, it is much more pronounced in Marathi, Telugu, Kannada, Tamil, and Hindi. It is definitely catching on in Malayalam, Gujarati, Punjabi, and Urdu.

Ambedkar and the Dalit Movement

Although the Dalit movement is hugely diversified today – and has been so in the past as well – with distinct conceptions of ideological frames, social coalitions, strategies, and programmes of action, it is not merely a collective endeavour to transform the diverse domains of social life but also calls for a reconstitution of the Dalit self. With the rise of this movement, different social and political forces have bestirred themselves to ideologically shape it. Ambedkar continues to be a towering influence on the movement across India.

His sweeping presence has only been reinforced in the decades under consideration, as the movement has inched towards shared concerns and marked off adversarial insinuations. This is reflected in several studies of the last three decades such as those by Murugkar (1991), Narain and Ahir (1994), Omvedt (1994), Michael (1999), Shah (2001, 2002), Beltz and Jondhale (2004), Waghmore (2013), Zelliot (1996, 2004), Jaoul (2006), V. Kumar (2006), Bellwinkel-Schempp (2007), Wankhede (2008), Pai (2013), and Bhattacharya and Rao (2017).

It is important to recognise that there are deep cleavages within the Dalit movement today, and the appeals to Ambedkar from its varying registers are often highly scattered (see Y.C. Rao 2009). Hindu right-wing nationalist forces, such as the Rashtriya Swayamsevak Sangh (RSS), have appropriated Ambedkar to present themselves as socially inclusive entities fighting against untouchability and the perversion of the caste system. This has involved a 'rebranding' of Ambedkar as a national hero.[25] While the Indian National Congress and the Communist left have begun to invoke Ambedkar in recent years, the RSS and its political affiliate, the Bharatiya Janata Party (BJP), had begun to sense his importance much earlier (see Guru 1991). The BJP has really intensified its outreach in recent years. The Indian prime minister Narendra Modi, heading the BJP-led government, inaugurated the ambitious Dr Ambedkar International Centre in New Delhi on 7 December 2017. He had laid the foundation stone for this centre in April 2015.

It is widely felt that the powerful portrayal of untouchability in films such as Shyam Benegal's *Ankur* (1977) and Satyajit Ray's *Sadgati* (1981) did not have a sustained impact afterwards. There is, however, a renewed interest in this theme. Increasingly, caste and caste relations, factors that shape people's life prospects, are not being papered over, and several directors are very consciously exploring the cultural domain that both sustains as well as ghettoises Dalits and their communities. Anand Patwardhan's *Jai Bhim Comrade* (2011) has been widely acclaimed for its depiction of the Ambedkar-inspired struggle of Dalits in an urban setting. Some of Ambedkar's central concerns have been expressed vibrantly in regional language films – these include Lalji George's *Chithariyavar* (2004) and Jayan K. Cherian's *Papilio Buddha* (2013) in Malayalam; Nagraj Manjule's *Fandry* (2013) and *Sairat* (2016) in Marathi; and K. Jyothi Pandian's *Ore Oru Gramathile* (1989) and Pa Ranjith's *Kabali* (2016) in Tamil. Neeraj Ghaywan's *Masaan* (2015) and Amit V. Masurkar's *Newton* (2017) have attempted to break the mould in which Dalit characters, and their cultural milieu, have been cast in mainstream Hindi cinema.

The Ambedkar-inspired Dalit movement, particularly religious conversion, has given rise to many kinds of creative expression – songs, popular painting and sculpture – redrawing community fault lines and leading to the emergence of new sacral sites and festivals as well as ritual communities, which have replaced/displaced the existing ones despite all their significance. Every year, thousands of Ambedkarites and Dalits visit Deekshabhoomi in Nagpur, where Ambedkar embraced Buddhism, and Chaityabhoomi in Dadar, Mumbai, where he was cremated. Ambedkar is remembered on 14 April (his birth anniversary), 14 October (*deeksha* [religious initiation] to Buddhism) and 6 December (*parinibbana* or death anniversary). Some existing festivals, such as Buddha Purnima/Vesak, have acquired added significance,[26] while Ram Navami and Durga Puja have become contentious.[27]

These expressions have produced distinct registers of popular culture. Sometimes Ambedkar has made his way into the existing iconography, among the deities adorning the walls of houses, and in the *viharas*. In the popular *deras* (abode or dwellings of the guru) in western India, Ambedkar makes his appearance with one or more Sikh gurus, Sant Raidas, and sometimes Kabir. In the Tamil country he appears alongside Periyar Ramasamy Naicker, although the internal disputes in the Tamil Dalit movement have made this contentious. The Bahujan Samaj Party (BSP), particularly the Mayawati-led BSP government in Uttar Pradesh, has associated Ambedkar with Kanshiram, Jotirao Phule and Periyar Ramasamy Naicker in an attempt to set up a new political lineage through sprawling monuments, giant statues and parks with red stone panels. These representations can take myriads of forms across the country, sending different signals in concrete socio-political settings. Some aspects of such creative expressions have been studied by Gopal Guru (1997) and Sharmila Rege (2013a). In 2012, Gary Tartakov published a collection dedicated to the theme of the Navayana Buddha (see also Tartakov 1994).[28] Johannes Beltz (2005, 2015) has extensively documented the changing trends in Ambedkar representations, although his study is focused on Maharashtra. Photographic representations of Ambedkar have also proliferated, beginning with the publication of Dhananjay Keer's collection in 1982. Ambedkar's statues, some patronised by the state but most of them erected through the contributions of Dalit communities, adorn not merely seats of power but even small hamlets inhabited by Dalits. Their significance alongside emerging Dalit art forms has been studied by Fitzgerald (1994), Tartakov (2012) and Komath (2015).

Philosophical and Methodological Studies

Scholars such as Queen (1994), Gokhale (2008), Guru and Sarukkai (2012), Guru (2017), Rodrigues (2017a), and Govind (2018) have examined the important implications of Ambedkar's thought on the central categories of social understanding and practices in India, and have tried to facilitate a broader dialogue with public concerns across the world. Anupama Rao (2011) makes a noteworthy contribution by tracing the journey of Dalit agency through rich ethnographic accounts. Meera Nanda, in many of her writings, has argued for the congruence between Ambedkar's ideas and a scientific spirit, pitting them against religious obscurantisms (see Nanda 2007). Ajay Skaria (2015) explores Ambedkar's argument that societies need to have a moral grounding, even though they believe themselves to be driven by the ideas of justice and equality. Aakash Singh Rathore considers Ambedkar central to the project of redefining the framework of our public life from the global South through his concept of *svaraj* (2017: 147–205). Cosimo Zene's edited volume (2013) sets up a conceptual and praxiological engagement with two central categories of marginality, Dalit and subaltern, through the writings of Ambedkar and Antonio Gramsci.

Ambedkar's philosophical concerns have led several thinkers to view him as a liberal figure. While the conceptual framework for his philosophical thinking overlaps with liberal thought – and occasionally borrows its vocabulary – Ambedkar reconstructs the latter to produce a framework distinctly his own.

The Idea of the Human

Ambedkar employs three concepts – *neech*, *achhut* and *bahiskrit* ('low', 'polluting' and 'socially excluded' respectively) – to denote an Untouchable's attributes, which represent a human being in whom extreme lowliness and social contempt intersect from birth. The Untouchable is supposed to have these primary attributes throughout his/her life. He/she is not just 'outside the fold' but is also bound by the reproduction of the existing social order, along with its category of the low and despised. As a Dalit, Ambedkar attempts to speak both of and to this human condition, and to explore strategies of emancipation from it. Do we have a site that testifies to this struggle to be human? Dalit autobiographies serve as an important testing ground. They reveal the enormity of the challenge faced by a Dalit in trying to be simply human.

The autobiography – a mode of expression for the struggle to reconstitute the Dalit self – initially made inroads into the Marathi literary scene. It soon extended its reach to other Indian languages and English. While there are Dalit autobiographies which draw little attention to Ambedkar,[29] many of those that came out after the 1970s invoke Ambedkar as an important inspiration for their rebellion against social codes as well as their refusal to be subsumed within a hierarchically bound cultural matrix. The autobiographies of Vasant Moon (2001), Narendra Jadhav (2003), Siddalingaiah (2006), Baby Kamble (2009), and Nimgade Namdeo (2010) bear testimony to this.

For Ambedkar, the restoration of a broken self engenders human agency. Sometimes he sees the two as mutually reinforcing processes shaping each other. It has been argued that the remarkable social agency engendered by Dalits through their struggles before independence was later co-opted by the constitutional-legal apparatuses of the state.[30] However, the argument seems not to hold if we consider the success with which the Dalit movement has contended with the multiple modes of marginality and offered imaginative alternatives.[31] The complexity, literary flair and experimentation seen in the Dalit literary output, particularly in the regional languages, is remarkable.[32] At the same time, the state's attempt to contain and manage Dalit assertions – through constitutional devices, preferential measures and ideological means – is written all over the political face of India. There have been quotidian resistances to the inclusion of Dalits as equals in all social layers; the middle classes have not warmed to the idea, and the state is concerned more about law and order than fairness. Marc Galanter (1984) and Gopal Guru (2010) have drawn attention to this, and studies by Thorat and Newman (2010), Deshpande (2011) and Mendelsohn (2014), among others, have corroborated the complex challenges that Dalits confront in being equally human.

Human Equality

It can be said that India has been waging a war for equality after freedom from colonial rule. While, in some respects, the state in India has supported this struggle through its constitutional-legal framework, it has also tried to contain and regulate this claim for equality. Scholarly works, on the other hand, have focused on preferential regimes or the reservation policy rather than grappling with this struggle for equality and its implications.

Ambedkar, however, gave centrality to this struggle for equality. He proposed a concept of equality and gave a set of arguments in its defence. He argued that the Indian independence movement had focused on only one dimension of inequality, which was related to colonial rule. There were four other sites of inequality: untouchability, caste, class, and gender (Thorat and Kumar 2009). Ambedkar's idea of equality has drawn some reflective consideration from scholars in recent years. Aishwarya Kumar (2015) has drawn our attention to the complex legacies in which Ambedkar's idea of equality was steeped as well as his disagreement with Gandhi.

Caste and Social Transformation

The salience of caste and its supposed affront to greatly sought-after values, such as non-domination, freedom of choice, equality of consideration, democracy, and citizenship, have attracted much scholarly attention over the years. This has only become more pronounced in recent years with the global interest in caste as a mode of discrimination. The contours of this debate have traversed predictable lines of enquiry: What are the specificities of the mode of social discrimination that informs caste and the caste system? What is the role of power in institutionalising and displacing the caste system? How do class and democracy bear upon caste and the caste system? What has been the impact of law and constitutional-ism on the caste system in general and practices of untouchability in particular? What kind of intra-caste dynamics (within the Untouchable castes) have unfolded in the wake of democracy and preferential measures? Ambedkar's thought is built around a conjunction of these questions. This is explored by Ganguly (2005), A. Rao (2009), Cháirez-Garza (2014), and Gupta (2016), among others.

Social Justice

India crafted a distinct regime of preferential consideration which involved setting aside, through constitutional mandate, a fixed proportion of seats in legislatures, public employment and higher education to denoted disadvantaged low castes and ethnic groups. This was in addition to the affirmative measures for these castes and groups alongside other disadvantaged groups in public policy. The proportion of seats set aside for these castes and ethnic groups was roughly equivalent to their proportion in the population, and they were treated as distinct wholes.[33] The preferential regime in India is primarily the product of Ambedkar's lifelong labour. He also situated this regime within the larger canvas of equal liberties and rights, equality of citizenship, group differences, and the rule of law. While the complex relationship that he set up among these ideas and policy measures has not been explored fully, Ambedkar's idea of social justice has drawn much scholarly attention in the last three decades, particularly with the global interest in matters of social justice. Studies in this area include those by Mendelsohn and Vicziany (1998), Guru (2002), Weisskopf (2004), Acharya (2008), Hasan (2009), and Stroud (2016).

Constitutionalism and Rights

From early on, the courts have referred to Ambedkar's interventions in the Constituent Assembly debates while justifying their verdicts. Many legal and political scholars, for their part, have been prompt in invoking Ambedkar to highlight the distinctiveness of the Indian Constitution, and how it marks a break with the existing frames of liberal constitutionalism. While many of these studies limit themselves to the substantive innovations that characterise Indian constitutionalism, a few seem to go further and argue that Indian constitutionalism represents a paradigmatic break from the existing modes of constitutionalism and law. The works of Marc Galanter (1984), Upendra Baxi (1995, 2008; see also Mendelsohn and Baxi 1994), S. Narula (2008), Pratap Bhanu Mehta (2010),[34] André Béteille (2012), and J. Soske (2013) are significant in this regard.

Economic Thought and Policy

Approaches to public policy formed the central concern of Ambedkar's early studies in economics.[35] His focus later shifted to discrimination and the social context of its reproduction, including economic opportunities. Studies undertaken by Sukhdeo Thorat, particularly those exploring the implications of caste for market access and opportunities, have been a significant development in this regard (see Thorat 1998, 2002, 2009; Thorat and Aryama 2007; Thorat and Attewell 2007; Thorat and Newman 2010; Thorat and Dubey 2012). Others too have focused on market discrimination, such as Ashwini Deshpande (2011). It is, however, worth noting that Narendra Jadhav (1991, 1992, 2015) draws attention to the neglect of Ambedkar's economic thought. Abraham (2002), Thorat (2006), as well as Arya and Choure (2014) draw attention to some specific dimensions of Ambedkar's economic thinking, such as public policy, planning, ecology, and redistribution, which need further consideration keeping in view his thinking on such issues as democracy, equality, constitutionalism, and the state.

The Gender Question

Ambedkar is credited with examining closely the intersection of caste and gender through the mode of thinking employed by Jotirao Phule and Periyar E. V. Ramasamy Naicker. Geetha (2007), John (2008) and Rege (2013a, 2013b), among others, have systematically explored this aspect in several studies. There are autobiographies by Dalit women that show how seriously they have anchored themselves in Ambedkar's thought (see, for instance, Pawar 2008). Irudayam et al. (2006) demonstrate how Dalit women have been at the forefront of the struggles against the violation of women's rights. The relation between the gender question, caste and law that centrally informs the Ambedkar-drafted Hindu Code Bill, and which invoked widespread protests from the Hindu orthodoxy, has not drawn much scholarly attention so far.

The Idea of Democracy

Several studies allude to Ambedkar's idea of democracy, which, despite being radical, held on to the constitutional frame. Studies also suggest that Ambedkar linked nationalism to the idea of both fraternity and democracy. Until now, the most important works on these conceptual links have been those of Mukherjee (2009), A. Kumar (2015) and Rodrigues (2017b). Lenart Skof (2011) has attempted to bring Ambedkar to the forefront of the contemporary debate on democratic theory.

Nationalism and Community

Not much scholarship has been devoted to Ambedkar's distinct conception of nationalism and the links he forges between this idea and democracy. The outpouring of literature on identity in India has not sufficiently engaged with the conceptual axis that Ambedkar sets up between nationalism, community, minority, and democracy. Dara (2009), Sarangi (2006) and Bharadwaj (2015) are some exceptions. Chris Bayly (2012: 297–98, 300–8) and Perry Anderson (2012), however, feel that Ambedkar proposed a refreshingly new liberal imaginary.

Scholars such as Luis Cabrera (2017) have argued that Ambedkar pitched for a distinctively universalistic approach to democratic citizenship and legitimacy, in opposition to the nationalist rooting of political communities. Kamala Visweswaran (2010: 131–63), on the other hand, argues that Ambedkar's subaltern sociology paves the way for transformative social linkages over concerns shared worldwide.

Gandhi and Ambedkar

One of the hotly contested relationships in modern Indian politics has been that between Gandhi and Ambedkar, an issue that touches upon the relation between Hinduism and Indian nationalism, the relation of the Dalits, Scheduled Tribes and minorities to the national question, the place of religion in public life, the role of the state in social transformation, and even abstract concerns such as the philosophy of public action, the concept of the human, the nature of modernity, ideas of swaraj and representation, etc. Some of the important recent works addressing this dynamic are Nagaraj (2010), Anderson (2012), Vajpeyi (2012: 208–41), Roy (2014), A. Kumar (2015), and Palshikar (2015). The lively debate between Rajmohan Gandhi (2015) and Arundhati Roy (2015) in the *Economic and Political Weekly* is also worth mentioning in this regard.

Ambedkar's idea of a separate electorate for Dalits became a bone of contention between him and Gandhi from 1931. The issue reflected their major disagreements with regard to the future of the Indian polity. Raja Sekhar Vundru (2018) has produced a detailed study of the points of contention in this debate and the bearing they have on the electoral system in India.

State and Power

A sustained interrogation and reflective consideration of the state, *qua* state, was somewhat missing from nationalist thought in India. Conceptions about the nature of public power and its relation to other contenders for fealty and authority were not given much attention in modern Indian thought, or later in academia.[36] This is surprising given the fact, and there is universal agreement in this regard, that India had a distinct tradition with regard to the state in such relational conceptions as *brahma-*

kshatra (knowledge and authority) and *dharma-danda* (righteousness and power),[37] and some of the most creative dimensions of Muslim political thought in India came to be centred on the nature of sovereign authority.[38] Ambedkar is one of the first modern Indian thinkers to dwell on this subject at length; he made the state and public power the subject matter of reflection in his early writings on the colonial state, and subsequently in his reflections on the nature of public authority.[39] Unfortunately, there has been little scholarly focus on this issue.

History and Culture

Ambedkar could not simply endorse the emerging discourse on the past in which the nationalist imagination in India had revelled. The latter valorised certain moments in the past, and the texts and traditions associated with such conjunctures.[40] He was at the same time becoming increasingly uneasy with those who embraced a linear, progressive conception of history that would sweep away all the vestiges of the past, redefining social relations and even human beings. The protagonists of such a position, he felt, did not see anything morally reprehensible in Indian social institutions, and he considered them to have mistaken epistemic issues with positivist historiography. In the latter half of the 1940s till his death in 1956, Ambedkar wrote several books and essays that had a strong angularity with history.[41] While historians generally have not given much thought to these relatively tentative writings, which Ambedkar himself considered conjectural, Sharmila Rege (2013a) in *Against the Madness of Manu* suggests that there are good reasons to view these works as integral to Ambedkar's larger and more comprehensive arguments against the Brahmanical and caste project. She also disparages the remarks of the historian R.S. Sharma, who in his book *Shudras in Ancient India* (1958) discounts Ambedkar's (1946b) work *Who Were the Shudras?* Sharma describes the latter as a 'political work' and observes that Ambedkar 'seems to have worked with a fixed purpose of proving a high origin for the shudras', a tendency 'much in evidence among the educated sections of the lower-caste people of the times' (Rege 2013a: 5). Rege, however, argues that Ambedkar 'sought a more robust and thorough critique of periodisation, sources and methodology deployed in studying Indian history' (*ibid.*: 73).

Religion and Morality

Ambedkar's ideas on religion, his critique of Hinduism, and his distinctive reconstruction and embrace of Buddhism have received sustained attention from scholarly circles; this attention has not diminished in the last 30 years. Ambedkar's choice of Buddhism itself has been explored from several perspectives. Such studies include those by Sangharakshita (1986), Rodrigues (1993), Queen and King (1996), Kadam (1997), Nanda (2001), Fuchs and Linkenbach (2003), Omvedt (2003), Fiske and Emmrich (2004), Queen (2004), Bellwinkel-Schempp (2007), Joseph (2012, 2013, 2014), Guru (2015), Dhar and Chakrabarti (2017), and Fuchs (2001, 2004, 2017). While Ambedkar's critique of Hinduism has not received equal critical attention, a few pointers can be found in Omvedt (2004) and Nanda (2016).

Ambedkar Memorial Lectures: Issues and Concerns

It might be worthwhile to locate the Ambedkar Memorial Lectures in the tradition of Ambedkar as a scholar, and the kind of scholarship that has sprung up around his ideas and concerns. Those who have delivered these lectures are not necessarily known for being Ambedkar scholars or for pursuing any of the themes outlined above. However, they are renowned scholars or public figures, from India or elsewhere, who have made a distinctive contribution in their respective fields. It is their contribution to their fields that establishes an intimate bond between them and the ideas and concerns of Ambedkar. While some of the scholars reflect on certain important facets of Ambedkar's thought or his persona from the vantage point of their own scholarship, others have pursued a theme they are known for as scholars. Together they set up an interlocutory field of shared concerns, engaging with both Ambedkar and one another. We have, therefore, called this volume *Conversations with Ambedkar*.

In the inaugural lecture of the series, 'Ambedkar's Legacy', Professor Bhikhu Parekh argues that the approach to this legacy should involve neither vilification nor deification of Ambedkar. Rather, Ambedkar should be understood 'on his own terms and in his context'. In his view, '[w]e need to elucidate, re-examine and even question the questions he asked, challenge what is dubious in his answers, and build on his profound insights' (p. 52). Parekh thinks that Ambedkar's distinctive contribution lies in four areas: his response to the problem of untouchability, conception of democracy, idea of nationalism, and approach to Buddhism.

For Ambedkar, untouchability was a distinct form of social inequality, deeply bound with the caste system, explains Parekh. A social revolution was required to uproot both, resulting in 'a radical restructuring of the very foundations of Hindu society'. Ambedkar also laid down a roadmap for the same by invoking the requisite agency from the untouchables, founded on self-respect and self-evaluation, making them 'the vanguard of the oppressed groups in the Hindu society'. This required precipitating a 'sense of crisis' in the Hindu society, demanding 'intense introspection'. It also called for 'concentrating on strategically significant issues, mounting carefully planned struggles throughout the country, and refusing to be satisfied with concessions and compromises' (p. 58). This crisis, Ambedkar felt, would throw open the pathway for a democratic polity. While only a democracy could be conducive to the emancipation of the Untouchables, India did not have the wherewithal for a 'mature liberal democracy', as the majority in the country was 'communal'. In this context, Ambedkar suggested two devices: 'the policy of reservation' and 'weighted representation in the legislature' (p. 59). Although he agreed to a joint electorate in the Poona Pact, he argued that only separate electorates would ensure that the representatives continued to be responsive to the concerns and interests of Dalits.

According to Parekh, Ambedkar supported 'a social democracy' constituted around the ideas of liberty, equality and fraternity. Ambedkar understood fraternity as a 'fellow feeling, a sense of concern for and an active interest in the well-being of other human beings'. Parekh rightly points out that '[f]or Ambedkar, fraternity gave depth to liberty and equality and realised them in areas lying beyond the reach of the law' (p. 64). In its absence, the rule of law would be merely the icing on the cake. Referring to Ambedkar's distinction between political democracy and social democracy, Parekh perhaps takes a debatable stance:

> For Ambedkar, the contradiction could only be resolved by the state dominating society and moulding it in a particular direction. And since the values inspiring the state were all Western, it could do so only if it was led by a determined westernised elite. If the state became a hostage to society, as it had done for centuries in pre-modern India, and was led by men and women with no commitment to these values, Ambedkar saw no hope for the country. (Parekh, p. 66)

According to Parekh, Ambedkar closely linked his idea of democracy to the idea of nationhood. A nation was 'not an abstraction, a transcendental entity hovering over its members. Rather, it was nothing other than its members in their intricate relations and interdependence' (p. 68). Parekh highlights Ambedkar's critique of Hinduism and his conversion to Buddhism as the latter was 'a truly "egalitarian" religion which had emerged in direct opposition to Hinduism without losing its Indian roots' (p. 62).

Parekh lavishes generous praise on Ambedkar for his intellectual depth, erudition, argumentative ability and boldness, passion, and commitment to principles. While appreciating the originality and boldness of Ambedkar's thought, he underscores three criticisms against him:

(*a*) Ambedkar 'relied too heavily on institutional mechanisms to protect and promote the interests of the Untouchables, and did not fully appreciate the importance of changing the moral culture of the wider society' (p. 68). Such reliance, Parekh feels, also led to inadequate appreciation of Gandhi's efforts to transform Hinduism; (*b*) Ambedkar's approach 'suffered from a strong statist and elitist bias' (p. 69); and (*c*) Ambedkar 'homogenised both the Untouchables and caste Hindus' (p. 70) and saw himself as the 'only true spokesman' of the former.

It is important to point out that the three criticisms that Parekh makes against Ambedkar have been the major hurdles confronting the Dalit movement, and are echoed in other lectures of this series as well. Parekh's lecture also connects to some of the key themes of scholarly writing on Ambedkar. At the same time, we have to take into account that Ambedkar's *legacy* encompasses a much wider field than what Parekh could highlight in the scope of a lecture.

In the second lecture, 'Citizenship as a Claim, or Stories of Dwelling and Belonging among the Urban Poor', Professor Veena Das argues how those in distress employ citizenship as a claim to circumvent the rule of law or tweak law itself to claim a rightful legal belonging. Drawing her evidence from fieldwork in a slum in NOIDA on the outskirts of Delhi, she demonstrates how those on the margins have been able to garner for themselves a modicum of basic claims, precarious though they are, and how they are always looking to reinforce these claims. Through this argument she attempts to substantially shift or even counter the widely held views on life, law and 'exception' that allude to a denial of agency, the power of the sovereign, and a loss of hope in politics – her interlocutors being Michel Foucault, Roberto Unger and Giorgio Agamben, among others. She finds that, '[i]nstead of a panoramic view of State and citizenship through the Hegelian lens of civil society or the Habermasian notion of public sphere, the attention to the minutiae of everyday life allows us to bring into view the complex agencies at play here in the claim to citizenship' (p. 96).

In the course of her argument, Das considers the distinction that Partha Chatterjee (2004) makes between civil society and political society, and argues that these are contested domains that are deeply enmeshed: citizens' agency operates by tapping resources belonging to civil society to wade through political society. She also argues that the notions of law and the state do not have homogeneous meanings, but hold forth other possibilities, although sometimes they are couched in the language of exception. She pitches Manu's concept of *apaddharma* (rule to be followed during distress) as a potential state of being, rather than such situations being read through the analogy of *homo sacer*. Apaddharma consists of 'substitute rules' that respond to 'states of emergency in which the life of both the individual and the community is to be preserved' and that 'allow a new set of rules to be formulated rather than a simple suspension of laws' (p. 84).

Das finds that the rural poor employ judicial pronouncements such as 'constitutional right to life' to imply not merely non-deprivation of life without due process, but also the obligation of the state to sustain conditions of livelihood, and to ensure that their *jhuggi-jhopdi*s (hutments) are not demolished by the authority concerned. Such an understanding is mediated through intermediaries who enjoy a modicum of trust in the community concerned. In the everyday interactions of the community with state functionaries and political parties, these intermediaries detect opportunities to reinforce these claims and subject recipients of their trust to accountability. This is a dynamic configuration as 'new forms of politics open up the space for continuous surveillance through governmental tactics', while the collective agency of residents establishes 'incremental citizenship, that creates new forms in which citizenship can be actualised' (p. 96). Some claims made in the name of citizenship have little sanction in law, but simply cannot be denied as they 'exist within the wider fields of normativity that structure everyday relations' (p. 80).

Although Das's lecture focuses on a different problematic, the appreciation of human agency and acknowledgement of the wider field of normativity that she underscores in her lecture are central considerations in Ambedkar's thought. While acknowledging the autonomous domain of the state and law, Ambedkar also underlined the porosity within this domain and the space it offered for the working of democracy. However, he was not enthusiastic about the possibility of a local initiative sustaining itself over time, leave alone turning modular and spilling over into a large-scale social transformation on its own, particularly in social contexts of gradation and ranking such as those in India.

The third lecture in this series, titled 'Discrimination and Justice: Beyond Affirmative Action', was delivered by Professor Deepak Nayyar. It explores the significance of the concept of social justice in our times and evaluates existing affirmative action practices in terms of how they measure up to this norm. It is Nayyar's contention that 'affirmative action is necessary but cannot be sufficient in the quest for social justice' (p. 102).

Nayyar makes a distinction between social inequality, social exclusion and social justice. Presuming social inequality as characteristic of all societies that we know, Nayyar thinks that discrimination has its origins in the division of labour and the conflict it engendered. While the 'forms of discrimination changed over time and differed across societies . . . the essential attributes of discrimination . . . are similar in their manifestations of inequality and injustice in societies' (p. 102). He sees social exclusion as a wider process which 'excludes individuals or groups from communities, livelihoods and rights, thus depriving them of freedoms that are constitutive of and instrumental in development, which is a source of well-being for people' (p. 103). The different forms of exclusion, economic, social and cultural, are interconnected. While certain modes of exclusion and inclusion may not necessarily be welcome, what is reprehensible is coercive inclusion and involuntary exclusion. Generally, the exclusion that we speak of begets a spiral of discrimination, and, to those included, privileges.

Social justice is closely bound with discrimination. While discrimination is present in many societies, social justice is not something fortuitous but has 'to be discovered and established' as something new. It is 'motivated by a concern which arises from the observed reality that society does not provide rights and opportunities for a significant proportion of people who are subjected to discrimination in one form or another' (p. 106). Therefore, it emerges not so much from a sense of egalitarianism but from perceptions of injustice. While the nation-state and political democracy as institutions, and capitalism and socialism as ideologies, succeeded to an extent in the quest for social justice, their impact has created 'new forms of privilege and exclusion'.

The quest for social justice needs some form of affirmative action. Where discrimination takes place against identifiable social groups, such as those based on race or caste, social legislation is necessary. But it may not be sufficient where discrimination has deep roots in history. Affirmative measures are always conceived of as a 'transitional remedy that would end once there are equal opportunities for all citizens' (p. 108). But this is not the case, since discrimination is often 'embedded in beliefs and ideologies' which affirmative action can scarcely undo. Therefore, it is essential that affirmative action 'be transformed into a claim from below'. For this, political democracy is essential. Therefore, there is a 'strong correlation between the idea of justice and the practice of democracy' (p. 108). Democracy 'increases political consciousness among voters' and 'increases participation in political processes'. This process begets opportunities. But, for the realisation of such opportunities, two conditions are essential: social consciousness among the included, and rights consciousness among the excluded. Since the first is difficult to come by, what is needed is 'social consciousness on the part of individuals and collective action on the part of communities' (p. 110).

Nayyar argues that the reservation policy in India has succeeded partly, and the situation would have been far worse without it, but it has not succeeded in the sphere of higher education. Further, the benefits of reservation have accrued mostly to the better off and the more educated among Dalits and Adivasis who form a 'creamy layer', but an overwhelmingly large proportion of Dalits and Adivasis remain outside the net. Those left out also include groups based on gender, religion, location, and income. At the same time, merely addressing group inequalities cannot resolve the problem of inequality among individuals.

In the US, which started a programme of affirmative action in 1964 after the civil rights movement, the idea of equal opportunities caught the imagination of the public. The attitude of the elites changed from that of hostility to one of acceptance if not enthusiasm, and the sanctity of the glass ceiling was eroded. The favourable factors have been the legal framework, the common schooling system, the spread of education and levels of income, and a relatively smaller percentage of the population facing discrimination. In South Africa, affirmative action after the end of apartheid focused on improvement in the quality of life of the disadvantaged groups and redressal of past discrimination. The Economic Equity Act of 1994 and the Employment Equity Act of 1998 stipulated that private sector firms must make their workforces demographically more representative. Under Black Economic Empowerment, white-owned firms were urged to transfer portions of their equity to black people, without which firms would not be eligible for government contracts. But there has not been much progress as yet.

Nayyar argues that it is important not merely to learn from these comparative profiles but also from our own past. There needs to be a long-term perspective. Words cannot be a substitute for action. There has to be parity in school education; we need to recognise that discrimination is a multidimensional phenomenon and needs a complex index of deprivation; affirmative action should be limited to the first generation; and there needs to be an equal opportunities commission to ensure implementation and adjudication of conflicting claims. The aim should be 'to progressively reduce and eliminate discrimination' rather than think of a perfect solution.

The argument that Nayyar makes is integral to Ambedkar's lifelong endeavour, which however begets its own conundrum: while affirmative action is called for to counter the effects of discrimination and social exclusion, the success of such action crucially depends upon wider support for it, which might be rare to come by. If discrimination and social exclusion are deeply embedded in beliefs and values, affirmative measures may have little impact in radically altering them. The beneficiaries of affirmative action can argue that the benefits of affirmative action should accrue to them as long as dominant beliefs and values persist!

Professor Ashis Nandy delivered the fourth lecture in the series, entitled 'Theories of Oppression and Another Dialogue of Cultures'. He advances a series of interrelated arguments, even against the so-called 'theories of oppression', to make the case that the alternative lies in the cultures of the oppressed.

The theories of 'secular salvation' upheld by the social sciences, Nandy feels, are deeply caught in 'a regime of narcissism': a common feature of these human sciences was 'their eroticised investment in themselves and in the cultural zone where they were born' (p. 123). They confined 'non-European knowledge systems within hermeneutically sealed academic vaults, open to only anthropologists and historians' (p. 123). They 'broke with traditions that drew their values from multiple sources, such as transcendental or divine injunctions, compassion, empathy, aesthetics, and reason' (p. 125). Most of these theories translated 'geographical space into chronological time', 'to see distant countries outside Europe and North America not as culturally, ecologically and socially different, as their forefathers did, but as an earlier stage of history, as in fact an earlier phase of the history of Europe' (pp. 123–24). Even those theories which posited themselves as opposed to the existing order and claimed to speak for the poor and the oppressed were 'aggressively global' with little consideration to 'the lifestyles of individual communities'.

The Enlightenment 'began its career in India on the wrong foot; almost by default, it established a powerful, social alliance with the existing social stratarchy' (p. 126). This was done by reading Enlightenment reason into traditional learning such as 'Navya Nyaya'. A similar pattern was at work in the colonised world. In the name of development, many radical voices supported assaults on societies and cultures, since the categories they employed were drawn from 'the imperium of knowledge' (p. 128). Even dissent itself was clearly managed. The radical agendas have sought to do to Dalits, tribals, and even to a significant proportion of Muslims, what the western intellectual establishment did to them.

Instead of trying to rescue the cultures of the oppressed, what is important is to listen to these cultures and learn from them. It requires 'opening a dialogue with the oppressed and cornered cultures in India first, and then – only then – with other countries and civilisations' (p. 130). Tribal and Adivasi cultures have come to reject their description as 'the poor and the exploited', charting their right to imagine and write their own futures. A dialogue with them can help us rediscover ourselves, from the inner recesses of our own colonised selves.

While Nandy opens up a new binary between the authentic and its other, Ambedkar's relationship to this argumentative cleavage charts a markedly different course. While he argued that emancipation is never a gift but collective self-definition of the oppressed, he felt, alongside Jotirao Phule, that the Enlightenment project has much in it that can be an invaluable resource in such an endeavour. He also felt that there are parallels to some of the insights of this project in the indigenous traditions, such as in the teachings of the Buddha. Besides, whatever evidence we have suggests that social institutions such as untouchability did not bear down on its victims less harshly in pre-modern times than when it came to be challenged by tapping, in no small measure, resources central to the Enlightenment project.

The fifth lecture in the series by Professor Upendra Baxi, entitled 'Restoring "Title Deeds to Humanity": Lawless Law, Living Death, and the Insurgent Reason of Babasaheb Ambedkar', puts the prevailing regime of law itself on trial through a reading of Ambedkar. Baxi sees hope in what he calls the Critical Ambedkar Studies Movement (CASM), pioneered by scholars such as Gopal Guru and Sharmila Rege. He views his own work as a furtherance of this endeavour.

Baxi highlights certain questions before CASM that await exploration: 'how may conferment of power (and *nothing else*) ever rectify millennial harms and injustices?'; 'how does one socially learn to "take responsibility for the past"?'; does Babasaheb 'provide us with any silhouette of a theory of justice across generations?'; 'did Babasaheb have a notion of justice that addressed affirmative action?'; 'is *intragenerational* justice to be considered an integral aspect of *intergenerational* justice'?; 'what did Babasaheb have to say about individuals and groups other than the Untouchables, such as Muslims, indigenous peoples or sexual minorities?'; 'how does the corpus of Ambedkar deal with the now insistent claim of "reasonable pluralism", advanced notably by John Rawls?'; 'what role, as an instrumentality of social control and change, does religion (as compared to the law) play in Ambedkar's life and thought?'; does the 'embittered renunciation of Hinduism' by Ambedkar 'mark merely the rejection of inegalitarian religion encouraging exclusion' or is it also a 'disenchantment with, and distancing from, constitutional legality'? and, 'how does one read and extend Ambedkar's theory of inclusion (and representation) to dignitarian considerations for some non-human animal persons and objects in natural nature?' Baxi himself feels that 'Dr Ambedkar speaks to us much beyond the conventional languages of contemporary human rights and salient ways of theorising "justice"' (p. 137).

In pursuit of CASM, Baxi finds significant conceptual resources to be tapped in the works of Georgio Agamben and Hannah Arendt, particularly in concepts such as 'bare life' and 'living death' in the former, and 'radical evil' and the 'banality of evil' in the latter. Agamben's notion of *homo sacer* and his disagreement with Foucault's theory of biopower/biopolitics too, he feels, resonates with Ambedkar's perspective on the caste system as productive of the conditions of the 'living dead'. Baxi brings in Gandhi as an interlocutor, and sees a deficit in Gandhi's employment of the term 'swaraj' as 'just freedom' against Ambedkar's '*just* freedom', and in Gandhi's assessment of 'caste as anachronism' against Ambedkar's terming it an 'evil'. While Ambedkar found 'the given model of constitutional liberalism and the normative device of fundamental rights [to be] a solvent of the problem of violent social exclusion' (p. 136), he also felt that these were inadequate, argues Baxi.

Baxi brings these conceptual resources and critiques to bear on Ambedkar's conception of 'lawless law' and its reduction of the Untouchable, the 'eternal scavenger', to the 'living dead'. The conception of 'lawless law', instead of being an oxymoron, allows Ambedkar to subject 'the very form of law' to a profound critique. Ambedkar spells out this critique in five sites of law: (*a*) the fact that the lives of Dalits are still caught in an order of normativity that prescribes conditions of living death, such as the *Dharmashastra* and *Arthashastra* traditions that 'perpetuate violent social exclusion' and the 'Hindu living law', which are in open defiance of the Constitution of India; (*b*) customs and practices, including their interpretation, that sanctify and fortify myriad forms of 'lawless law' as 'dharma'; (*c*) the '*micro-fascism* of the local acts/performatives' (p. 140) that reinforce caste apartheid, such as preventing Dalits from drawing water from the sole village well, etc.; (*d*) the clever disguise of the obfuscation of law that manifests in acts of omission and commission relating to employment, sale/purchase, evictions, etc. In all such instances, lawlessness of law is pursued by using the normal provisions of the law. The law does not look into motives and the injury they spell out; and (*e*) lawlessness of law 'as a sphere and a theatre constitutive of biopolitics', expressed in such manifestations as Gandhi's fast unto death.

Given that law proves itself helpless before 'lawless law', Ambedkar's horizon was not limited to jurisprudence but encompassed *demosprudence*. This can be seen in his attempt to convert certain needs into rights. While he saw the need to develop jurisprudence, i.e., 'principles which will inform the conduct of governance' (p. 142), he also considered it essential to employ the weapon of radical criticality.

Baxi's lecture is a significant addition to the Ambedkar scholarship outlined earlier in this Introduction. While it is important to recognise the centrality of the 'Untouchable' to the Ambedkar problematic, it is also important to note that Ambedkar speaks as the other to mainstream nationalism in India, engaging with the entire conceptual baggage that it deployed. *What Congress and Gandhi Have Done to the Untouchables* (Ambedkar 1945), which Baxi sees as raising some fundamental questions, together with *Pakistan, or the Partition of India* (Ambedkar 1946a), is a key statement of his conception of the 'other'. Ambedkar refused to be shunted to the barricades as a critic, and wanted to be at the centre of public affairs, truly in the spirit of republicanism.

The sixth lecture in the series, by Gopalkrishna Gandhi, entitled 'Leading India', dwells on the challenges and pitfalls of leadership in India, while at the same time admitting its indispensability. Commenting on the continued and growing presence of Ambedkar in the public imagination of India, Gopalkrishna Gandhi iterates an observation frequently made by ethnographers these days, that Ambedkar 'remains more alive, more invoked, more honoured than any political leader, dead or living' (p. 147) in India, even after six decades of his death. The image of Ambedkar reigns 'in the unbounded commons of India . . . not by official leave or institutional facilitation, but by the granite strength of popular will' (p. 147). This commemoration of Ambedkar is 'powered by Dalit India' while 'the India of the so-called higher castes stands by, cautiously if courteously distant, acknowledging him half-heartedly, even absent-mindedly'. Given the neglect that Ambedkar suffered at the hands of 'official India' and 'Hindu India', Dalits have rallied for his legacy, but in a mode of hero worship, with which Gopalkrishna Gandhi feels Ambedkar would have been uncomfortable. On the other hand, political India has used Ambedkar's legacy self-servingly. The state also exalts him 'out of a sense of respectful obligation and intelligent "play-safe-ness"'.

In Gopalkrishna Gandhi's view, Ambedkar's significance was not appropriately recognised by the political dispensation of his time. He should have been the natural choice for the vice-president of India, and for succeeding to the presidency of India after Rajendra Prasad. But he was not even backed by the Congress in his first electoral contest in 1952. Ambedkar's leadership was palpable across his political career, particularly in the way he steered the proceedings of the Constituent Assembly away from some of the diehard apologists of the past. He combined in himself both rage and calm, often begetting an 'impassioned dispassion'. Today, the time has come to make him the 'helmsman' for the whole of India instead of confining him as a leader of the marginalised.

Gopalkrishna Gandhi draws attention to the shift in the idea of leadership from the time of India's national movement. There was much that was reprehensible in the national movement – communal tendencies, factionalism and cliques – but it was not comparable to the current situation. Today, leading India has become about 'leading a community, then a faction within the party, then a conglomerate of factions within that party, then the party with fault lines sharp and ready to tear and then, if at all and very optionally, a vision that is all-India' (p. 152). Leadership is largely confined to the adherents of 'regressed wedges of belonging'. Gandhi feels that most Indians today are more comfortable with 'capsular coda' than with having reasoned and argumentative encounters. This tendency has made Indians 'better disciples than analytics, better followers than equals, and better imbibers than reflecting listeners' (p. 152).

What would leading India mean? Gopalkrishna Gandhi lays stress on the following ingredients: (*a*) identification with the people without ignoring their shortcomings; (*b*) challenging those misleading India, and consequently risking widespread opposition, unpopularity and violent intolerance; (*c*) creating counter-helms that interrogate and excoriate the official helm; (*d*) farsightedness and not entrapment by 'a narrow-eyed, pinch-hearted and stunningly bigoted ideology' or a 'dictatorial creed . . . of nationalistic strength and patriotic virility', which is deeply entrenched in 'political giantism'.

Since one does not decide one's birth, a person should not be condemned by it. Therefore, political inheritance cannot be disparaged. A political life in India invariably draws the family into the public domain. Entering a political legacy is not always a bed of roses. It can be a privilege as well as a punishment. In India, caste, community, kinship, and family have often joined hands. At the same time, truly transformational leadership has come from beyond kinship, as demonstrated by Gandhi, Ambedkar, etc.

At a moment when ethnic prejudice has turned out to be the nationalist ideology, leading India has come to mean 'stoking subliminal prejudices, creating new bogeys, mixing ancient biases with new and imagined insecurities, superimposing, on new manifestoes, old testaments with rings that stir subconscious memories of mythic wrongs and legendary vistas' (pp. 159–60). In this understanding, leading India has become a matter of survival rather than service, 'placing faction above party, party above politics, and politics above nation'. Leadership has become a matter of desperation, of packaging money, deals, prejudices, polarisation, and fault lines.

In the context of this lecture, it is important to recall that Ambedkar held a distinct set of views on the idea of leadership, some of which he came to express in his address 'Ranade, Gandhi and Jinnah', delivered at the Gokhale Memorial Hall, Poona, in 1943 (Ambedkar 1979b). Gopalkrishna Gandhi hits the nail on the head when he talks of the slide of leadership in India today. But one could argue that this is a macro view, and there are new sprouts all across the country searching for their own place under the sun. Increasingly, 'leading India' may signify being at the helm of this democratic ferment. For Ambedkar, the question of leadership is also deeply bound with the larger philosophical and political concerns of the day, a perspective that he derived from his exposure at Columbia University and LSE.

In the seventh lecture in the series, Aruna Roy explores the question, 'Is Unbridled Capitalism a Threat to Constitutional Democracy in India?' She argues that the neoliberal turn of the Indian economy is irreconcilable with Indian constitutional democracy. Under 'neoliberal globalisation' there has been 'manipulation of democratic institutions and instruments', and 'the guiding principles enshrined in the Indian Constitution are being systematically eroded'; 'growth rates in [GDP] are presented to the country as the only defining principle of "development"' (p. 164). While capitalism has claimed 'a symbiotic relationship' with democracy, the processes unfolding in India demonstrate that democracy is being 'converted into a marketplace where money and capital will decide policies and only those with money will have voice' (p. 164).

The independence movement had created 'a powerful legacy of civil disobedience, struggle and political protest' (p. 172). The Indian Constitution was a product of struggles against both external powers and internal domination. Ambedkar drew attention to the abyss that existed between political equality and social and economic inequality in India. After independence, and except during the period of Emergency, in spite of ideological differences, the sanctity of free speech, expression and democratic space has been intact. An earnest effort was under way to secure 'freedom from want and access to the basic necessities; dignity and the equality of all; and the freedom to speak out, convey disagreement and express dissent' (p. 169). Equality, although fragile, had offered 'a new space for millions of people' that was constitutionally guaranteed.

It is important to bear in mind that the poor in India have not merely been the greatest defenders of democracy but also its most creative theoreticians and practitioners. The legacy of satyagraha and constitutional rights has been their bedrock of support. In the wake of neoliberal expansion, marginalised communities have sought a deepening of democracy and democratic rights on the political plane, and on the economic side, 'universal basic development rights', using the new paradigm of the 'rights-based approach' (p. 170). It is the people's struggles that had sought the right to information and transparency and accountability. As a result of their struggles, there emerged a slew of right-based entitlements such as the Right to Information Act (RTI), the Mahatma Gandhi National Rural Employment Guarantee Act, the Forest Rights Act, the Right to Education Act, and the National Food Security Act. For the implementation of these measures, issues of democratic governance too became a matter of concern. The rights-based legislations were not merely 'social safety nets'. Basic economic and political rights, alongside monitoring accountability and implementation, denoted a battle for a share of national resources. They have led to assertive democratic movements. Citizens have come to realise the importance of the vote and governance while at the same time challenging the hollow rhetoric of election promises.

Such an inheritance has been supplanted by a ruling class that has 'no experience of struggle in their personal or political lives' (p. 166). There is a close congruity between the interests of this class and capital. Capital has come to regard laws to ensure equality, justice and constitutional guarantees as impediments. The state has often allowed an alliance between the market and communal forces to thrive. Economic growth has become the sole justification of state policy. While there is a rage against subsidies to the poor, the rich themselves walk off with tax reductions and waivers. Those in the civil services find popular demands an irritant, and have become increasingly patronising, arbitrary and aggressive. The corporate-monopolist control over the media is carefully nurturing an acquiescent public.

While the hiatus between the poor and the rich has increased, and the middle classes and farmers are increasingly being pushed to the margins, the state has enormously increased its expenditure on security and surveillance. While intolerance has steadily become worse over the last fifteen years, dissent and opposition are now being obliterated. New slogans and metaphors are pressed into service in the public domain for this purpose. The leaders are projected on giant screens and invested with indomitability. The propaganda machine is working overtime. Larger-than-life images are crafted through the virtual domain. There are calls for 'strong leaders', while the voters are scattered along the fault lines of class, caste, gender, and religious discrimination. The Constitution itself has been subjected to piecemeal erosion. There are direct attacks on citizens' fundamental rights to equality, liberty and fraternity through executive and legislative measures. The state responds to popular movements by using violence and considers dissent anti-development and anti-national. Middle- and upper-caste groups are clamouring for reservations in what seems to be a parody of the genuine demands of marginalised communities, mocking at the just claims of the oppressed. The fringe elements, in fact, reflect some of the priorities of the ruling regime. The theoretical principles of both Gandhi and Ambedkar are under attack with the shift of emphasis 'from empowerment to growth at any cost' (p. 173).

Ambedkar, who had personal experience of discrimination, realised that a strong legal framework of equality is a sine qua non to fight for social justice. The legal domain, which guaranteed rights to people, has itself become a terrain of struggle. Basic constitutional rights have become the first port of call of popular struggles. Our striving today should not be to lay down a roadmap, but to invite people for dialogue and discussion to fashion 'a world of equality and reason', where the assertion of the larger good defined by people will shape political structures and economic policies. In spite of the designs of capital, the sharp political wisdom of the poor has not been subdued yet. The RTI should be seen as embodying 'the right to know and the right to decide; and democratic accountability to the people on the part of all those in positions of power' (p. 191).

Aruna Roy rightly draws our attention to the wider public culture engendered by the nationalist struggle that came to inform India's constitutional democracy. She thinks that it is being eroded with the triumph of the neoliberal dispensation. But it is necessary to draw attention to the fact that most of the rights-based legislations, including RTI, were enacted by the very same regime that also opened the floodgates of neoliberalism. We need to know why the rights-based order is suddenly on the wane, if it was the product of people's struggles. While Ambedkar definitely played a major role in instituting a 'strong legal framework of equality', he also drew our attention to the hiatus between political democracy and public culture in India. Should we then say that a public culture that has remained immune to the promptings of democracy, consorting with neoliberalism, is posing a major threat to constitutional democracy in India?

The eighth lecture in the series was by Professor Romila Thapar, on 'Rethinking the Concept of Civilisation as History'. The historians' concept of civilisation, Thapar suggests, 'implies a kind of package with specific characteristics': the territory of a civilisation is demarcated and its history is identified with a period of high intellectual and aesthetic achievement. In addition, civilisation is articulated in a particular parent language; it is symbolised by a single religion; it assumes that society is stratified and there is evidence of a state and governance; its elite is distinctive and dominates its surroundings; there is a marked presence of aspects of culture – art, monuments, literature, music, all of a sophisticated form; and, above all, 'a civilisation records its knowledge of the world and attempts to advance it'. The definition, therefore, is expansive and covers many aspects of the life of a society (p. 194). However, such a concept of civilisation needs to be subjected to evaluation from a twofold perspective: Who decides what is a civilisation? What is encompassed in the idea of civilisation in context?

The concept of civilisation that was formulated in the 18th century was closely tied to the Enlightenment understanding of history and later with social Darwinism. In 'colonial thinking', the idea of civilisation went through a specific mutation and, in conjunction with disciplinary learnings such as anthropology and archaeology, a topology of progress came to be mapped. Certain stages came to be regarded as dominant patterns, with urbanism, literacy and the existence of the state identified as the highest stage of evolution. This set up new hierarchies across peoples, dividing them into savages, barbarians and the civilised. However, it is important to note that it was not a wholly reductive binary, as can be seen in the stances of the orientalists and the utilitarians on the question in India. The orientalists considered some social formations as civilisations and ignored others. While Islam with the Arabic language, Sanskritic Hinduism and Confucian China came to be regarded as civilisations, Buddhism which set up interconnecting bonds across these formations was not generally regarded as a civilisation. Colonial thinking concurred with the orientalists that Indian civilisation was monolithic with its beginnings in the Vedic period.

It is not merely the concept of civilisation bequeathed by colonial thinking that is under attack today, but also what is to be encompassed in it. There has been new data, such as the discovery of Harappan cities with complex urban planning and writing skills; they predate Vedic culture. The colonial notion of civilisation popularised in the 19th century was fixed within territorial boundaries, while this civilisation itself developed across fragile boundaries with shifting frontier zones. It hosted 'a variety of cultures', with all the changes to which they were susceptible. The significance of a language as a mark of a civilisation too underwent changes as we can see in the axis between Prakrit-Sanskrit-regional languages. The same could be said about religion. Most of the colonial scholars who wrote on religions in India saw them as monolithic, in the mirror image of their counterparts in Europe, while in fact they were manifested 'through a range of sects'. The prevalent understanding of Indian civilisation barely touches and generally ignores 'contributions beyond those of the elite and the upper castes' (p. 204). While civilisations came to flourish in a demarcated territory informed by specific cultures, many of their achievements were the outcomes of the commingling of groups, elites and non-elites, from within and outside the territorial zones.

Given this shift in perspective as well as in the substantive under-standing of civilisation, Thapar argues, if the concept is to be retained today, it should be subjected to a 'peeling' by which certain determinations of this notion have to be shed, and others have to be fused. Further, it should be able to encompass the history of the labouring masses. The territorially bound and culturally hegemonised concept needs to speak to intersecting zones, because cultures were never staid waters but hugely porous entities, with their own give and take, that redefined themselves over time. It is important to recognise the porosity of civilisations and the self-perception of the actors themselves. Such an understanding cannot be squared with the colonial understanding of civilisation and the clash of civilisations to which it lends itself.

While Ambedkar employs the concept of Hindu/Aryan civilisation generally to decry its negative attributes, and attempts to bring to the fore Buddhism and its impact as the core of Indian civilisation, Thapar's exposition of the concept subjects Ambedkar's thought to much critical scrutiny. This is not on account of the impact of colonial thinking, and its associated disciplines, on a wide array of the learning to which Ambedkar was exposed, probably more than anyone else in India. Ambedkar was able to escape the entrapment of this thinking more than many others due to the epistemic reflectivity and methodological rigour that inform his work. His political stance too made him cautious of the idea of civilisation, given the power and status that it conferred on some to the exclusion of others. At the same time, it has to be noted that Ambedkar often employs categories to demarcate social reality, be it dharma/dhamma, caste, community, religion, or language, etc., that were deeply caught up in the colonial discourse. However, Ambedkar was conscious of the porosity of these categories as can be seen in his writings on untouchability, Hindu–Muslim relations and so on. One of the great challenges that he confronted was social demarcation, and the necessity of proposing social categories to understand the distinctiveness of the social reality in which experiences of marginality and exclusion, domination and subalternity, etc., are enmeshed.

The ninth lecture in the series, entitled 'Is There a Conception of the Exemplar in Babasaheb Ambedkar?', was delivered by Professor Gopal Guru. Guru argues that Ambedkar rejects himself as an exemplar. However, for Dalits, exemplars are needed, and they have not merely sourced them from the historical past but have turned to Ambedkar as an exemplar par excellence.

An exemplar offers benchmarks for our understanding and action. Dalits regard Ambedkar as their exemplar, almost by convention, without thinking it through much. He becomes the first to reach out to in 'everyday forms of inspiration and resistance' (p. 212). This is particularly the case with regard to the Dalit masses. There is a big difference between the trust that Dalits repose in Ambedkar, and Dalit intellectuals who 'governmentalise' him for policy purposes and employ him as an instrument to combat adversaries. For the masses, Ambedkar connotes their struggle for *manuski* (dignity).

According to Guru, Ambedkar's status as an exemplar has been contested from three sites. 'Right-wingers' and defenders of the caste system are not prepared to accept Ambedkar as an exemplar. Following Manu, they think that a Shudra cannot be an exemplar, and upper castes cannot accept the fact that a Dalit can rise to the level of an exemplar. What irritates these sections most is the fact that, for Dalits, Ambedkar is not the historical past but their present existence, their own self, their pride. On the contrary, the former want to make good 'their deficit modern self by claiming to be socially superior'. With Ambedkar on the side of Dalits, it does not seem to be working for them since he rejects ranking people as superior and inferior.

The poststructuralist scholars place other exemplars alongside Ambedkar. Such a stance has some advantages: it brings to the fore other benchmarks, and has the possibility of 'democratising' the Dalit cultural imagination. However, the protagonists of this stance would not place their exemplars alongside those of the upper castes such as Gandhi and Tagore. Their stance effectively results in lessening the significance of Ambedkar before the Dalit masses, by making him one among many.

Liberal conservatives deny that Ambedkar has universal signifi-cance and limit him to the Dalit world. They think that Ambedkar is good as an exemplar, but only for Dalits and not for the rest. They see Ambedkar only as 'a Dalit thinker, or as a messiah of the Dalits, or as a social reformer' (p. 217). They 'filter' down Ambedkar, compromising his universality. In the process they inflict enormous sacrifices and challenges on Dalits in their striving towards universality. Those who subscribe to this stance, thereby, delimit the 'cultural aspirations of Dalits'.

In the political space of India, there are a large number of claimants for social justice from the upper castes (Brahmins, Jats, etc.). But they do not invoke Ambedkar, the architect of social justice, to justify their claims. If they were to do so, they would not merely have risen above their caste, they would also have acknowledged Ambedkar as their path to universality. Needless to say, in the process, their claims for social justice would have to be justified through the reasoning of Ambedkar.

Given these dispositions, Guru seeks to know whether there is a notion of the exemplar in Ambedkar's own thought. His own answer to this query is yes, 'it is present [but] only as an initial condition. In the final analysis, Ambedkar discounts the need for an exemplar' (p. 219).

Guru argues that, for Ambedkar, a concrete human being is the product
of the ethical relationship among human beings and not of myths. He
admits certain exemplars such as the Buddha, Kabir and Phule, who are
historical and moral figures, and not mythological. Potential exemplars
are embedded in social relationships, but also dare to take up the cudgels
against concrete modes of dominance. Ambedkar acknowledges some of
his contemporaries as exemplars to the extent that they share common
concerns, but they are exemplars for others, not for Dalits. Gandhi is an
exemplar, not for Dalits, but for upper-caste Hindus. Ambedkar sets the
benchmark for the status of exemplar for those in the mainstream of social
life in terms of the extent to which they share his concerns, interrogating
their conceptions such as Ramarajya and their claims to exemplar status.

Ambedkar himself did not inherit an exemplar figure. He
therefore employs the term 'instructive' rather than 'imitative' to denote
the relationship with the exemplar. Why instruction? A person has to
take moral responsibility for their actions. In imitation, such moral
responsibility is avoided by attributing it to the authoritative promptings
of the exemplar. An exemplar, according to Ambedkar, is called for only as
an 'initial condition' and not as an 'essential condition'. The principle that
Ambedkar advances is *atta dippo bhava* (be your own guide). It involves
moving from truth to truth by a radical overcoming of self-limits. 'Atta
dippo bhava' consists in not remaining content with one's self-limits, but
reaching out to make the concerns of others one's own. This is done through
maitree, or unconditional friendship. 'Atta dippo bhava' is autonomous
consciousness with a self-generating moral and intellectual power. A person
has complete autonomy to adopt a new description of the self for reflective
re-description from the point of view of this autonomy. It involves living
by one's self-definition rather than by the description of others. While such
a stance can lead to solipsism or selfishness and egoism, Ambedkar thinks
that maitree is the essential precondition in the pursuit of self-definition.

While Ambedkar himself disclaims exemplar status, Dalits
claiming Ambedkar as their exemplar par excellence find much support in
Ambedkar's writings and in the Dalit movement that we have outlined in
an earlier section; the same cannot be said about the other arguments that
Guru makes. If Ambedkar recognises exemplars, but only for non-Dalits,
and at the same time sets limits to what it means to be an exemplar, then
Ambedkar cannot escape being a universal exemplar, like the Buddha. If
human beings constitute themselves through their relations with other
beings, then the principle of 'atta dippo bhava' cannot be an overriding
principle, but only a principle that acts as a guide in these relations. In

fact, the principle of 'atta dippo bhava', taken in the way Guru argues for it, militates against Ambedkar's idea of democracy. 'Atta dippo bhava' therefore is either an enabling principle or, at most, a principle of last resort.

The tenth Ambedkar Memorial Lecture was delivered by Professor Homi Bhabha on the theme 'The Burdened Life: Ambedkar, Arendt and the Perplexity of Rights'. Bhabha argues that we are increasingly witnessing a world where the link between 'territory and belonging' is snapped for a large number of people. The migrant, the refugee, the outsider, and those in similar conditions are paradoxically in search of a homeland, while being marked and categorised, at the same time, by habitats they are made to flee from. The sense of otherness in which the everyday experiences of these people is caught, be it on grounds of migration, race, caste, belief, or disputes on political status, 'creates a cleft subject caught in-between agonistic self-identification and ambivalent civic recognition' (p. 230). Toni Morrison's *Home* speaks to this condition where sites of belonging seem strange, and belonging itself becomes a lingering presence. This feeling of being a 'foreigner in my own home' reflects the conditions of minorities and the socially excluded, such as the Untouchables.

This eerie 'double consciousness' in which a large part of humanity is caught today denotes a human condition that highlights a citizen's alterity, where, as Arendt suggests, 'difference is inserted in my oneness'. This 'ontological' shift in the conception of the self calls for a distinct 'political and ethical agency'. The social contractualists constructed a citizen-subject, attributing to him/her dignity and respect, cutting across space and time. In this perspective, a moral universalism grounded on human equality came to be the ethical imperative that bonded a citizen-community, and found its classic expression in the Universal Declaration of Human Rights. The alterity in which vulnerable subjects are caught today makes citizens dubious bearers of these rights. At the same time, 'alterity makes possible other ways of thinking about the rights of belonging and the wrongs of sovereign citizenship' (p. 232).

Bhabha finds such an ethical stance expressed by Mohamed Trabelsi of the Tunisian Red Crescent, active among the refugees in Zarzis in Tunisia, which has become a 'beach-head for beleaguered refugees' from all corners of the world. Unlike the local community of citizenry which wished to remain as distant as possible from the scourge of mutilated and rotting bodies of refugees, Trabelsi argued that the dead and the disdained deserved the 'dignity of human rights' because 'we never know how our lives can change at some point and we can become those people' (p. 235). Trabelsi, according to Bhabha, expresses an ethical stance that exceeds 'the "moral intuitionism" that underscores the concept of universal human values' (p. 236). It invokes the principle of 'ethical alterity': the imperative arising from being in the same potential condition as the other.

> Such a mode of identification is founded on a subject caught in a proleptic temporality – a future conditional – in which the citizen-subject is moved by an affective empathy with the 'other' premised on a radical internal 'unknowability'. . . . It is the very opposite of deferral or irresponsibility; it emphasises the dire necessity of taking imminent action *in the present* (in the interest of an-other) . . . (Bhabha, p. 236)

Bhabha finds parallels to the human condition that he has charted for refugees and those who wish to flee from their homelands in the conditions of Dalits. He uses Marathi writer Avinash Dolas's story 'Refugee' to illustrate this. In the story, Santu, a Mahar Dalit fleeing upper-caste vengeance 'for having struggled against the stranglehold of caste injury and its prejudicial laws', encounters Surji, a Bangladeshi refugee who is in search of his relatives, on a train to Bombay. Eventually, both of them find their precarious habitat in a blue-roofed *basti* (shelter) in Bombay.

In arguing his case for contextually grounded ethical alterity, Bhabha thinks that certain notions of moral universalism need to be revisited. Freedom of movement is integral to the very idea of freedom of thought or liberty itself. He feels that Ambedkar found dignity as associated with the idea of universal citizenship deeply problematic: dignity was employed by upper castes to keep the Untouchables in their place and was 'opposed to the freedom of movement'. It upheld 'caste carcerality'. Against such an appropriation, Ambedkar argued for a dignity *in extremis*: it 'was not what you were born with; dignity was how you learned to bear the burden of disrespect and dehumanisation and still take that 1 per cent chance to survive' (p. 245).

Even if we admit that the phenomenological reality that Bhabha traces is the existential future that confronts us all, it cannot be presumed that it would invoke a singular moral response from all. There could be all kinds of subterfuges and shortcuts, as the debate between Ambedkar and Gandhi highlights with regard to issues of moral disagreements (Ambedkar 1979a: 81–96). Given reasonable pluralisms, wherein adherents to different doctrines pursue their distinct beliefs and ways of life, it would be near impossible to bring them together on a single regulative moral norm. Any attempt in such a direction would grossly violate the freedoms that are central to Bhabha's argument. Besides, why would people feeling secure in their contexts and enjoying the benefits of this security seek precarious 'alterity'? They might do everything they can to ensure their security.

While Ambedkar sought a moral dispensation, it was strongly grounded in a hermeneutic of cultural tradition, and secured in a responsive political community. Bhabha may have to tell us much more about the moral anchor that can sustain 'burdened lives' if he wants to place Ambedkar on his side.

I have chosen to cull out these lengthy summaries of the lectures and offer a few critical comments on each one to demonstrate the ground they share in common with the scholarly concerns that take off from Ambedkar and the themes that his intellectual scholarship has provided to a collective academic endeavour centred around India today. These lectures, with their focus on democracy and social inequality, practices of untouchability, citizenship and rule of law, discrimination and exclusion, modernity and its travails, justice and constitutional democracy, the idea of civilisation, the challenges of leadership, the ideal of the exemplar, and the response that the burdened lives of our time await, are much more caught up in Ambedkar's concerns than they initially seem. At the same time, the differences in perspective, concept usage and policy stance in the lectures will continue to generate productive debate around these concerns.

Notes

[1] Established under the Dr B. R. Ambedkar Vishwavidyalaya Act, 2007, notified on 29 July 2008.

[2] One of the earliest formulations on Fordism was offered by Antonio Gramsci, a Marxist philosopher and working-class leader of Italy, in his writings on 'Americanism and Fordism', in which he saw Fordism as a specific mode of forging hegemony. See Gramsci (1971: 561–622). Also see Jessop (1992).

[3] For an account of Columbia University, see McCaughey (2003).

[4] Ambedkar too bore the marks of this pedagogic approach even as he challenged some of its assumptions as well as political options. In this context, it is important to distinguish between the intervention of Columbia University and the impact it had in realigning class and race relations in the early 20th century, and the response of the faculty members to these issues. Several leading universities in the US in the early part of the 20th century emphasised a social science that ignored or sidelined a social reality deeply marked by race and class; see, for instance, Vitalis (2015: 1–24). However, many academics in the same universities, including Columbia, refused to toe the dominant line on social issues that informed the university.

[5] For Dewey's social involvement in New York, see Ryan (1995).

[6] Ambedkar told the *New York Times* in 1932 that 'the best friends I have had in my life were some of my classmates at Columbia and my great professors, John Dewey, James Shotwell, Edwin Seligman and James Harvey Robinson' (Columbia University 1995).

[7] The insights obtained through these studies made the Webbs the leading founders of LSE to emphasise concrete empirical studies to assess social conditions based on verifiable data. The school sought to investigate social and economic problems, particularly poverty and economic inequality, to further the Fabian aim of bettering society, focusing on research on issues of poverty, inequality and related issues. The Webbs argued that poverty is preventable and can be reduced,

and social cooperation can be enhanced through adequate and effective social services and public control. One of the initial objectives of the LSE was to renew the training of Britain's political and business elite, on the assumption that they were exposed to inadequate teaching and research (see Dahrendorf 1995).

[8] Numerous Dalit autobiographies are replete with poignant accounts of such quotidian practices. See Valmiki (1997), also Tulsiram (2012) (both in Hindi). One of the best attempts to grapple with this social reality is Geetha (2009).

[9] For an account of the social existence of working masses in suburban Bombay in the early 20th century, see Chandavarkar (1994); see also Chandavarkar (2004).

[10] C. B. Khairmode (1953–55) highlights the themes of both 'devotionalism' and 'penury' in his 12 volumes of Ambedkar's biography (in Marathi). See in particular volumes 1 and 2.

[11] Ambedkar's work, *What Congress and Gandhi Have Done to the Untouchables* (1945), captures these concerns very vividly.

[12] Two works are worth mentioning in this context: Rattu (1997) and Beltz and Jondhale (2004).

[13] The debate between Ambedkar and Gandhi following the publication of *The Annihilation of Caste* (Ambedkar 1979a) was mainly procedural, dwelling on the nature of the data, the framework employed for investigation, and the kind of disposition that is suited to different kinds of investigation.

[14] A second edition of this volume was published under the title *Pakistan or the Partition of India* (Ambedkar 1990).

[15] In this study, Ambedkar sometimes draws attention to what he deems the unsavoury side of Muslim behaviour, such as religious fanaticism, the hold of religion on Muslim life, etc. However, we cannot conclude from this that he was anti-Muslim. He is, in fact, much more critical of Hindus and the Hindu leadership than he is of Muslim behaviour in this text.

[16] At its Lahore session in 1940, the Muslim League, led by Mohammad Ali Jinnah, took the stand that the Muslims of India were a separate nationality and demanded a separate state for them. The Indian National Congress, however, insisted that Indians, irrespective of their religious affiliation, shared a thick world in common and formed a single nationality. Ambedkar discussed the stances of the two parties in *Thoughts on Pakistan*, published a few months after the Lahore resolution. He tried to assess the strengths and weaknesses of their respective claims without taking a definitive stand on the question. In the second edition of the book, retitled *Pakistan or the Partition of India*, Ambedkar added a section to present his own views 'on the various issues involved in the problem of Pakistan' (Ambedkar 1990: 1). He justified these changes in the introduction to this edition, arguing that he had advanced a set of arguments in *Thoughts on Pakistan* without stating his own position. He also refers to the political impact of the book; how both Gandhi and Jinnah cited it when they met in Shimla in 1945; and how the book had proved to be a mirror of the 'Indian political what is what'. About his disposition, he said it was not necessarily dispassionate but above prejudice, and that he strove to construct a 'perfectly accurate' and 'suggestive picture' of the situation (*ibid.*: 2).

[17] I am using the concept of oppression the way Iris Marion Young does in *Justice and the Politics of Difference* (1990).

[18] In *What Congress and Gandhi Have Done to the Untouchables* (1945), Ambedkar presents this contention as the dividing line between his and Gandhi's approaches to the matter.

[19] The studies by Gail Omvedt (1966), Rosalind O'Hanlon (1985) and Eleanor Zelliot (1996), among others, testify to this.

²⁰ One such important campaign site is the National Campaign on Dalit Human Rights (www.ncdhr.org.in). It made a major intervention at the Durban Conference in 2001.

²¹ For an early account, see Hardtmann (2009).

²² See, for instance, Ambedkar Age Collective (2015).

²³ The Ambedkar-related literature cited here is mainly from the 1990s onwards (studies available in English). For earlier literature, see Rodrigues (2002: 535–52).

²⁴ *Dr Babasaheb Ambedkar: Writings and Speeches*, vols 1–21, published by the Government of Maharashtra, Department of Education, from 1979 to 2003. The same committee has brought out other collections related to Ambedkar. The Ministry of Social Welfare and the Ministry of External Affairs, Government of India, have reprinted volumes 1–17 from the Government of Maharashtra series.

²⁵ Rakesh Sinha, one of the ideologues of the RSS, has argued that Ambedkar's 'canvas was much bigger and the role was epochal. "Nation building" can be considered his core project' (2015: 21). The *Organiser* published a special issue on 17 April 2016 in commemoration of the 125th birth anniversary of Ambedkar under the title 'Ultimate Unifier, Dr Ambedkar'. The *Economic and Political Weekly* has highlighted this process of 'rebranding' and co-option through extensive comments; see, for instance, Teltumbde (2015).

²⁶ This added significance is on account of the construction of the Buddha–Ambedkar legacy through manifold representations in song, dance, artefacts, painting, design, etc.

²⁷ In anti-caste writings and imagery, particularly in southern India, Ravana, whom Rama killed in the epic battle of the *Ramayana*, is increasingly seen as thwarting Aryan dominance and the primacy of caste. Similarly, the so-called demon king Mahisha, whom Durga slew, has emerged as a non-Brahmin hero.

²⁸ The relationship between 'village Buddhism' and intellectual and soteriological Buddhism has been explored by Fitzgerald (1988, 1994).

²⁹ In *Viramma*, one of the very powerful portrayals of a Dalit woman that provides a graphic account of the quotidian workings of caste and untouchability, the agency of a Dalit woman and her zest for life stand out (Viramma and Racine 2000). Tulsiram's *Murdahiya* (2012) focuses on the reproduction of social relations within a village economy informed by untouchability and the growing up of an Untouchable boy in this setting. An ardent Marxist perspective informs this account. Its sequel, *Manikarnika* (Tulsiram 2014), highlights the specific marginality that an Untouchable young man experiences in a large and well-known university setting, as well as the hopes and solidarities it engenders. Ambedkar does not figure prominently in these accounts.

³⁰ Anupama Rao takes this stand in her work on the Dalit movement in Maharashtra, arguably one of the best documentations of the movement (see A. Rao 2009).

³¹ For a vivid account of this see, Channa and Mencher (2013).

³² An inkling of this may be had in Satyanarayana and Tharu (2009, 2013).

³³ Over the years, other disadvantaged groups have been extended preferential consideration in public employment and/or higher education but not in legislative representation. The proportion of such benefits has also remained fairly low compared to their share in the population on account of the legal ceiling of 50 per cent on all reservations.

³⁴ In a large number of his writings, Mehta has drawn attention to the seminal role that Ambedkar played in including the subaltern masses within the framework of constitutional democracy.

³⁵ His most important studies in this area include his PhD dissertation at Columbia

University, *The Evolution of Provincial Finance in British India* (1925), and his DSc thesis at London School of Economics, *The Problem of the Rupee* (1923).

[36] Uday S. Mehta (2010), however, argues that Indian constitutional debates threw up precisely such an idea, an idea that pitted itself against the colonial charge of Indian fragmentariness, drawing its justification from it. He sees the invocation of this idea as revolutionary, a break from history and time, making the political foundational to the reimagination of the life of the nation. Such an imagination of power, he argues, limits the domain of liberty, towards which paradoxically the anti-colonial movement was directed.

[37] Power institutionalised in the concept of *kshatra* has been an issue of continued debate and deep contention in India. It is kshatra which wields *danda* (coercive power). The sustenance of dharma, or ethical life, is dependent on who wields the danda and how.

[38] The work of Ziauddeen Barani, particularly the *Fatwa-i-jahandari*, and Abul Fazl, particularly the *Ain-i-Akbari*, are significant in this regard.

[39] Nationalist thought and the conception of the political owe much to the hostile 'othering' of the colonial state in India. Eventually, when the nationalist leaders had to exercise power, they simply caved in to the demands of the state, as they had thought over it little. It is the state which had the last laugh, rather than those who wanted to tear it apart. It was people like Ambedkar, and probably Rammanohar Lohia, who developed an alternative mode of formulating the idea of the 'common' and ascribing authoritative significance to it.

[40] There was broad agreement across differences that the Vedic period and the epics represented the high tide of Indian culture. Thinkers such as Ranade, Tilak, Bankim Chandra Chattopadhyaya, and Jawaharlal Nehru broadly converged on this issue.

[41] They include: *Who Were the Shudras? How They Came to Be the Fourth Varna in Indo-Aryan Society* (1946b); *The Untouchables: Who Were They and How They Came to be Untouchables?* (1948); 'The Rise and Fall of Hindu Women: Who Is Responsible for It?' (1951); 'Revolution and Counter-Revolution' (1987a); and *Riddles in Hinduism* (1987b).

References

Abraham, P. 2002. 'Notes on Ambedkar's Water Resources Policies', *Economic and Political Weekly*, 37(48): 4772–74.

Acharya, A. 2008. 'Affirmative Action for Disadvantaged Groups: A Cross-constitutional Study of India and the US', in Rajeev Bhargava (ed.), *Politics and Ethics of the Indian Constitution*, pp. 267–94. New Delhi: Oxford University Press.

Ambedkar, B. R. 1923. *The Problem of the Rupee*. London: King & Co.

———. 1925. *The Evolution of Provincial Finance in British India*. London: King & Co.

———. 1945. *What Congress and Gandhi Have Done to the Untouchables*. Bombay: Thacker & Co.

———. 1946a. *Pakistan, or the Partition of India*, 3rd edn. Bombay: Thacker & Co.

———. 1946b. *Who Were the Shudras? How They Came to Be the Fourth Varna in Indo-Aryan Society*. Bombay: Thacker & Co.

———. 1948. *The Untouchables: Who Were They and How They Came to Be Untouchables?* New Delhi: Amrit Book Co.

———. 1951. 'The Rise and Fall of Hindu Women: Who Is Responsible for It? *Mahabodhi*, May–June.

———. 1979a. *Annihilation of Caste*, in *Dr. Babasaheb Ambedkar: Writings and Speeches*, vol. 1, pp. 23–96. Bombay: Education Department, Government of Maharashtra.

————. 1979b. 'Ranade, Gandhi and Jinnah', in *Dr. Babasaheb Ambedkar: Writings and Speeches*, vol. 1, pp. 211–40. Bombay: Education Department, Government of Maharashtra.

————. 1987a. 'Revolution and Counter-revolution', in *Dr. Babasaheb Ambedkar: Writings and Speeches*, vol. 3. Bombay: Education Department, Government of Maharashtra.

————. 1987b. *Riddles in Hinduism* in *Dr. Babasaheb Ambedkar: Writings and Speeches*, vol. 4. Bombay: Education Department, Government of Maharashtra.

————. 1990. *Pakistan or the Partition of India* in *Dr. Babasaheb Ambedkar: Writings and Speeches*, vol. 8. Bombay: Education Department, Government of Maharashtra.

————. 2011. *The Buddha and His Dhamma: A Critical Edition*, eds Aakash Singh and A. Verma. New Delhi: Oxford University Press.

————. 2014. *Annihilation of Caste: The Annotated Critical Edition*, ed. S. Anand. New Delhi: Navayana. With an introduction by Arundhati Roy titled 'The Doctor and the Saint'.

Ambedkar Age Collective. 2015. *Hatred in the Belly: Politics behind the Appropriation of Dr Ambedkar's Writings*. Hyderabad: The Shared Mirror.

Anderson, Perry. 2012. *The Indian Ideology*. Gurgaon: Three Essays Collective.

Arya, Rajendra Kumar, and Tapan Choure. 2014. 'The Economic Thoughts of Dr. Bhimrao Ambedkar with respect to Agriculture Sector', *Developing Country Studies*, 4(25): 84–86.

Baxi, Upendra. 1995. 'Emancipation and Justice: Babasaheb Ambedkar's Legacy and Vision', in Upendra Baxi and Bhikhu Parekh (eds), *Crisis and Change in Contemporary India*, pp. 122–49. New Delhi: Sage.

————. 2008. 'Outline of a Theory of Practice of Indian Constitutionalism', in Rajeev Bhargava (ed.), *Politics and Ethics of the Indian Constitution*, pp. 92–118. New Delhi: Oxford University Press.

Bayly, Chris. 2012. *Recovering Liberties: Indian Thought in the Age of Liberalism and Empire*. Cambridge: Cambridge University Press.

Bellwinkel-Schempp, Maren. 2007. 'From Bhakti to Buddhism: Ravidas and Ambedkar', *Economic and Political Weekly*, 42(23): 2177–83.

Beltz, Johannes. 2005. *Mahar, Buddhist and Dalit: Religious Conversion and Socio-political Emancipation*. New Delhi: Manohar.

————. 2015. 'The Making of a New Icon: B.R. Ambedkar's Visual Hagiography', *South Asian Studies*, 31(2): 254–65.

Beltz, Johannes, and Surendra Jondhale (eds). 2004. *Reconstructing the World: B. R. Ambedkar and Buddhism in India*. New Delhi: Oxford University Press.

Béteille, André. 2012. *Democracy and Its Institutions*. New Delhi: Oxford University Press.

Bharadwaj, V. 2015. 'Ambedkar's Paradox of Differentiation: Language, Nation and Recognition of States in Post-colonial India', *Indian Economic and Social History Review*, 52(1): 79–108.

Bhattacharya, Sabyasachi, and Yagati Chinna Rao (eds). 2017. *The Past of the Outcaste: Readings in Dalit History*. New Delhi: Orient BlackSwan.

Cabrera, Luis. 2017. '"Gandhiji, I Have No Homeland": Cosmopolitan Insights from B. R. Ambedkar, India's Anti-caste Campaigner and Constitutional Architect', *Political Studies*, 65(3): 576–93.

Cháirez-Garza, J. F. 2014. 'Touching Space: Ambedkar on the Spatial Features of Untouchability', *Contemporary South Asia*, 22(1): 37–50.

Chandavarkar, Rajnarayan. 1994. *The Origins of Industrial Capitalism in India: Business Strategies and the Working Class in Bombay, 1900–1940*. Cambridge: Cambridge University Press.

————. 2004. 'From Neighbourhood to Nation: The Rise and Fall of the Left in Bombay's

Girangaon in the Twentieth Century', in Meena Menon and Neera Adarkar, *One Hundred Years, One Hundred Voices: The Millworkers of Girangaon: An Oral History*. Calcutta: Seagull Books.

Channa, Subhadra Mitra, and Joan P. Mencher. 2013. *Life as a Dalit: Views from the Bottom on Caste in India*. New Delhi: Sage.

Chatterjee, Partha. 2004. *The Politics of the Governed*. New Delhi: Oxford University Press.

Columbia University. 1995. 'Bust of Ambedkar Given to Columbia', *Columbia University Records*, 21(9), 3 November, http://www.columbia.edu/cu/record/archives/vol21/vol21_iss9/record2109.21.html (accessed on 8 July 2018).

Dahrendorf, Ralf. 1995. *LSE: A History of the London School of Economics and Political Science, 1895–1995*. Oxford: Oxford University Press.

Dara, Krishnaswamy. 2009. *The Idea of Minority in Ambedkar's Thought: Equality and Differential Rights*. Germany: VDM Verlag Publishers.

Deshpande, Ashwini. 2011. *The Grammar of Caste*. New Delhi: Oxford University Press.

Dhar, Anup, and Anjan Chakrabarti. 2017. 'Sriniketan Encounters Ambedkar: Whither the Political', *Economic and Political Weekly*, 52(19): 53–56.

Fiske, Adele, and Christoph Emmrich. 2004. 'The Use of Buddhist Scriptures in Dr B. R. Ambedkar's *The Buddha and His Dhamma*', in Johannes Beltz and Surendra Jondhale (eds), *Reconstructing the World: B. R. Ambedkar and Buddhism in India*, pp. 100–122. New Delhi: Oxford University Press.

Fitzgerald, Timothy. 1988. 'Buddhism and Social Change in Maharashtra', *Bulletin of Humanities*, 18: 50–73.

———. 1994. 'Buddhism in Maharashtra: A Tri-partite Analysis – A Research Report', in A. K. Narain and D. C. Ahir (eds), *Dr. Ambedkar, Buddhism and Social Change*, pp. 17–34. New Delhi: Buddhist World Press.

Fuchs, Martin. 2001. 'A Religion for Civil Society? Ambedkar's Buddhism, the Dalit Issue and the Imagination of Emergent Possibilities', in Vasudha Dalmia, Angelika Malinar and Christof Martin (eds), *Charisma and Canon: Essays on the Religious History of the Indian Subcontinent*, pp. 250–73. New Delhi: Oxford University Press.

———. 2004. 'Ambedkar's Buddhism', in T. N. Madan (ed.), *Indian Religions*, pp. 307–25. New Delhi: Oxford University Press.

———. 2017. 'Dhamma and Common Good: Religion as Problem and Answer, Ambedkar's Critical Theory of Social Relationality'. Unpublished manuscript.

Fuchs, Martin, and Antje Linkenbach. 2003. 'Social Movements', in Veena Das (ed.), *The Oxford India Companion to Sociology and Social Anthropology*, pp. 1524–64. New Delhi: Oxford University Press.

Galanter, Marc. 1984. *Competing Equalities: Law and Backward Classes in India*. New Delhi: Oxford University Press.

Gandhi, Rajmohan. 2015. 'Independence and Social Justice: The Ambedkar Gandhi Debate', *Economic and Political Weekly*, 56(15): 35–44.

Ganguly, Debjani. 2005. *Caste, Colonialism and Countermodernity: Notes on a Postcolonial Hermeneutics of Caste*. New York: Routledge.

———. 2008. 'Vernacular Cosmopolitanism: World Historical Readings of Gandhi and Ambedkar', in D. Ganguly and J. Docker (eds), *Rethinking Gandhi and Nonviolent Relationality: Global Perspectives*, pp. 245–64. London: Routledge.

Geetha, V. 2007. *Patriarchy: Theorizing Feminism*. Kolkata: Stree.

———. 2009. 'Bereft of Being: The Humiliations of Untouchability', in Gopal Guru (ed.), *Humiliation: Claims and Context*, pp. 95–107. New Delhi: Oxford University Press.

Gokhale, Pradeep. (ed.). 2008. *The Philosophy of B. R. Ambedkar*. Pune: Sugava.

Govind, Rahul. 2018. 'Ambedkar's Lessons, Ambedkar's Challenges', *Economic and Political Weekly*, 53(4): 80–92.

Gramsci, Antonio. 1971. *Selections from the Prison Notebooks*, eds Quentin Hoare and Geoffrey Nowell Smith. London: Lawrence and Wishart.

Gupta, Charu. 2016. *The Gender of Caste: Representing Dalits in Print*. Ranikhet: Permanent Black.

Guru, Gopal. 1991. 'Hinduisation of Ambedkar in Maharashtra', *Economic and Political Weekly*, 26(7): 339–41.

————. 1997. *Dalit Cultural Movement and Dialectics of Dalit Politics in Maharashtra*. Mumbai: Vikas Adhyayan Kendra.

————. 2001. 'The Language of Dalit-Bahujan Political Discourse', in Ghanshyam Shah (ed.), *Dalit Identity and Politics*, pp. 97–107. New Delhi: Sage.

————. 2002. 'Ambedkar's Idea of Social Justice', in Ghanshyam Shah (ed.), *Dalits and the State*, pp. 40–50. New Delhi: Concept Publishing.

————. 2007. 'Twentieth Century Discourse on Social Justice: A View from Quarantine India', in Sabyasachi Bhattacharya (ed.), *Development of Modern Indian Political Thought and the Social Sciences*, pp. 221–38. New Delhi: Oxford University Press.

———— (ed.). 2009. *Humiliation: Claims and Context*. New Delhi: Oxford University Press.

————. 2010. 'Social Justice', in Niraja Gopal Jayal and Pratap Bhanu Mehta (eds), *The Oxford Companion to Politics in India*, pp. 361–80. New Delhi: Oxford University Press.

————. 2015. 'Bhimrao Ambedkar's Modern Moral Idealism: A Metaphysics of Emancipation', in Jonardon Ganeri (ed.), *The Oxford Handbook of Indian Philosophy*, pp. 737–49. New Delhi: Oxford University Press.

————. 2017. 'Ethics in Ambedkar's Critique of Gandhi', *Economic and Political Weekly*, 52(15): 95–100.

Guru, Gopal, and Sundar Sarukkai. 2012. *The Cracked Mirror: Debate on Experience and Theory*. New Delhi: Oxford University Press.

Hardtmann, Eva-Maria. 2009. *The Dalit Movement in India: Local Practices, Global Connections*. New Delhi: Oxford University Press.

Hasan, Zoya. 2009. *Politics of Inclusion: Castes, Minorities, and Affirmative Action*. New Delhi: Oxford University Press.

Irudayam, A., J. P. Mangubhai and J. G. Lee. 2006. *Dalit Women Speak Out: Violence against Dalit Women in India*, vols 1–2. New Delhi: National Campaign on Dalit Human Rights.

Jadhav, Narendra. 1991. 'Neglected Economic Thought of Babasaheb Ambedkar', *Economic and Political Weekly*, 26(15): 980–82.

————. 1992. *Dr. Ambedkar's Economic Thoughts and Philosophy*. Mumbai: Popular Prakashan.

————. 2003. *Outcaste: A Memoir. Life and Triumphs of an Untouchable Family in India*. New Delhi: Penguin.

———— (ed.). 2013. *Ambedkar Speaks: 301 Seminal Speeches*, vols 1–3. New Delhi: Konark.

————. 2014. *Ambedkar: Awakening India's Social Conscience*. New Delhi: Konark.

————. 2015. *Ambedkar: An Economist Extraordinaire*. New Delhi: Konark.

Jaffrelot, C. 2005. *Dr Ambedkar and Untouchability: Analysing and Fighting Caste*. New Delhi: Permanent Black.

Jaoul, Nicolas. 2006. 'Learning the Use of Symbolic Means: Dalits, Ambedkar Statues and the State in Uttar Pradesh', *Contributions to Indian Sociology*, 40(2): 175–207.

Jessop, Bob. 1992. 'Fordism and Post-Fordism: A Critical Reformulation', in Michael Storper and Allen J. Scott (eds), *Pathways to Industrialization and Regional Development*, pp. 42–62. London: Routledge.

John, Mary. 2008. 'Reservations and the Women's Movement in Twentieth Century India', in Meena Dhanda (ed.), *Reservations for Women*, pp. 29–58. New Delhi: Women Unlimited.

Joseph, M. T. 2012. 'Buddhists: The Political Dynamics of Conversion and Caste', in R. Robinson (ed.), *Minority Studies: Oxford India Series on Contemporary Society*, pp. 138–59. New Delhi: Oxford University Press.

———. 2013. 'Dr B. R. Ambedkar's Views on Religion: A Sociological Analysis', *Indian Anthropologist*, 43(2): 43–44.

———. 2014. '"Identity Religion" or "Religion for Engagement in Civil Society": A Study of the Ambedkarite Buddhists of Maharashtra', in V. K. Annakutty et al. (eds), *He Is Not Far from Any of Us: Festschrift for Hans-Juergen Findeis*, pp. 551–57. Bonn: Bier'sche Verlagsanstalt.

Kadam, K. N. 1997. *The Meaning of Ambedkarite Conversion to Buddhism and Other Essays*. Mumbai: Popular Prakashan.

Kamble, Baby. 2009. *The Prisons We Broke* [Marathi title: *Jina Amucha*]. New Delhi: Orient BlackSwan.

Keer, Dhananjay. 1982. *Dr Ambedkar: A Memorial Album*. Bombay: Popular Prakashan.

Khairmode, C. B. 1953–55. *Babasaheb Ambedkaranche Charitra*, vols 1–2. Pune: Sugava Publication.

Komath, Rajesh. 2015. 'Ambedkar Will Teach the Nation from His Statues', *Economic and Political Weekly*, 50(25–26): 48–58.

Kshirsagar, Ramchandra K. 1992. *Political Thought of Dr Babasaheb Ambedkar*. New Delhi: Intellectual Publishing House.

Kumar, Aishwarya. 2010. 'Ambedkar's Inheritances', *Modern Intellectual History*, 7(2): 391–415.

———. 2015. *Radical Equality: Ambedkar, Gandhi, and the Risk of Democracy*. Palo Alto, CA: Stanford University Press.

Kumar, Vivek. 2006. *India's Roaring Revolution: Dalit Assertion and New Horizons*. New Delhi: Gagan Deep.

McCaughey, Robert A. 2003. *Stand, Columbia: A History of Columbia University in the City of New York, 1754–2004*. New York: Columbia University Press.

Mehta, Pratap Bhanu. 2010. 'What Is Constitutional Morality?', *Seminar*, 615: 17–18.

Mehta, Uday S. 2010. 'Constitutionalism', in Niraja Gopal Jayal and Pratap Bhanu Mehta (eds), *The Oxford Companion to Politics in India*, pp. 15–27. New Delhi: Oxford University Press.

Mendelsohn, Oliver. 2014. *Law and Social Transformation in India*. New Delhi: Oxford University Press.

Mendelsohn, Oliver, and Upendra Baxi. 1994. *The Rights of Subordinated Peoples*. New Delhi: Oxford University Press.

Mendelsohn, Oliver, and Marika Vicziany. 1998. *The Untouchables: Subordination, Poverty and the State in Modern India*. Cambridge: Cambridge University Press.

Michael, S. M. 1999. *Dalits in Modern India*. New Delhi: Vistaar.

Moon, Vasant. 2001. *Growing Up Untouchable in India*. New Delhi: Vistaar.

Mukherjee, A. 2009. 'B. R. Ambedkar, John Dewey and the Meaning of Democracy', *New Literary History*, 40(2): 345–70.

Murugkar, Lata. 1991. *Dalit Panther Movement in Maharashtra: A Sociological Appraisal*. London: Sangam Books.

Nagaraj, D. R. 2010. *The Flaming Feet and Other Essays: The Dalit Movement in India*. New Delhi: Permanent Black.

Namdeo, Nimgade. 2010. *In the Tiger's Shadow*. New Delhi: Navayana.

Nanda, Meera. 2001. 'A "Broken People" Defend Science: Reconstructing the Deweyan Buddha of India's Dalits', *Social Epistemology*, 15(3): 335–65.

———. 2007. *Breaking the Spell of Dharma and Other Essays*. Gurgaon: Three Essays Collective.

————. 2016. 'Ambedkar's Gita', *Economic and Political Weekly*, 51(49): 39–45.

Narain, A. K., and D. C. Ahir (eds). 1994. *Dr Ambedkar, Buddhism and Social Change.* New Delhi: Buddhist World Press.

Narula, S. 2008. 'Equal by Law, Unequal by Caste: The "Untouchable" Condition in Critical Race Perspective', *Wisconsin International Law Journal*, 26: 255–343.

Natrajan, Balmuri, and Paul Greenough (eds). 2009. *Against Stigma: Studies in Caste, Race and Justice Since Durban.* Hyderabad: Orient BlackSwan.

O'Hanlon, Rosalind. 1985. *Caste, Conflict and Ideology: Mahatma Jotirao Phule and Low Caste Protest in Nineteenth-Century Western India.* Cambridge: Cambridge University Press.

Omvedt, Gail. 1966. *Cultural Revolt in a Colonial Society: The Non-Brahman Movement in Western India.* Kolhapur: Scientific Socialist Education Trust.

————. 1994. *Dalits and the Democratic Revolution: Dr Ambedkar and the Dalit Movement in Colonial India.* New Delhi: Sage.

————. 2003. *Buddhism in India: Challenging Brahmanism and Caste.* New Delhi: Sage.

————. 2004. 'Confronting Brahmanic Hinduism: Dr Ambedkar's Sociology of Religion and Indian Society', in Johannes Beltz and Surendra Jondhale (eds), *Reconstructing the World: B.R. Ambedkar and Buddhism in India*, pp. 49–62. New Delhi: Oxford University Press.

————. 2008. *Ambedkar: Towards an Enlightened India.* New Delhi: Penguin.

Pai, Sudha. 2013. *Dalit Assertion.* New Delhi: Oxford University Press.

Palshikar, Suhas. 2015. 'Ambedkar and Gandhi', *Economic and Political Weekly*, 50(15): 45–50.

Parekh, Bhikhu. 2015. 'Ambedkar and the Pursuit of Fraternity', in *Debating India: Essays on Indian Political Discourse*, pp. 93–124. New Delhi: Oxford University Press.

Pawar, Urmila. 2008. *The Weave of My Life: A Dalit Woman's Memoirs*, trans. Maya Pandit. Kolkata: Stree.

Queen, Christopher S. 1994. 'Ambedkar, Modernity and the Hermeneutics of Buddhist Liberation', in A. K. Narain and D. C. Ahir (eds), *Dr Ambedkar, Buddhism and Social Change*, pp. 99–122. New Delhi: Buddhist World Press.

————. 2004. 'Ambedkar's Dhamma: Source and Method in the Construction of Engaged Buddhism', in Johannes Beltz and Surendra Jondhale (eds), *Reconstructing the World: B. R. Ambedkar and Buddhism in India*, pp. 132–50. New Delhi: Oxford University Press.

Queen, Christopher S., and Sallie B. King (eds). 1996. *Engaged Buddhism: Buddhist Liberation Movements in Asia.* New York: SUNY Press.

Rao, Anupama. 2009. *The Caste Question: Dalits and the Politics of Modern India.* Berkeley: University of California Press.

————. 2011. 'Minority and Modernity: B. R. Ambedkar and Dalit Politics', in Saurabh Dube (ed.), *Modern Makeovers: Oxford Handbook of Modernity in South Asia*, pp. 93–109. New Delhi: Oxford University Press.

Rao, Yagati Chinna (ed.). 2009. *Dividing Dalits: Writings on Sub-categorisation of Scheduled Castes.* New Delhi: Rawat.

Rathore, Aakash Singh. 2017. *Indian Political Theory: Laying the Groundwork for Svaraj.* London: Routledge.

Rattu, Nanak Chand. 1997. *Last Few Years of Dr Ambedkar.* Wolverhampton: Amrit Publishing House.

Rege, Sharmila. 2013a. 'Introduction', in Sharmila Rege (ed.), *Against the Madness of Manu: B. R. Ambedkar's Writings on Brahmanical Patriarchy.* New Delhi: Navayana.

————. 2013b. *Writing Caste/Writing Gender: Narrating Dalit Women's Testimonies.* New Delhi: Zubaan.

Rodrigues, Valerian. 1993. 'Making a Tradition Critical: Ambedkar's Reading of Buddhism', in Peter Robb (ed.), *Dalit Movements and the Meanings of Labour in India*, pp. 299–336. New Delhi: Oxford University Press.

———— (ed.). 2002. *The Essential Writings of B. R. Ambedkar*. New Delhi: Oxford University Press.

————. 2017a. 'Ambedkar as a Political Philosopher', *Economic and Political Weekly*, 52(15): 101–7.

————. 2017b. 'A Radical Conception of Democracy: Its Promise and Limits', in Avatthi Ramaiah (ed.), *Contemporary Relevance of Ambedkar's Thoughts*, pp. 24–49. Jaipur: Rawat.

Roy, Arundhati. 2014. 'The Doctor and the Saint', introduction to B. R. Ambedkar, *Annihilation of Caste: The Annotated Critical Edition*, ed. S. Anand. New Delhi: Navayana.

————. 2015. 'All the World Is a Half Built Dam', *Economic and Political Weekly*, 50(25): 165–73.

Ryan, Alan. 1995. *John Dewey and the High Tide of American Liberalism*. London: W. W. Norton & Company.

Sangharakshita. 1986. *Ambedkar and Buddhism*. Glasgow: Windhorse.

Sarangi, Asha. 2006. 'Ambedkar and the Linguistic States: A Case for Maharashtra', *Economic and Political Weekly*, 41(2): 151–57.

Satyanarayana, K., and Susie Tharu (eds) 2009. *No Alphabet in Sight: New Dalit Writings from South India*. New Delhi: Penguin.

———— (eds). 2013. *Steel Nibs Are Sprouting: New Dalit Writing from South India*. New Delhi: Harper Collins.

Shah, Ghanshyam (ed.). 2001. *Dalits and State*. New Delhi: Concept Publishing.

———— (ed.). 2002. *Dalit Identity and Politics*. New Delhi: Sage.

Sharma, R. S. 1958. *Shudras in Ancient India*. New Delhi: Motilal Banarsidass.

Shourie, Arun. 1997. *Worshipping False Gods: Ambedkar, and the Facts Which Have Been Erased*. New Delhi: ASA Publications.

Siddalingaiah. 2006. *Uru Keri: Atmakathana* (Kannada). Bangalore: Ankit.

Sinha, Rakesh. 2015. 'Dr Ambedkar: A Misunderstood National Leader', *Organiser*, 7 June.

Skaria, Ajay. 2015. 'Ambedkar, Marx and the Buddhist Question', *South Asia*, 38(3): 450–65.

Skof, Lenart. 2011. 'Pragmatism and Deepened Democracy: Ambedkar between Dewey and Unger', in Akeel Bilgrami (ed.), *Democratic Culture: Historical and Philosophical Essays*, pp. 122–42. New Delhi: Routledge.

Soske, J. 2013. 'The Other Prince: Ambedkar, Constitutional Democracy and the Agency of Law', in Cosimo Zene (ed.), *The Political Philosophies of Antonio Gramsci and B.R. Ambedkar: Itineraries of Dalits and Subalterns*, pp. 59–71. London: Routledge.

Stroud, Scott R. 2016. 'Pragmatism and the Pursuit of Social Justice in India: Bhimrao Ambedkar and the Rhetoric of Religious Reorientation', *Rhetoric Society Quarterly*, 46(1): 5–27.

Tartakov, Gary Michael. 1994. 'Art and Identity: The Rise of a New Buddhist Imagery', in A. K. Narain and D. C. Ahir (eds), *Dr Ambedkar, Buddhism and Social Change*, pp. 175–94. New Delhi: Buddhist World Press.

————. 2012. *Dalit Art and Visual Imagery*. New Delhi: Oxford University Press.

Teltumbde, Anand. 2015. 'In Thy Name Ambedkar', *Economic and Political Weekly*, 50(40): 10–12.

————. 2016. *Mahad: The Making of the First Dalit Revolt*. New Delhi: Aakar.

Thorat, Sukhdeo. 1998. *Ambedkar's Role in Economic Planning and Water Policy*. New Delhi: Shipra.

————. 2002. 'Oppression and Denial', *Economic and Political Weekly*, 37(6): 572–78.

————. 2006. *Ambedkar's Role in Economic Planning, Water and Power Policy*. New Delhi: Shipra.

————. 2009. *Dalits in India: Search for a Common Destiny*. New Delhi: Sage.

Thorat, Sukhdeo, and Aryama (eds). 2007. *Ambedkar in Retrospect: Essays on Economics, Politics and Society*. New Delhi: Rawat.

Thorat, Sukhdeo, and Paul Attewell. 2007. 'The Legacy of Social Exclusion', *Economic and Political Weekly*, 42(41): 4141–45.

Thorat, Sukhdeo, and Amaresh Dubey. 2012. 'Has Growth Been Socially Inclusive during 1993–94 to 2009–10', *Economic and Political Weekly*, 47(10): 43–53.

Thorat, Sukhdeo, and Narendra Kumar (eds). 2009. *B. R. Ambedkar: Perspectives on Social Exclusion and Inclusive Policies*. New Delhi: Oxford University Press.

Thorat, Sukhdeo, and K. Newman (eds). 2010. *Blocked by Caste: Economic Discrimination in Modern India*. New Delhi: Oxford University Press.

Tulsiram. 2012. *Murdahiya* (Hindi). New Delhi: Rajkamal Prakashan.

————. 2014. *Manikarnika* (Hindi). New Delhi: Rajkamal Prakashan.

Vajpeyi, Ananya. 2012. *Righteous Republic: The Political Foundations of Modern India*. Cambridge, MA: Harvard University Press.

Valmiki, Omprakash. 1997. *Joothan*. New Delhi: Rajkrishna.

Verma, Vidhu. 1999. 'Colonialism and Liberation: Ambedkar's Quest for Distributive Justice', *Economic and Political Weekly*, 34(39): 2804–10.

————. 2010. 'Reinterpreting Buddhism: Ambedkar on the Politics of Social Action', *Economic and Political Weekly*, 45(49): 56–65.

Viramma, Josiane Racine and Jean-Luc Racine. 2000. *Viramma: Life of a Dalit*, trans. Will Hobson. New Delhi: Social Science Press.

Visweswaran, Kamala. 2010. *Un/Common Cultures: Reason and Rearticulation of Cultural Difference*. Durham: Duke University.

Vitalis, Robert. 2015. *White World Order, Black Power Politics*. Ithaca: Cornell University Press.

Vundru, Raja Sekhar. 2018. *Ambedkar, Gandhi and Patel: The Making of India's Electoral System*. New Delhi: Bloomsbury.

Waghmore, Suryakant. 2013. *Civility against Caste: Dalit Politics and Citizenship in Western India*. New Delhi: Sage.

Wankhede, Harish. 2008. 'The Political and the Social in the Dalit Movement Today', *Economic and Political Weekly*, 43(6): 50–57.

Weisskopf, Thomas. 2004. *Affirmative Action in the United States and India: A Comparative Perspective*. London: Routledge.

Young, Iris Marion. 1990. *Justice and the Politics of Difference*. Princeton, NJ: Princeton University Press.

Zelliot, Eleanor. 1996. *From Untouchable to Dalit: Essays on the Ambedkar Movement*. Delhi: Manohar.

————. 2004. *Ambedkar's World: The Making of Babasaheb and the Dalit Movement*. New Delhi: Navayana.

————. 2008. 'Understanding Dr B. R. Ambedkar', *Religion Compass*, 2(5): 804–18.

Zene, Cosimo (ed.). 2013. *The Political Philosophies of Antonio Gramsci and B. R. Ambedkar: Itineraries of Dalits and Subalterns*. London: Routledge.

1

Ambedkar's Legacy

Bhikhu Parekh

I would like to begin by thanking the Vice Chancellor for inviting me to deliver the inaugural Ambedkar Memorial Lecture (AML). Infant mortality among our institutions is fairly high and I like to hope that the AML will prove to be an exception.

The lecture gives me the opportunity to express my great admiration for and deep gratitude to Babasaheb for the way in which he shook up the Hindu society and shaped the destiny of our country. He was one of the finest social and political thinkers of 20th-century India. From extremely humble origins he rose to be one of the most highly educated Indians of all time, with an MA and a PhD from Columbia University, a DSc from the London School of Economics, and a bar-at-law from Gray's Inn in London. Ambedkar wrote more scholarly books than almost all other Indian leaders, and that without the forced leisure offered by the prisons in which many of our leaders wrote their books. His collected *Writings and Speeches* run into over a dozen bulky tomes and still exclude much. He kept thinking and writing until the very end of his life. *The Buddha and His Dhamma*, on which he was working a day before he died, is a text of considerable scholarship. It explores Buddhism from an activist perspective, gives new meanings to the ideas of *karma*, *dukkha* and *nirvana*, and represents an ingenious attempt to construct a social and political philosophy on Buddhist foundations.[1]

Ambedkar was also one of the major architects of our Constitution. Even when the drafting committee lost half of its seven members through death, resignation or long absences, and they were not replaced, Ambedkar carried on the work with great energy. The Constitution was obviously framed within the limits set by the consensus prevailing in the Constituent Assembly and did not represent Ambedkar's own long-held views on several important issues. However, it could not have been what it is without his labours.[2] He drafted and piloted the Hindu Code Bill through the Parliament and, although the delay in its passage disappointed him and led to his resignation, what emerged in the end carries his imprint. He also set up many institutions of higher education, more in fact than many other leaders, and saw to it that they flourished, represented his views on education, and contributed to the uplift of the Dalits.

Thanks to the causes for which he fought and the way in which he did so, he was much underrated and even maligned during his lifetime. Gandhi did not seek him out until August 1931, nearly eight years after Ambedkar had entered public life,[3] and in his first interview took a highly patronising attitude towards him. He even mistook him for a Brahman and discovered his real identity only during the Second Round Table Conference![4] Pandit Nehru did not meet him until as late as October 1939 and did not think much of him.

M. R. Jaykar thought that Ambedkar was a 'destructive' force bent on creating what Jaykar called 'Maharistan', a separate land for the Mahars along the lines of Pakistan. Subhas Bose expressed a widely held view when he observed that 'Ambedkar had his leadership thrust upon him by the benign British government because his services were necessary to embarrass the nationalist leaders' (2012: 29). Some other leaders of the independence movement were even more unkind in their assessment of him. Even today some continue to see him as a person who could not look beyond the interests of the Dalits and rise above his sense of deep personal hurt and pain, and who as a result allowed his great talents to be misdirected, even distorted, by bitterness and hatred against the Hindu society. Some resent that, like Jinnah, he made no personal sacrifices for the independence struggle, including going to prison, and was a political freerider.

As I shall argue later, these and other criticisms are largely misguided. However, Ambedkar was not an easy person to understand and deal with. His intellectual arrogance and dismissive attitude towards those who disagreed with him, hurt and alienated them. He was in my view unduly aggressive in his attacks on Gandhi, and did not fully appreciate either Gandhi's complex style of operation or the constraints under which he had to function. If Dhananjay Keer is right, he was, in private conversations, dismissive of Pandit Nehru, whom he called a 'fourth standard boy', viewing him as just another Brahman (Keer 1971: 327). He was equally dismissive of Jinnah and several other leaders, including the communists, whom he dismissed as 'mostly a bunch of Brahman boys' (Harrison 1960: 190–91).

While Ambedkar bears some responsibility, much of the underestimation of his great contribution was and is due to several factors such as a deep and sometimes wilful misunderstanding of his ideas, casteist prejudices and resentment against his attack on Hindu society and Gandhi. Although Ambedkar worked closely with the British government and lobbied it to get what he wanted, he was not at all its stooge, as is seen in his vigorous attacks on it. He was no less patriotic or committed to India's independence than any other leader, including the Mahatma, as he showed by his words and actions on several occasions. Unlike many of them, however, he drew an important distinction between independence of the country and independence of its people. An independent India might mean little more than transfer of power from one set of masters to another, and make no difference to and even worsen the condition of the oppressed classes, especially the Dalits. Ambedkar therefore insisted that the latter could not be expected to throw their weight behind the independence movement unless the Congress made an explicit commitment to their cause and to the institutional safeguards and policies that it entailed. Ambedkar rightly argued that what he called the 'weapon of nationalism' was often a device to equate majority interests with those of the country as a whole, and was used all too freely to suppress minority interests and views. He was also right to argue that the question of untouchability was not just a social question like child marriage or a ban on widow remarriage, as Gandhi and others had argued. It was fundamentally an economic and a political problem requiring a radical restructuring of not just the Hindu but the Indian society as a whole.

While for these and other reasons Ambedkar unjustifiably remained a controversial and grudgingly recognised figure for long, the pendulum swung to the other extreme from the 1980s onwards. Largely as a result of the better historical perspective offered by the passage of time, continuing atrocities against Dalits even 60 years after independence, and the growing political visibility of the Other Backward Classes and those sections of the Scheduled Castes who have acquired status and dignity because of, among other things, the reservation policy, Ambedkar is now almost deified in some circles. Across many states in India his statues, portraits, posters bearing his image, and schools and parks named after him have proliferated. Finely framed photos of him in immaculate western attire are lovingly garlanded and placed in prominent places. In some parts of India there is even a competition to build bigger and bigger statues of Ambedkar. All this is perfectly understandable and, within limits, even proper. It is one way in which long-suppressed communities express their pride in the achievements of someone who did so much for them at such a high personal cost. It is also a way of establishing collective solidarity among them and firming their resolve to fight for a better life. In any case, such worshipful adoration is not limited to Ambedkar. Gandhi has long been a recipient of it, and it is consistent with the traditional Hindu practice of honouring men and women of great qualities or *vibhuti*s, remembering them daily, and drawing inspiration and strength from them.

While the adoration of Babasaheb is understandable, it has its dangers. It turns him into a Dalit hero and diminishes his stature as a great national and international thinker and leader. It is striking that as his life was coming to an end, another great minority leader in the shape of Martin Luther King was emerging in the United States. Both had similar concerns, and Ambedkar was in some respects a greater thinker than Martin Luther King. And yet, while King enjoys an iconic international status, much admired and even revered by those fighting for minority rights, Ambedkar sadly remains a local and a rather dated figure – partly because of India's low political and intellectual visibility in the world, and partly because of the tendency to reduce him to a Dalit spokesman.

Uncritical adoration of Ambedkar also puts him on a pedestal and discourages a critical engagement with his thought. It denies his historicity, the fact that he thought and acted in a particular historical context, and turns him into a timeless figure whose ideas do not need to be contextualised and adapted to changing historical circumstances and challenges. Above all, uncritical adoration does him grave injustice. Ambedkar was and saw himself as an 'iconoclast' who took 'nothing for granted or on authority', and demanded 'a consistent and critical interrogation of inherited dogmas'. As he remarked in 1933 when he was praised by his grateful followers in superlative terms, 'you are deifying a common man like you. These ideas of hero worship will bring ruin on you if you do not nip them in the bud' (Keer 1971: 234). He put it even more bluntly in his winding-up speech in the Constituent Assembly on 25 November 1949:

> [I]n India, Bhakti or what may be called the path of devotion or hero-worship, plays a part in its politics unequalled in magnitude by the part it plays in the politics of any other country in the world. Bhakti in religion may be a road to the salvation of the soul. But in politics, Bhakti or hero-worship is a sure road to degradation and to eventual dictatorship.[5]

As Ambedkar said of the Buddha, the latter was not a '*Mokshadata* (Saviour)' but a '*Margadata* (Guide)' (Keer 1971: 420). The Buddha only showed the way, and left it to his followers to decide on the basis of their own experiences whether the destination was right, the path correct, and at what pace to travel along it. It was because, among other things, Buddhism was non-authoritarian and non-dogmatic that Ambedkar said that he was drawn to it in the first instance.

What strikes even a casual student of Ambedkar's thought is his unquenchable intellectual curiosity and the concomitant intellectual restlessness which led him to change his views on several subjects when required to do so by arguments or evidence. In the 1920s, he thought that the *Manusmriti* sanctioned, even enjoined untouchability. Hence on 24 December 1927, he burnt a copy of it – it must be said not alone but joined by a Brahman friend G. N. Sahasrabuddhe. As he thought further about the historical causes of untouchability and undertook a detailed study of the *Dharmashastra*s, he took a different view. He concluded in his book *The Untouchables: Who Were They and Why They Became Untouchables?* (Ambedkar 1990a) that the *Manusmriti* was written around the 2nd century CE whereas untouchability began around 400 CE. He concluded that the *Manusmriti* could not have sanctioned, let alone enjoined, untouchability. Ambedkar associated the rise of untouchability with a ban on cow slaughter and beef eating, neither of which was prohibited by Manu.

Ambedkar changed his views on several other subjects as well, such as whether independent India should opt for socialism and whether that should be enshrined in the Constitution, the importance of temple entry, and whether the Untouchables should engage in a nationwide civil rights movement. He also changed his views on whether they should campaign for their own segregated villages and how they should cooperate with other backward castes. This does not mean that he was inconsistent or confused, though that too was the case sometimes, but rather that as his insights into a problem deepened or the historical circumstances changed, he appreciated that his goals and principles called for different strategies.

I suggest that the best and fairest way to respond to Ambedkar is neither to marginalise nor to deify him, neither to dehistoricise him nor to reduce him one-dimensionally to Gandhi's sparring partner, but rather to judge him on his own terms and in his context, and critically interrogate his thoughts and actions. We need to elucidate, re-examine and even question the questions he asked, challenge what is dubious in his answers, and build on his profound insights. Such an approach shows that we consider him big enough both to be worthy of a critical engagement and to continue to be relevant to our concerns. This is how Gandhi, Nehru and others are being currently reassessed, and this is how Ambedkar himself approached the Buddha. Ambedkar deserves nothing less, and that is what I shall do in the rest of the lecture.

Untouchability

Although Ambedkar's intellectual interests covered a wide range, including religion, philosophy, political theory, sociology, social psychology, history, and economics, the practice of untouchability was at their centre. It was the prism through which he looked at almost all other issues, and he brought to it his deep knowledge of various disciplinary perspectives. Untouchability was obviously a form of inequality, but it did not obtain anywhere else except in Hindu India. It was a product of the uniquely Hindu form of inequality as embodied in the caste system, and could not be analysed in terms of a general theory of equality. Ambedkar therefore analysed untouchability at two levels. First, he inquired into the nature of the caste system, how it differed from other kinds of inequality, how it was sustained for centuries and shaped the Hindu self-consciousness. Second, he asked why it had taken the perverse form of untouchability, whether this was adventitious or integral to the caste system, and how it originated, was maintained and could be ended. He also asked the related question of why caste Hindus did not feel ashamed of or even embarrassed by it and had continued with it for centuries without significant opposition. Indeed, Ambedkar was struck by the fact that there was no traditional discourse on the history and development of untouchability during the entire history of Hindu society.[6] He thought that this was so because Hindu thinkers had taken it for granted and assumed that it was self-evident or a part of the natural order of things. Ambedkar asked why they held such a view.

While inequality, be it social, political or economic, was to be found in all societies, the caste system represented a historically unique form. For Ambedkar, it had six distinguishing features.[7] First, it was based on birth, was articulated into self-contained groups, and adhered to their members until their death. Second, although they were self-contained, castes were not distinct social groups like classes and tribes, but were embedded in and formed part of a wider social whole which graded and related them in a hierarchical manner. Third, the ideas of purity and pollution lay at the centre of hierarchy. Hierarchy itself was common to many unequal societies, but hierarchy involving purity and pollution was unique to the Hindus. Higher castes felt defiled and their social standing was lowered in their own and others' eyes when they came into contact with the lower castes, especially in such culturally significant areas as commensality and marriage.

Fourth, each caste had a name which gave it 'fixity and continuity and individuality' (Ambedkar 1987: 145). It was unambiguously bounded, internally homogeneous, and had public marks of identification. Indeed, it was carried over into the surnames of its members who could not therefore hide their caste and hope to pass off as someone else. All this made caste inequality easy to enforce, difficult to escape, and highly oppressive.

Fifth, inequality in Hindu society was minutely graded. It was not like two or more unequal or sharply separated groups facing each other in their stark hostility, but rather an elaborate and carefully delineated hierarchy based on 'an ascending scale of reverence and a descending scale of contempt' (Das 1963: 23–24). Every caste had some subcastes that were superior and others that were inferior to it. Even the Untouchables had their Untouchables and their own internal hierarchy. Since the contours of inequality were blurred, it did not appear to be as stark and unbearable as it did in a slave-owning or a racially or class-divided society. Furthermore, every caste could live with its inferior status and the contempt it entailed because it found compensating satisfaction in enjoying and exercising its superiority over others. Such a minutely graded system made it exceedingly difficult for the oppressed groups to unite, let alone take a holistic view of and mount a challenge to the entire social order.

Finally, according to Ambedkar, caste profoundly shaped the Hindu's identity or sense of himself. The Hindu defined himself in terms of his place in the hierarchy, and could not think of and relate to others without viewing them as superior or inferior to him. And if he ever sought to establish some kind of equality with them, he did so by seeing them as superior in some and inferior in some other real or imaginary respects. For the Hindus, society meant status, and the latter, hierarchy. These ideas had struck such deep roots in their psyche, argued Ambedkar, that they were incapable of entertaining the interrelated ideas of unique individuals sharing a common humanity. Since Hindu inequality was not just a matter of status but of identity, and was tied up not only with the social but also personal identity, it required the resources of not only sociology but also social psychology to unravel its nature and sources of appeal.

For Ambedkar, inequality in this exceedingly complex form was the pervasive organising principle of Hindu society. As he put it on several occasions in moments of despair, 'Hindu, thy name is inequality.' Inequality was neither incidental nor a historical excrescence but lay at the very heart of Hindu society. To be a Hindu was to belong to a particular caste, and to belong to a particular caste was to get caught up in the system of inequality. One could not escape the system of inequality without escaping the caste, and one could not do the latter without ceasing to be a Hindu.

In Ambedkar's view, the practice of untouchability was a necessary product of the caste system. The latter involved hierarchy and the Untouchables occupied its lowest rung. It involved purity and pollution, and the Untouchables represented the most impure group, contact with whom brought the highest degree of pollution. In these and other ways, untouchability was the concentrated expression of the spirit informing the caste system. The two were inseparable, and untouchability could not be abolished without abolishing the caste system and radically restructuring the very basis of the Hindu social order. In some of his writings Ambedkar thought that the caste system could be eradicated within the Hindu framework.[8] In others he argued the opposite, that since Hindu society was structured in terms of the caste system, to destroy the latter was to put an end to Hindu society itself. It would create a new society but that would not be Hindu. Ambedkar's view made sense only if one accepted his identification of Hindu society with the caste system, and defined the term 'Hindu' in a particular way. There are no good reasons to accept such a view, and Ambedkar offered none. Vivekananda, the older Gandhi and many others defined the 'Hindu' in civilisational or cultural terms, as someone sharing a particular view of man and the world and the tradition that had grown up around it, and did not think that the end of the caste system spelt the end of Hindu society, identity or even religion.

Ambedkar traced the beginnings of untouchability to around 400 CE. He was not sympathetic to the widely held view that the Untouchables were pre-Aryans, and explained the origin of the practice in terms of the Brahmanic struggle for domination. Marginalised groups, who had converted to Buddhism and whom Ambedkar called 'broken men', resisted Brahmanic hegemony and attempts to bring them within the Brahmanic fold. The frustrated Brahmans devised ways of humiliating them by placing them outside the mainstream society and preventing all forms of contact with them. The 'broken men' ate meat, including beef. Although the Brahmans themselves used to eat meat, including beef, they became vegetarians and made it a mark of purity and status. Over time, meat, especially beef eating, became the strongest taboo, and those engaged in meat eating came to be seen as the lowliest of the lowly or the Untouchables (Ambedkar 1946). As to why the 'broken' men did not give up beef, Ambedkar argued that they were extremely poor and survived on dead cows, which no one else would eat. Like other Hindu practices, the ban on beef was a case of culture being used to legitimise domination. The motive behind the practice of untouchability was political, namely to subdue the 'broken men', eliminate potential competitors for resources, and to declare a war on the Buddhists.

Ambedkar explained the continuation of untouchability for nearly 1,600 years in terms of three mutually reinforcing factors, namely the ideological, the economic and the political. Untouchability was sanctioned by religion or religiously inspired culture, and the entire weight of the structure of dominant beliefs and practices was deployed to convince its victims that this was their 'inescapable destiny'. Caste Hindus also commanded economic power, which they used freely to exploit the Untouchables and keep them in degrading and dehumanising conditions.

As Ambedkar put it, untouchability was a 'gold mine' for caste Hindus (Ambedkar 1945: 196). It fed their pride and sense of self-importance, provided cheap labour and a pool of people to do the dirty work for them, and avoided competition by limiting the supply of talented people. The economically powerful castes not only defined merit in a convenient manner but also systematically discouraged it. Finally, caste Hindus controlled the institutions of government and terrorised people into obedience by imposing the most horrendous forms of punishment on even the smallest deviations from caste norms and the feeblest expressions of defiance. For Ambedkar, the three agencies of control worked in tandem and formed part of an oppressive system.

Ambedkar asked why caste Hindus never protested against or even felt embarrassed by the practice of untouchability. In his view several factors played a part, of which three were particularly important. Caste Hindus shared the dominant ideology and its justification of untouchability in terms of the doctrine of karma. Their economic and political interests too pulled in the same direction. The third factor had to do with the absence of what Ambedkar called 'public conscience', that is, 'conscience which becomes agitated at every wrong, no matter who is the sufferer' and leads an individual to join the struggle to remove that wrong (Ambedkar 1976: 3; see also Kshirsagar 1991: 61).[9] Public conscience is the product of what Ambedkar called 'fellow feeling' or a 'sense of fraternity'. Ambedkar sometimes used this term widely to refer to a sense of concern for one's fellow human beings, and sometimes narrowly to refer to the 'disposition' to identify with and feel concerned about other members of one's society. Thanks to the caste system, which fragmented society into self-contained and mutually indifferent groups, such a fellow feeling did not develop among Hindus. Indeed, the very term 'Hindu society' was an oxymoron because there could be no 'society' in the absence of shared sympathies. In India, people were treated with contempt, yet it did not sicken an Indian with disgust and 'rouse his sense of justice and fair play'; 'his humanity [did] not rise in protest' at 'his fellow men treated as being less than human' (Das 1963: 34–35).[10] Being entrenched in a way of thinking that reduced human beings to their membership of particular castes, caste Hindus could not see the Untouchables as human beings like them, let alone as fellow members of a shared community. Not surprisingly, they rarely took interest in, let alone campaigned against, the degrading and inhuman status of Untouchables.

Ambedkar's analysis of how untouchability had been enforced for so long shaped his views on how it could be ended. For him, its eradication amounted to nothing less than a social revolution, a radical restructuring of the very foundations of Hindu society. It involved 'relentless struggle', an uncompromising, determined, organised, and occasionally even violent movement by the Untouchables. The struggle was to be mounted at various levels among the Untouchables as well as within the wider society. Its ultimate goal was to acquire political power, 'the key to all social progress' (Keer 1971: 405). Political power consisted in controlling the institutions of the state and using them to create an egalitarian and casteless society. He told his followers, 'You should realise what our object is. . . . It is not fighting for a few jobs and for a few conveniences. It is the biggest cause that we have ever cherished in our hearts. That is to see that we are recognised as the governing community' (quoted in Jaffrelot 2003: 105).

The Untouchables needed to see through and break the hold of the dominant ideology, and realise that their lowly status was not their destiny or a result of their karma, but the product of an externally imposed unjust and exploitative system. As Ambedkar observed on several occasions, slaves must be convinced that they need not be slaves,[11] that their slavery can be ended, and that it is within their power to do so, as the necessary first step towards their emancipation.

For Ambedkar, it was equally important that the Untouchables should develop a sense of self-respect, which alone could generate a 'divine discontent' with their current condition and a burning desire to change it (Keer 1971: 143).[12] He stressed that '[s]elf-respect is a most vital factor in life. Without it man is a mere cipher' (*ibid.*: 127). The Untouchables must realise that they were fighting not so much to 'improve' their material condition as to regain their 'honour' and 'dignity' and reclaim the 'title deeds' of their humanity that had been taken away by their masters (Ambedkar 1945: 281; see also Ambedkar 1946; Keer 1971: 143).

Dignity and self-respect were acquired, Ambedkar argued, not just by claiming that one is a human being like others, but rather through a struggle in which one asserts them, fights for and makes sacrifices for them, mobilises one's moral and emotional energies behind them, and tests and intensifies one's commitment to them. In such a struggle one also develops a sense of agency and power, builds up one's strength, stands up to one's opponent, proves to him that one will not be taken for granted or dismissed as inconsequential, and secures his respect and recognition. Every gain in the struggle further reinforces one's self-respect and generates the energy to continue and intensify the struggle. As Ambedkar put it, 'it is out of hard and relentless struggle that one derives strength, self-respect, self-confidence and recognition' (quoted in Keer 1971: 127).

For Ambedkar it was important that the Untouchables should also take a critical look at themselves, and ensure that they were worthy of respect in their own and others' eyes. Over the centuries they had developed 'evil habits' and 'bad ways of living', ugly customs, passivity, a sense of helplessness, the tendency to pursue their narrow self-interest, hierarchical gradation among themselves, low ambition, and so on (Keer 1971: 143). Thanks to all this, they were unable to unite for a common cause. More importantly, they were unable to respect themselves and command the respect of others. They had developed deep, subtle and often unconscious self-contempt, and half-believed that they were worthy of nothing better. While fighting against the wider society, and as a necessary precondition of it, the Untouchables must also fight against themselves and acquire the intellectual and moral qualities of free men.

Ambedkar thought that while concentrating on their own struggle, the Untouchables should also aim higher. Like Marx, by whom he was deeply influenced, he thought that the Untouchables constituted a negative class, a concentrated expression of the evil of the prevailing system, and should become the vanguard of the oppressed groups in Hindu society.[13] They should form alliances with them and set up a political party committed to the cause of social and political revolution. This is what his Independent Labour Party and later the Republican Party of India, in their own different ways, were meant to do. Once the oppressed groups were united, the state was theirs to take. As he put it in one of his optimistic moods: 'the scheduled castes and the backward classes form majority of the population of the country. There is no reason why they should not rule the country. All that is necessary is to organise for the purpose of capturing political power which is your own because of adult suffrage' (Choudhary 1987: 288).

Ambedkar argued that the Untouchables could not change Hindu society without forcing caste Hindus to rethink their traditional beliefs and practices. Like all privileged groups, the latter would not do so unless they felt convinced that the Untouchables would not rest until the prevailing social order was radically restructured, and they must change quickly or face the consequences. For Ambedkar, a 'sense of crisis' brought about changes in days which slow reformist pressure could not achieve in decades. 'The great defect in the policy of least resistance and silent infiltration of rational ideas', on which, in his view, Gandhi and the liberals respectively relied, 'lies in this that they do not *compel* thought, for they do not produce crisis' (Ambedkar 1945: 136). The Untouchables were to create a sense of crisis by concentrating on strategically significant issues, mounting carefully planned struggles throughout the country, and refusing to be satisfied with concessions and compromises. While violence was to be scrupulously avoided, some violence might regrettably occur. Ambedkar thought that such a determined challenge to Hindu society was bound to trigger intense introspection and throw up radical movements for change. That should in turn pave the way for a democratic polity in which all citizens, including the Untouchables, enjoyed equal civil and political rights. For Ambedkar, democracy was the sine qua non of the liberation of oppressed groups.

Universal adult franchise marked an important step towards the empowerment of the Untouchables, but it was no more than that. Although the Untouchables would have the vote, they were a minority and powerless before the Hindu majority, which could use the 'weapon' of democracy to continue to oppress them. In a mature liberal democracy, the dangers of this happening were minimised by two factors. First, the majority was 'political', that is, made up of shifting alliances and interest groups, and hence contingent and fluid. Second, it had at least some fellow feeling for the oppressed minorities and could be depended upon to pay due regard to their interests. These conditions did not obtain in India where the majority was 'communal', and hence permanent and entrenched, and did not share a fellow feeling with the minorities. It was a 'vested corporate interest group', a 'closed governing class', before which the minorities, including the Untouchables, were totally helpless. Ambedkar wondered how to cope with such a situation.

Ambedkar was convinced that the principle of majority rule lay at the heart of democracy and must be respected by anyone who valued democracy. The ideas of consociational democracy, giving the minorities a veto in certain areas, etc., that had been tried out in other societies were either unfamiliar or did not find favour with him. He thought that the best way to guard against majority domination was to devise an institutional mechanism under which the majority could not rule on its own and needed to accommodate and share power with the minorities, that is, to make it what Ambedkar called a 'relative majority'. He suggested two devices, the policy of reservation which was already in force in colonial India, and weighted representation in the legislature.

The policy of reservation involved giving the Untouchables a proportionate number of constitutionally guaranteed seats in the legislature. Similar reservations in the administrative structure gave them some control over the formulation and implementation of government policy and generated confidence in the legitimacy of the political system (Ambedkar 1978: 47). Reservations in educational institutions, especially their higher echelons, ensured that they were able to acquire the qualifications necessary to rise to the highest positions in all areas of life.

Since the danger of minorities being systematically outvoted by the majority remained, Ambedkar proposed weighted representation to reduce the gap between the numbers of majority and minority representatives. The majority was to be given fewer seats than its number warranted, and the minorities were to receive more seats than their proportion in the population, their share being in 'inverse proportion to their social standing, economic position and educational condition' (Ambedkar 2010: 50). Ambedkar proposed that the Hindus who constituted 55 per cent of the population should have 40 per cent of the seats in the legislature. By contrast, Muslims, who were just over 28 per cent of the population, were to be allocated 32 per cent of the seats; the Scheduled Castes, which were just over 14 per cent of the population, 20 per cent of the seats, and so on. Under this scheme, the majority still remained a majority, but it was no longer an 'absolute' majority. As to why it would accept such a reduced political representation and power, Ambedkar argued that it would otherwise face minority resistance and likely civil unrest.

Although weighted representation did not violate the democratic principle of 'one person one vote', it did violate the equally, perhaps even more important principle of the equal value of votes, or what Ambedkar called 'one vote one value'.[14] Ambedkar had no well-worked-out answers to this criticism. He invoked a rather different group-based view of democracy, according to which democracy implied a form of government in which all major groups were involved in the exercise of power as part of the process of self-government, and the majority did not rule supreme. In a communally based society like India, Ambedkar argued, democracy needed to take account of and balance both the individual and the group. Since the system of weighted representation checked the abuse of majority power, involved minorities in the government of the country, and safeguarded their interests and rights, it was wholly consistent with the basic principles of democracy.

For Ambedkar, this was not however the end of the matter. While it placed minorities at the centre of the political system, there was always the danger that their representatives might not reflect the views and promote the interests of their communities. Since they depended on the majority community to get elected, they had every reason to court its goodwill even at the expense of their own communities. The only way to guard against this was to ensure that they were rooted in and fully accountable to their communities. Ambedkar thought that a separate electorate for the Untouchables was the best way to achieve this, and made it one of the major planks of his political strategy.

Ambedkar insisted on a separate electorate for the Untouchables at the Second Round Table Conference, and secured it in the Communal Award of 1932. When Gandhi opposed it and embarked on an indefinite fast, Ambedkar accepted a compromise in which the number of Untouchable representatives was to be increased and they were to be elected in two stages. In the primary election, four Untouchable candidates were to be selected by the Untouchables themselves. Whoever secured a majority in the general election based on a joint constituency was the winner.[15] Although Ambedkar accepted the compromise, he continued to feel unhappy about it because, among other things, the election of 'Untouchable' representatives still remained in the hands of the Hindu majority. He began to demand that the winning candidate must secure at least a certain percentage of 'Untouchable' votes, but found no support from the Congress.

Ambedkar refused to give up and made his last attempt to secure such a provision by getting Sardar Nagappa to introduce a bill in the Constituent Assembly (Kshirsagar 1991: 89). Since the term 'separate electorate' aroused deep fears, Nagappa said that his bill involved a 'qualified joint electorate'. It required that a successful Scheduled Caste parliamentary candidate should secure not less than 35 per cent of the Scheduled Caste votes. Voters were to be issued two ballot papers, a white one for the general and a coloured one for the Scheduled Caste voter. Candidates securing the minimum of 35 per cent of the Scheduled Caste votes were 'qualified' candidates. Their general votes were then counted, and the one who got the majority was declared elected. Nagappa's bill met with strong opposition and was dropped, to Ambedkar's great disappointment. As he watched the developments in post-independence India, he became bitterly disillusioned with the careerism and hunger for power of the Scheduled Caste representatives and their neglect of their communities.[16] It seems that he was no longer sure that a separate electorate would remedy the situation.[17] He urged the Scheduled Castes to choose their representatives with great care, to remain vigilant, and to bring sustained pressure on them by means of organised campaigns.

Conversion

As we saw earlier, Ambedkar took the view that untouchability was bound up with the caste system, that the latter was integral to Hindu society, and that the Untouchables would always remain such within the Hindu social framework. Ambedkar however did not entirely give up on Hindu society, and hoped to transform it from within. He knew it had thrown up some reformist movements in the past, and Gandhi's vigorous campaign against untouchability from 1932 onwards gave him some hope. He supported temple entry satyagrahas, joined the popular Ganapati festivities in Bombay, arranged inter-caste dinners and meetings, and so on. Increasingly, he came to feel that all this was leading nowhere. Gandhi's Harijan Sevak Sangh, which replaced the more radical Anti-Untouchability League, had neither involved the Untouchables in their own emancipation nor confronted caste prejudices. Even that alarmed the orthodox Hindus who intensified their resistance, and Gandhi's life was threatened. Although Gandhi's campaign created a widespread reformist movement among caste Hindus, Ambedkar concluded that Hindu society was not going to change and that the Untouchables had no hope of achieving social equality with caste Hindus. As he remarked, '[T]here can be a better or a worse Hindu. But a good Hindu there cannot be' (Ambedkar 1979a: 89).

From around 1935 onwards, Ambedkar began to lose interest in temple entry satyagrahas and fostering better inter-caste understanding, and talked of converting to another religion. Pride and self-respect also played a part, for he felt that a religion that had for centuries treated him and other Untouchables so abominably did not deserve their allegiance. As he said on several occasions, he was born a Hindu but did not wish to die as one. Since one was a Hindu by virtue of birth and not because of subscription to certain beliefs, he could cease to be one not by rejecting his religion publicly, but only by explicitly joining another religious community.

Ambedkar asked what religion the Untouchables and even perhaps other backward castes should convert to. He ruled out Christianity and Islam, the choice of many of them in the past, on several grounds. They were not themselves free of the caste system. Since they had engaged in mass conversions, they had to accommodate the caste consciousness of their new converts, and were deeply infected by it. Furthermore, Christianity was tainted by its colonial connections, and Islam had been caught up in the surcharged inter-communal conflict and the movement for the separate state of Pakistan. Ambedkar also thought that these two religions tended to 'denationalise' converts. Religion in India was not a matter of personal belief but of membership of a particular community. It was bound up with the latter's history, culture, language, customs, rituals, way of life, etc., and had a strong cultural and political content. In other words, it was inseparable from and signified a particular nationality. Rather surprisingly, Ambedkar took the view that Islam and Christianity were 'foreign' religions, so that converts to them did not in their own and especially in others' eyes feel an integral part of their mainstream. For the Untouchables to convert to either of them was to step out of not only the Hindu society but also the Indian nation, something they did not and should not wish to do.

Ambedkar's choice of religions was limited to Sikhism and Buddhism. He was sympathetic to the former in his early years, but felt that it too was tainted by the caste system, though not to the same extent as Christianity and Islam, and carried a good deal of Hindu philosophical and cultural baggage. Ambedkar preferred Buddhism, a truly 'egalitarian' religion which had emerged in direct opposition to Hinduism without losing its Indian roots. It placed morality, not God, at its centre, and concentrated on man and the righteousness between man and man, rather than problems of the soul and of worship as other religions did. Since Ambedkar took the view that the Untouchables were originally Buddhists and had been made Untouchable because of that, conversion to Buddhism also had the advantage of returning them to their roots and settling old historical scores with Brahmanic Hinduism.[18] Ambedkar converted to Buddhism himself and encouraged thousands of his followers to do the same in Nagpur in October 1956, nearly 20 years after he had first raised the subject. He called the conversion 'rebirth', an end to one form of life and mode of existence and the beginning of another.

Vision of India

Ambedkar's vision of independent India was articulated in terms of the three interrelated ideas of liberty, equality and fraternity, familiar since the French Revolution, but to which he gave somewhat different meaning and content. The three together constituted the basis of what he called 'social democracy'. Liberty stood for self-determination and the ability to lead a life of one's choice. It required a constitutionally guaranteed body of legal, political and other rights, and depended on a well-structured state. Equality meant 'one man one value'. It involved not only political equality or equality of rights and political power, but also social and economic equality. For Ambedkar, the three were closely related and reinforced each other. Social equality referred to equality of status and respect based on acknowledgement of the equal dignity and shared humanity of all human beings, and absence of all forms of discrimination, hierarchy and exclusion in their formal and informal relations. Economic equality meant equality of life chances and a broad equality of economic power. It required that no individual or group should be at the mercy of others or exercise disproportionate power over them. Ambedkar called this 'socialism' or 'state socialism' and distinguished it from the welfare state, which provided a safety net to the poor but took little interest in the inequality of economic power and wealth. The programme of the Independent Labour Party on which the Scheduled Castes fought the elections of 1937 comprised a planned economy, nationalisation of key industries, including land and insurance, extensive state-supported industrialisation, agricultural cooperatives, land mortgage banks, guaranteed workers' rights, land settlement and public works to relieve unemployment, free and compulsory primary education, and so on. Ambedkar wanted socialism to be enshrined in the Constitution so as to place it 'beyond the reach of a parliamentary majority to suspend, amend or abrogate it' (Ambedkar 1978: 46). He later changed his views on both constitutionally mandated socialism and limits on parliamentary democracy. He diluted the socialist programme when he set up the Republican Party of India. And in the course of commending the draft Constitution to the Constituent Assembly on 19 November 1948, he said that it had 'deliberately' excluded a particular economic system in order to respect genuine differences of views on the subject and to allow the electorate to make its own choice.

For Ambedkar, fraternity meant fellow feeling, a sense of concern for and an active interest in the well-being of other human beings, especially the members of one's own society. Although he sometimes used the term interchangeably with a sense of nationhood, for the most part he thought that fraternity presupposed and grew out of the latter. Nationhood, or what following John Stuart Mill he also called a 'sentiment of nationality', implied a sense of common belonging, 'a longing not to belong to any other group' but this one, a 'corporate sentiment of oneness which makes those charged with it to feel that they are kith and kin' (Ambedkar 1979c: 143). Unlike nationalism, which was exclusive, aggressive and collectivist, nationhood represented mutual identification and commitment and a sense of being at home with people inhabiting a common territorial unit. For Ambedkar, the sense of nationhood and the concomitant sentiment of fraternity fostered social cohesion, mutual trust, willingness to make sacrifices for others, and above all, what he called 'public conscience'.

For Ambedkar, fraternity gave depth to liberty and equality and realised them in areas lying beyond the reach of the law. Take something as basic as the rule of law, which is at the heart of liberty and equality. It requires that the law should be fair and non-discriminatory in its content and implementation. In the absence of fraternity, it could be procedurally correct and satisfy all the formal requirements of fairness, but so designed as to serve the interests of a particular group and oppress others. Even if a law was just in its content, the judges and the police might subvert it. Judges necessarily enjoyed some degree of discretion in all legal systems, and had to decide whom to accept as witnesses, how much credence to give to their testimony, what counted as evidence, how to weigh it up, and so on. They might use their discretion to the detriment of certain groups, particularly those with whom they did not identify and against whom they entertained ill-feeling. Similarly, when they despised certain groups, the police might falsify evidence, record things that were never said, frame false charges, and harass them in ways too subtle to prove.

By its very nature, argued Ambedkar, the law cannot deal with many areas of human conduct, and leaves the individual at the mercy of his fellow citizens. If a fellow passenger vacates his seat or mumbles abuses when a member of the despised group sits next to him, or when a man gives all too familiar excuses for not selling his property to a member of the minority community, or if a teacher slights or humiliates the latter, law offers the victim no protection. Many ordinary social relations in civil society are of this kind, and beyond the reach of the law. As Ambedkar put it:

> [A]ll this injustice and persecution can be perpetrated within the limits of the law. A Hindu may well say that he will not employ an Untouchable, that he will not sell him anything, that he will evict him from his land, that he will not allow him to take his cattle across his field, without offending the law in the slightest degree. In doing this he is only exercising his right. The law does not care with what motive he does it. . . .
>
> Such are the forces which are arrayed against the struggling Untouchables. There is simply no way to overcome them because there is no legal way of punishing a whole society which is organized to set aside the law. (Ambedkar 1989: 270–71)

For Ambedkar, then, liberty, equality and fraternity were inseparable. Without equality, liberty was precarious and at the mercy of the dominant group. Conversely, without liberty, equality led to uniformity and killed individuality, initiative and creativity. Without fraternity, both equality and liberty were 'no deeper than coats of paints'. They were denied to minority groups or limited to the narrow area of the state and not extended to civil society. Indeed, they did not then become a 'natural course of things' and constantly required 'a constable to enforce them'.[19] Conversely, fraternity was impossible in the absence of liberty and equality. The latter removed artificial barriers between individuals and groups, facilitated easy interactions between them, encouraged democratic participation, placed all on an equal footing, gave equal dignity and status to marginalised groups, and fostered a common sense of belonging.

It is hardly surprising that the Preamble to the Constitution of India, in the drafting of which Ambedkar played an important role, commits the country to 'secure' justice, liberty and equality to all its citizens and to 'promote among them all fraternity'. Ambedkar felt confident that if independent India remained true to these values, it would make a decisive break with its divisive and hierarchical past. As he said in a much applauded speech in Parliament on 17 December 1946:

> I know today we are divided politically, socially, economically. We are a group of warring camps, and I may even go to the extent of confessing that I am probably one of the leaders of such a camp. . . . With all our castes and creeds, I have not the slightest hesitation that we shall in some form be a united people.[20]

That, however, was not going to be easy. India contained a contradiction at its very heart. Its Constitution committed it to the great ideals of liberty, equality and fraternity, but all the three were largely absent in its daily life. The state and society pulled in opposite directions. Ambedkar put the point well in his important speech in the Constituent Assembly on 25 November 1949:

> On the 26th of January 1950, we are going to enter into a life of contra-dictions. In politics we will have equality and in social and economic life we will have inequality. In politics we will be recognising the principle of one man one vote and one vote one value. In our social and economic life, we shall, by reason of our social and economic structure, continue to deny the principle of one man one value. How long shall we continue to live this life of contradictions? How long shall we continue to deny equality in our social and economic life? If we continue to deny it for long, we will do so only by putting our political democracy in peril. We must remove this contradiction at the earliest possible moment or else those who suffer from inequality will blow up the structure of political democracy which this assembly has so laboriously built up.[21]

For Ambedkar, the contradiction could only be resolved by the state dominating society and moulding it in a particular direction. And since the values inspiring the state were all Western, it could do so only if it was led by a determined westernised elite. If the state became a hostage to society, as it had done for centuries in pre-modern India, and was led by men and women with no commitment to these values, Ambedkar saw no hope for the country.

Critical Appreciation

Ambedkar's thought was born in the crucible of experience and shows remarkable originality and intensity. As I observed earlier, he was primarily concerned with analysing the causes, modes of legitimation, mechanisms of oppression, and ways of eradication of the practice of untouchability in particular and the problem of inequality in general.

He rightly located untouchability within the larger discussion of inequality, and analysed the latter without losing sight of the specific form it had taken in Hindu society. His analysis of the graded nature of Hindu inequality is profound, and explains why it was largely taken for granted for centuries and made organised opposition difficult. He traced its cultural, economic and political roots and showed how they reinforced each other. He rightly argued that Hinduism had a strong inegalitarian core and was used to justify an oppressive social order. Ambedkar was right to argue that the social fragmentation brought about by the caste system militated against taking an overall view of the society and mounting a critique of it. This partly explains why, in the traditional Hindu literature on the subject, there is no systematic and comprehensive critique of either the caste system or even the practice of untouchability. The critique was first offered by the Buddhists, and even they were not as radical as they could have been.

So far as the eradication of untouchability is concerned, Ambedkar rightly stressed that the Untouchables were not and should not see themselves as its passive victims waiting for others to liberate them. They must take their destiny into their own hands and organise themselves for collective action. Ambedkar's great contribution lay in giving them a clear collective identity that they had hitherto lacked. He traced their origins and gave them a sense of historical continuity and depth. He highlighted the specificity of their experiences, offered them a vision of their place in India, and gave them a social and political identity. He traced their centuries-old struggles and linked their current struggle with others that had gone before. He mounted a powerful critique of the *Dharmashastra*s and gave the Untouchables a critical perspective on them. In these and other ways, he raised their collective self-consciousness and made them a distinct cultural and political subject. This extraordinary achievement has largely been responsible for the most welcome emergence of a distinct body of Dalit literature and perspective on history, Hinduism and India.

Unlike many radicals, Ambedkar did not hesitate to criticise the Untouchables themselves and urged them to put their own house in order. He stressed too that their struggle had to be conducted on several levels, including the ideological, the social, the political, and the economic. He saw with great clarity that their struggle for liberation was closely bound up with the struggles of other backward castes. He strove all his life to bring them together within a single political party, and rightly stressed the critical need for a radical economic programme.

Approaching democracy, equality, nationhood, the state, etc., from his unique perspective, Ambedkar was able to highlight, and offer new insights into, their neglected dimensions. More than any other Indian leader, he stressed the vital importance of social equality, and showed how in its absence political equality remained purely formal and little more than a set of state-derived rights. As he argued, social inequality humiliates its victims, denies their humanity, undermines their pride, ambition and self-respect, and disables them from fighting against it. It also profoundly distorts interpersonal relations and makes the lives of its victims a veritable nightmare. While political and even economic equality can facilitate social equality, they cannot by themselves create and sustain it. This was why

Ambedkar was highly critical of liberals and Marxists who respectively put their faith in political and economic equality, took a reductionist view of social equality, and failed to appreciate its specificity and complexity.

The idea of fraternity is neglected in much of modern, especially liberal, thought, and Ambedkar was right to stress its importance without embracing a narrow nationalism. As a victim of social inequality himself, he saw the role that fellow feeling plays in inspiring struggle against injustices. Although one can be inspired by an abstract commitment to the ideals of equality and justice, one's struggle acquires energy and tenacity when one is able to see the victims in their concreteness, identify with them, feel their pain and sorrow and make them one's own; in short, when one is guided by what Ambedkar called 'fellow feeling'. He was right to stress the role of moral emotions and reject a narrowly intellectualist view of moral and political life.

Ambedkar's analysis of the nation, with which he associated the idea of fraternity, is equally rich and suggestive.[22] A nation for him was not an abstraction, a transcendental entity hovering over its members. Rather, it was nothing other than its members in their intricate relations and interdependence. To serve the nation was nothing more and nothing less than to serve its members and promote their well-being. This is why Ambedkar felt that India's independence struggle could not be conducted in isolation from the internal struggle against its own oppressive social order. As he observed, the nation is not a primordial entity but a collective creation of its members, and has claims on them only to the extent that it includes them all in its self-understanding. Like Tagore and Gandhi, Ambedkar's concept of nationhood has a humanist orientation and is remarkably free from the collectivism, narrowness and aggressiveness generally associated with it.[23]

While much in Ambedkar's social and political thought is valuable and needs to be built upon, it has its limitations. I shall highlight three of these. First, Ambedkar relied too heavily on institutional mechanisms to protect and promote the interests of the Untouchables, and did not fully appreciate the importance of changing the moral culture of the wider society. To be sure, he said repeatedly that the 'Hindu mentality' needed to change, but did not explore how this was to be done and what it entailed. Not all his institutional mechanisms could make much difference to the plight of the Untouchables if the Hindu majority remained ill-disposed to them. The majority would not agree to these mechanisms in the first instance and would deal with the likely resistance ruthlessly, or accept and then subvert such institutions in all too familiar ways. A profound cultural and moral change was needed in Hindu society in order to deal with the humiliations and privations of the Untouchables. And that required mobilising its reformist resources and delegitimising untouchability. Since Gandhi saw this, he rightly concentrated on transforming Hinduism from within, and Ambedkar was wrong to dismiss his work. Gandhi created among caste Hindus a deep sense of shame and guilt and awakened them to the egalitarian strand within their religion.[24] It is, of course, more than likely that he would not have given the subject high priority without Ambedkar's criticism and pressure. However, the latter would not have made much headway without Gandhi's efforts either. The two played complementary roles, one concentrating on caste Hindus and the other on the Untouchables, one attacking untouchability from a moral and cultural perspective and the other from an economic and political angle.

A second limitation of Ambedkar's thought, which is closely related to the first, is that Ambedkar's approach suffered from a strong statist and elitist bias. He was right to emphasise the importance of political power, but wrong to think that the state provided answers to all of society's problems. Like many modernists, he drew too neat a contrast between state and society, seeing the former as a rational progressive agency and the latter as reactionary and blighted, and relied on the state to transform society. The state could not do so unless it was led by a westernised elite, of whom Ambedkar saw himself as a member. It is striking that he valued university education as highly as and sometimes even higher than primary and secondary education, and set up more colleges and institutions of higher education than schools. True to the logic of his position, Ambedkar once suggested that the caste system and untouchability could be eradicated summarily and comprehensively, if India could throw up its equivalent of Mustapha Kamal Pasha or even Mussolini![25]

This view is flawed. The state cannot be as neatly separated, let alone insulated, from society as Ambedkar imagines. A colonial state run by outsiders might stand above society but not a democratic one, and that too only up to a point. Furthermore, society is never as pliable and passive as Ambedkar thinks; it imposes constraints upon and can frustrate the state at countless points. For its part, the state is vulnerable to its own pathology, and can easily become remote, bureaucratic and authoritarian. Suspicious of the dark forces lurking in society, it arrogates to itself more and more power, becomes self-absorbed, and loses touch with the very society it seeks to transform. Ambedkar was right to stress the state's emancipatory role but wrong not to see that it has its limits and must carry society with it by supporting and even encouraging radical reformist movements. To rely on the westernised elite is not only to condemn the vast majority of Indians to a subordinate position, but also to alienate them from the state and weaken the foundations of democracy. Ambedkar himself was rightly opposed to both the subordination of the majority to the minority and the alienation of the former from the state.

Third, Ambedkar homogenised both the Untouchables and caste Hindus, a tendency he shares with many radicals. He was convinced that the Untouchables had common interests and a common enemy, and that they should all unite behind the banner of 'one party, one leader, one programme'. He saw himself as their only true spokesman, the only genuine champion of their interests, and his programme as the master key to their liberation. Although he was one of their best spokesmen and rose above their other leaders, he was not the only one and his views were not shared by all. The Untouchables in different parts of India had different histories, different forms of interaction with caste Hindus, and, beyond a certain minimum, faced different problems. Their leaders also disagreed about the causes and best ways of eradicating untouchability. They differed on such issues as the separate electorate, the policy of reservation, socialism, the role of the state, and the nature of Hindu society. Ambedkar tended to challenge the representative credentials of his opponents, and sometimes dismissed them as Congress stooges or victims of false consciousness. Apart from being unfair, such an approach discouraged a vigorous and healthy debate among the Untouchables, suppressed genuine differences and hindered the development of an open and self-critical culture.

Ambedkar displayed the same homogenising tendency in his discussion of caste Hindus. Almost all his proposals, be they separate electorates, weighted representation, or that only the Untouchables could represent the Untouchables, were based on the assumption that caste Hindus were almost all hostile to the demands of the Untouchables, that they formed a solid bloc, and that no justice could be expected from them. This is why he talked of and feared the Hindu 'majority' and dismissed Nehru, the communists and others as unreliable friends.

Ambedkar's assumption had only limited validity. Hindus differed among themselves on many issues, including untouchability. While large sections of them approved of it, many did not. Among the latter, some were for the caste system, some against it, and yet others like Gandhi opposed its current form but not the allegedly egalitarian classical varnas. Furthermore, caste Hindus belonged to different castes, and had their own conflicts of interest as well as disputes about their relative hierarchical status. The same minutely graded inequality that hindered lower-caste unity also prevented the upper castes from uniting. Even when Hindus held common views on the caste system, they disagreed on the economic, the political and other questions, and belonged to different political parties.

Once one recognises this, caste Hindus no longer appear as the homogeneous and implacable enemy of the Untouchables. One appreciates that they have their deep internal differences and divisions, conflicting views and interests, and that they are not a permanent and deeply entrenched 'communal' but a fluid and malleable 'political' majority. One also recognises that caste Hindus have several identities of which the Hindu is only one, and that different groups of them privilege different identities in different contexts. They do not therefore act as a cohesive group and cannot in any meaningful sense even be called a majority. This is demonstrated by the experience of post-independence India, where Hindus have fought against the caste system and untouchability, though not always as vigorously as one might wish, and refused to throw their entire weight behind the Bharatiya Janata Party and its earlier incarnations. This is not to say that Ambedkar was wrong to fear Hindu domination, but rather that he was wrong to exaggerate it and base his entire emancipatory strategy on that fear.

Life

I have so far concentrated on Ambedkar's thought and highlighted its strengths and weaknesses. Like all great political leaders, he was far more than the totality of his thoughts and actions, and must be judged by the quality of his political life and his dominant passions and principles. Ambedkar exemplified the great virtues of intellectual and moral integrity, courage, and passion for equality. He had a remarkably open mind, and did not allow the fear of inconsistency to prevent him from changing his views on even the most important issues when required to do so by evidence and arguments. In his uncompromising commitment to the pursuit of equality, he stood up to the greatest man of his age. At his very first meeting with Gandhi on 14 August 1931, Ambedkar told him, 'You say I have got a homeland, but still I repeat that I am without it. How can I call this land my own homeland and this religion my own wherein we are treated worse than cats and dogs. . . . No self-respecting Untouchable worth the name will be proud of this land' (Keer 1971: 166–67).

He said so at the Second Round Table Conference. When in the aftermath of the Communal Award, Gandhi embarked on an indefinite fast, Ambedkar feared, wrongly as it turned out, that it would damage the 'Untouchable' cause. He did not hesitate to condemn it in the strongest possible terms, calling it 'a filthy and foul act', and braved the fierce opposition it provoked. Although his language was intemperate, he was right to stand up for his beliefs and to create the kind of crisis in Hindu society whose epistemological and political power he had long considered central to change. When enormous pressure was put on him to compromise, he did not give in as others of lesser calibre would have done. He bargained hard and secured the maximum possible concessions. As Ambedkar once said, words to which he remained true all his life:

> It is my solemn vow to die in the service and cause of all the down-trodden people among whom I was born, I was brought up and I am living. I would not budge an inch from my righteous cause and care for the violent and disparaging criticism of my detractors. (Quoted in Chentharassery 1998: 143)

After independence, Ambedkar felt strongly about the Hindu Code Bill which he saw as a long overdue opportunity to reform the Hindu family and undermine some aspects of the caste system. Although he was a little too dismissive of the powerful electoral and political constraints on Nehru, he remained true to his conviction and chose to resign rather than hang on to power by agreeing to what he thought to be an unacceptable compromise.

When Gandhi died, Ambedkar was one of the very few leaders, perhaps the only one, not to issue a public statement expressing sorrow. He followed the funeral procession for a few yards and then withdrew to his study as if nothing had happened. One might wish that he had been more generous and risen above his past conflicts with Gandhi. However, since this was how he felt about Gandhi, honesty required that he should not succumb to populist and opportunistic gestures. He was determined to be true to himself, to what he sincerely believed and felt, no matter what the world thought of him and what price he had to pay. Ambedkar's life, marked as it was by great personal tragedies[26] and bitter political struggles, had a rare wholeness, authenticity and intensity, and stands as a beacon to a country and indeed a world disillusioned and rendered cynical by a relentless decline in standards of public morality.

First Ambedkar Memorial Lecture, 14 April 2009, Ambedkar University Delhi.

Notes

[1] Ambedkar rejected many aspects of Buddhism, such as the idea of rebirth, life as dukkha (suffering), and the *sangha* as an organisation apart from society. He reinterpreted many of Buddha's ideas in socio-political terms. All suffering in the world was the result of conflict between classes; it consisted in exploitation; it could only be ended by restructuring the world on the principles of liberty, equality and fraternity. *Nibbana* (or nirvana) implied happiness in this world and self-control, and so on. Ambedkar's Buddha is a secular socialist. *The Buddha and His Dhamma* (1991 [first published in 1957]) was written in a hurry because

of severe ill-health and the fear of impending death. Ambedkar had said it would take at least a year, but finished it in two months. It was written for the benefit of poorly educated Untouchables, especially those disillusioned with Hinduism rather than Christianity.

2 During a heated discussion on 2 September 1953, Home Minister Katju reminded Ambedkar that he had drafted the Constitution. The latter responded: 'Sir, my friends tell me that I made the Constitution. But I am quite prepared to say that I shall be the first person to burn it out. I do not want it. It does not suit anybody' (Keer 1971: 149). He was particularly scathing about Article 31, which established the right to property and made it a fundamental right. It is 'a very ugly thing' and 'we do not take any responsibility for that' (Das 1979: 172).

The Constitution of the United States of India, which Ambedkar published in his *States and Minorities* (1978 [1947]), bears only a limited resemblance to the document he commended to the Constituent Assembly. The former advocated a non-parliamentary form of government: Parliament not being able to remove the executive by passing a no-confidence motion; the prime minister to be elected by the whole house; minority representatives to be included in the Cabinet and elected by their number in Parliament, and so on.

3 Ambedkar made his representation before the Southborough Committee on representation in 1919 and took much interest in making the Depressed Classes a distinct political constituency in 1920 and early 1921. He also started the journal *Mooknayak* in 1920. But his precarious financial condition and the demands of his research at the London School of Economics (LSE) gave him little time to be active in public life till 1923. In 1922, he submitted his DSc thesis to LSE, and in the same year was called to the bar at Gray's Inn, London. In 1923, he started his law practice at the Bombay High Court, a profession that gave him much more time to devote himself to public life.

4 Gandhi did not know Ambedkar was a Harijan till he went to London. He had thought Ambedkar was 'some Brahman who took deep interest in Harijans and therefore talked intemperately'. See Keer (1971: 165–68).

5 See Constituent Assembly Debates (CAD) (Proceedings), vol. XI, 25 November 1949, http://164.100.47.132/LssNew/constituent/vol11p11.html (accessed on 26 May 2018).

6 'In any other country the existence of these classes [the criminal tribes, the aboriginal tribes and the Untouchables] would have led to searching of the heart and to investigation of their origin. But neither of these has occurred in the mind of the Hindu . . .. The old orthodox Hindu does not think that there is anything wrong in the observance of Untouchability. To him it is a normal and natural thing. As such it neither calls for expiation or explanation. The new modern Hindu realizes the wrong. But he is ashamed to discuss it in public . . .. But what is strange is that Untouchability should have failed to attract the attention of the European student of social institutions' (Ambedkar 1990a: 239–41).

7 See 'Castes in India' (Ambedkar 1979b). See also *Annihilation of Caste* (Ambedkar 1979a). This essay was written as an address to a meeting of the Jat-Pat Todak Mandal, a body created under the auspices of the Arya Samaj to reform Hindu society. When the organisers saw his draft, they postponed the meeting! Ambedkar published his address as a brochure.

8 In the joint memorandum submitted to the Minorities Committee of the Round Table Conference, Ambedkar said that the Untouchables should be called 'non-caste Hindus', 'Protestant Hindus' or 'non-conformist Hindus' (see Keer 1971: 189). In his evidence to the Simon Commission in 1928, he said, 'It does not matter whether I call myself a Hindu or a non-Hindu, as long as I am outside the

pale of the Hindu community' (Ambedkar 1982: 477). Ambedkar increasingly dissociated himself from Hindu society, saying, 'even though I am Hindu-born, I will not die a Hindu' (Keer 1971: 502).

[9] For Ambedkar, 'active' conscience drives a man to 'undertake a crusade to eradicate the wrong' and fires him 'with a righteous indignation' (1945: 197).

[10] See also Ambedkar (1987: 44, 97), where he says that fellow feeling is 'a sentiment which leads an individual to identify with the good of others', a 'disposition to treat men as the object of reverence and love'.

[11] 'Tell the slave he is a slave and he will revolt' (see Keer 1971: 60).

[12] As Ambedkar said on 1 September 1951 at the laying of the foundation stone of Milind Mahavidyalaya at Aurangabad: 'The problem of [raising] the lower order is to remove from them that inferiority complex which has stunted their growth and made them slaves to others, to create in them the consciousness of the significance of their lives for themselves and for the country, of which they have been cruelly robbed by the existing social order. Nothing can achieve this purpose except the spread of the higher education' (from *Silver Jubilee Souvenir of the People's Education Society*, Bombay, January 1974, quoted in Lal 2002: 119).

[13] 'It is to the lower classes that we must look for the motive power of progress' (Rodrigues 2005: 82).

[14] Ambedkar wanted a proper admixture of different communities in the civil service. This might lead to a 'small degree of inefficiency' but it would correct caste biases of officers and inspire public confidence in the system.

[15] Under the Communal Award, the Untouchables voted in both the reserved and general constituencies and had two votes. Ambedkar thought that the value of the second vote 'as a political weapon was beyond reckoning', and that its loss under the Poona Pact did great damage to the cause of the Untouchables (Ambedkar 1945: 90).

[16] In 1956, Ambedkar complained to his secretary, Nanak Chand Rattu, that 'the educated few have proved to be a worthless lot, with no sympathies for their downtrodden brethren.' They were busy 'fighting among themselves for leadership and power' (Rattu 1997: 93).

[17] The working committee of his Scheduled Castes Federation resolved on 27 August 1955 that reservations for Scheduled Castes in the central and state legislatures should be abolished. In his *Thoughts on Linguistic States* written four months later, Ambedkar advanced a similar view and favoured plural-member constituencies (Ambedkar 1979c).

[18] Ambedkar had told Gandhi that though they had differences on the issue of untouchability, when the time came he would 'choose only the least harmful way for the country'. In keeping with that, he adopted Buddhism, 'for [it] is a part and parcel of Bharatiya culture. I have taken care that my conversion will not harm the tradition of the culture and history of this land' (Keer 1971: 498).

Conversion of Dalits to Buddhism on a mass scale goes back to 1901, when Iyothee Thass of Tamil Nadu, a Dalit leader, led his followers into Buddhism, saying that this was really a return to their ancient religion. Other Dalit leaders showed a similar inclination in the 1920s and later. See Omvedt (2004: 145).

[19] CAD (Proceedings), vol. XI, 25 November 1949, http://164.100.47.132/LssNew/constituent/vol11p11.html (accessed on 26 May 2018).

[20] See 'Parliament Speech', 17 December 1946, https://www.inc.in/en/media/speech/parliament-speech (accessed on 28 May 2018).

[21] CAD (Proceedings), vol. XI, 25 November 1949, http://164.100.47.132/LssNew/constituent/vol11p11.html (accessed on 26 May 2018).

22 'Without social union political unity is difficult to be achieved. If achieved, it would be as precarious as a summer sapling. . . . With mere political unity India may be a State. But to be a State is not to be a nation, and a State, which is not a nation, has only small prospects of survival in the struggle for existence' (Ambedkar 1990b: 193). Ambedkar thought that a multi-ethnic or 'composite' state should develop a strong sense of social unity to counter ethnic nationalism.

23 In spite of his strong commitment to a socialist economy, Ambedkar placed great emphasis on individual liberty and rights and called Article 32, which protected them, the soul of the Constitution (Keer 1971: 411).

24 For a critical assessment of Gandhi and Ambedkar in relation to untouchability, see Parekh (1999: ch. 7). Gandhi wrote to Sir Mirza Ismail: 'Having suffered like him in South Africa, Dr Ambedkar always carries my sympathy in all he says. He needs the gentlest treatment' (see M. K. Gandhi 1999: 208). Gandhi wanted Nehru to include Ambedkar in his Cabinet. When Nehru and others were reluctant because Ambedkar had been attacking and maligning the Congress, Gandhi rejoined that power was coming to India and not to the Congress. See R. Gandhi (1995: 260).

25 Ambedkar thought that India needed a strongman to abolish the caste system. He felt that it needed a dictator like Kamal Pasha or Mussolini in social and political matters. He was disappointed that Gandhi would not play that role (see Keer 1971: 258). For Ambedkar, a radical reform of Hinduism included such things as a single book acceptable to all Hindus; abolition of hereditary priesthood; passing an examination prescribed by the state and holding a *sanad* (certification) to qualify as a priest; limiting of the number of priests and regulation of their conduct by the state, and so on. Ambedkar did not ask whether such a programme might not provoke fierce Hindu resistance, whether a secular state could undertake it, whether and why it should be limited to Hinduism, what was to be done if Hindus disagreed about which 'text' was central and which religious ceremonies were 'proper', and so on. See Ambedkar (1979a: 76–77).

26 Ambedkar's four children died early. He wrote to his friend Dattoba Powar that 'he was a broken man' and that 'life to me is a garden full of weeds' (Keer 1971: 66). There were threats to his life, mostly through anonymous letters. He was also often subjected to vicious personal attacks. It is a measure of his great courage and uncompromising commitment to the cause of the Untouchables that he did not allow any of these to weaken his resolve.

References

Ambedkar, B. R. 1945. *What Congress and Gandhi Have Done to the Untouchables.* Bombay: Thacker and Co.

———. 1946. *Who Were the Shudras? How They Came to Be the Fourth Varna in the Indo-Aryan Society.* Bombay: Thacker and Co.

———. 1976. *Conditions Precedent for the Successful Working of Democracy.* Nagpur: Y. M. Panchbhai.

———. 1978 [1947]. *States and Minorities.* Lucknow: Buddha Vihar.

———. 1979a. *Annihilation of Caste,* in *Dr. Babasaheb Ambedkar: Writings and Speeches,* vol. 1, pp. 23–96. Bombay: Education Department, Government of Maharashtra.

———. 1979b. 'Castes in India', in *Dr. Babasaheb Ambedkar: Writings and Speeches,* vol. 1, pp. 3–22. Bombay: Education Department, Government of Maharashtra.

———. 1979c. 'Thoughts on Linguistic States', in *Dr. Babasaheb Ambedkar Writings and Speeches,* vol. 1, pp. 137–201. Bombay: Education Department, Government of Maharashtra.

———. 1982. 'Evidence of Dr. Ambedkar before the Indian Statutory Commission on

23rd October 1928', in *Dr. Babasaheb Ambedkar: Writings and Speeches*, vol. 2. Bombay: Education Department, Government of Maharashtra.

———. 1987. *Dr. Babasaheb Ambedkar: Writings and Speeches*, vol. 3. Bombay: Education Department, Government of Maharashtra.

———. 1989. 'Held at Bay', in *Dr. Babasaheb Ambedkar: Writings and Speeches*, vol. 5, pp. 259–71. Bombay: Education Department, Government of Maharashtra.

———. 1990a. *The Untouchables: Who Were They and Why They Became Untouchables?*, in *Dr. Babasaheb Ambedkar: Writings and Speeches*, vol. 7. Bombay: Education Department, Government of Maharashtra.

———. 1990b. *Pakistan or the Partition of India* (*Dr. Babasaheb Ambedkar: Writings and Speeches*, vol. 8). Bombay: Education Department, Government of Maharashtra.

———. 1991 [1957]. *The Buddha and His Dhamma* (*Dr. Babasaheb Ambedkar Writings and Speeches*, vol. 10). Bombay: Education Department, Government of Maharashtra.

———. 2010. *Words of Freedom: Ideas of a Nation*. New Delhi: Penguin.

Bose, Subhas Chandra. 2012 [1935]. *The Indian Struggle 1920–34*. http://www.induslibrary.com/wp-content/uploads/2015/07/the_indian_strugle_I.pdf (accessed on 18 July 2018).

Chentharassery, T. H. P. 1998. *History of the Indigenous Indians*. New Delhi: A. P. H. Publishing Corporation.

Choudhary, Valmiki (ed.). 1987. *Dr Rajendra Prasad: Correspondence and Select Documents*, vol. 9. New Delhi: Allied Publishers.

Das, Bhagwan (ed.). 1963. *Thus Spoke Ambedkar*, vol. 1. Jalandhar: Buddhist Publishing House.

——— (ed.). 1979. *Thus Spoke Ambedkar*, vol. 3. Bangalore: Ambedkar Sahitya Prakashan.

Gandhi, M. K. 1999. *Collected Works of Mahatma Gandhi*, vol. 48. New Delhi: Publications Division, Government of India.

Gandhi, Rajmohan. 1995. *The Good Boatman: A Portrait of Gandhi*. New Delhi: Penguin.

Harrison, Selig S. 1960. *India: The Most Dangerous Decades*. Princeton, NJ: Princeton University Press.

Jaffrelot, Christophe. 2003. *India's Silent Revolution: The Rise of the Lowers Castes in North India*. London: Hurst & Company.

Keer, Dhananjay. 1971. *Dr Ambedkar: Life and Mission*. Mumbai: Popular Prakashan.

Kshirsagar, R. K. 1991. *Political Thought of Dr Babasaheb Ambedkar*. New Delhi: Intellectual Publishing House.

Lal, A. K. 2002. *Protective Discrimination: Ideology and Praxis*. New Delhi: Concept Publishing.

Omvedt, G. 2004. *Ambedkar: Towards an Enlightened India*. New Delhi: Penguin.

Parekh, Bhikhu. 1999. *Colonialism, Tradition and Reform*. New Delhi: Sage.

Rattu, N. C. 1997. *Last Few Years of Dr Ambedkar*. New Delhi: Amrit Publishing House.

Rodrigues, Valerian (ed.). 2005. *The Essential Writings of B. R. Ambedkar*. New Delhi: Oxford University Press.

2

Citizenship as a Claim, or Stories of Dwelling and Belonging among the Urban Poor

Veena Das

It is a great honour and a privilege to be invited to deliver the Ambedkar Memorial Lecture this year.[1] My interactions in the last few days with the honourable Vice Chancellor Professor Shyam Menon and the faculty and students of Ambedkar University have been stimulating. Inspired not only by Ambedkar's contributions to our thinking on citizenship but also encouraged by his obvious irritation with setting up idols in the name of thinking, I am emboldened to offer a view of citizenship that privileges not the august halls in which Constitutions are made but rather the slums and squatter colonies in which constitutional provisions are animated through the labours of the poor. Even if Ambedkar, the lawmaker, might have issues with what I have to say, I feel that Ambedkar, the child, who could not turn on the tap in school even if he was dying of thirst, would agree that much is at stake in thinking of citizenship through the lives of the urban poor.

How might one then constitute the domain of politics in the lives of the poor? An obvious genealogy for tracing this question runs from Walter Benjamin (1978) and Hannah Arendt (1977) to Giorgio Agamben (1998), and settles on what Didier Fassin (2009, 2010) calls the politics of life. For these authors, as Fassin notes, the notion of life splits the human into two domains – that of physical and biological life that man has in common with animals, and of political life that separates man from animals and gives him a unique place in the scheme of things. But does society offer the same possibilities for engaging in politics to all sections? What about women, the poor and the dispossessed? Although there are important differences in the theoretical positions of these three authors, there is a general line of thought that postulates that the power of the exception invested in the sovereign can strip the lives of those living in abject conditions (such as in Nazi camps or in refugee camps) to 'bare life' that can be taken away by the mere will of the sovereign. In a related argument, it is asserted that the struggle for survival robs the poor of the capacity to engage in any deliberative form of politics and reduces the realm of politics to a sentimental humanitarianism. Arendt, for instance, argues that the historical example of the French Revolution shows the limits of the participation of the poor in the processes of politics. She attributes the 'failure' of the French Revolution to the poor who came in their multitudes onto the streets – making their plight public but also bringing the force of biological necessity into the realm of politics and ultimately 'dooming' the revolution itself. There is a second version of this story in which the leaders, out of pity for the driven poor – mixed with rage over hypocritical institutions – doomed the revolution by reducing 'politics to nature' (Pitkin 1998: 231). For Arendt, issues pertaining to poverty belong not to the realm of politics but rather to the household or the administrative wings of government, and when these issues enter the realm of politics, it ceases to be the free deliberation between equal citizens devoted to ensuring freedom.

Although Partha Chatterjee (2004) does not take direct issue with Arendt, his intervention on the politics of the governed is an attempt to think of politics and citizenship through a different theoretical lens. Chatterjee makes a distinction between 'civil society' and 'political society' to gesture towards the fact that the politics of what he calls 'the governed' is honed from the ground and makes use of whatever resources are available to secure goods necessary to preserve biological life. Yet, Chatterjee contends that what the poor engage in is politics, and not simply appeals to pity or the use of traditional patron–client relations. Much as I appreciate Chatterjee's work to restore politics to the poor, he tends to work with binaries of those who govern and the governed; legal and illegal; governmentally produced population and moral community; civil society and political society; whereas my attempt is to show that these concepts bleed into each other and produce the capacity to make claims on the State as a way of claiming citizenship. I too, then, come back to the politics of life, but rather than splitting life into the biological and the political, I argue that it is their mutual absorption that comes to inform the notion of rights in the sense of haq^2 (Cavell 1988; Das 2007; Fassin 2010).

Notions of Law, Life and Exception

This lecture puts three concepts into a dynamic, moving relationship – those of life, law and exception. I begin with a brief exposition of each concept and then argue – through an ethnography of struggles over securing a dwelling among a group of urban poor in a squatter colony on the periphery of Delhi, India – that it is the force that each of these concepts exerts on the others that comes to define the conditions of possibility for the emergence of claims over citizenship for the urban poor. In suggesting that citizenship is a claim rather than a status, that one either has or does not have it, I hope to show the precariousness as well as the promise for the poor of 'belonging' to a polity.

In a conceptual essay that appears in their influential book, *Law in Everyday Life* (1995), the editors Austin Sarat and Thomas R. Kearns usefully summarise the various ways in which legal scholars have looked at the relation between law and society. They divide these scholars into two dominant traditions: first, those who work with an instrumental understanding of the law, and, second, those who think of law as constitutive of social relations. They argue that though both kinds of scholars are interested in understanding the relation between law and society, one puts the weight on law's capacity to regulate social relations (instrumentalist view), while the other is interested in tracking the traces left by law on social relations (constitutive view). As Sarat and Kearns point out, the instrumentalist view of law is interested in law's effectiveness – the extent to which law is observed or not. This has inevitably led to an emphasis on certain kinds of legal objects, viz. rules, while ignoring other objects such as the symbolic performances by which the majesty or distance of law from everyday life is represented. The instrumentalist view is committed to a strict division between legal rules, and customs and habits, since law is distinguished in this view from other rules and norms operative in society by virtue of the fact that the former derives its authority from the State while the source of the latter are smaller groups in a society. Law in this picture is seen as a residual category whose role is episodic, artificial and often disruptive.

On the constitutive side, law is not experienced as episodic or artificial – it is not simply a set of rules that impinges on us from the outside. Rather, the most stunning example of law's constitutive power is to shape social relations in a way that its own traces are erased in the very process of creating persons as legal subjects. Social actors, in this view, internalise the images, meanings and even artefacts of law such that they appear as normal and natural. I am interested in the manner in which the notion of rights is now evoked among the urban poor, many of whom think that the State has promised them certain rights and that they have the standing (haq) to claim these rights. But where does the promise of the State to enhance life – as in quality of life or the good life – come from?

Foucault (2003) famously argued that the emergence of the bio-political State in a long transformation from the 18th to the 19th century marked a new understanding of the idea of life as it came to be seen as an entity to be managed by the State. Rabinow (2006) usefully summarises the movement from bio-power to bio-politics in Foucault as he shows how the two poles of bio-power – that of the anatomo-politics of the human body and that of the regulatory controls over population – came to be conjoined in the 19th century. A politics of 'bio' emerged so that life as a political object was turned back against the controls exercised over it in the name of claims over right to life, to one's body and to health. According to this view, bio-politics, as distinct from bio-power, refers not only to the regulatory power of the State as reflected in law, but must include truth discourses, strategies of intervention on collective existence in the name of life and health, and finally modes of subjectivation by which individuals are made to work upon themselves in subtle ways that make such pursuits as the desirability of preserving health a part of the common sense of the time (see also Rabinow 1992; Cohen 2004; Rose 2007).

In this picture of life, law is explicit and visible as a mode of regulation in such acts as that of passing health legislation, but it can also be discerned through its faint traces in the practices of other institutions such as the clinic and the school. It is striking to me that the concept of life at play in these theories is unambiguously that of biological life. *I am suggesting, instead, an idea of life, as in 'forms of life', in which the social and the natural absorb each other – forms referring to the dimension of social conventions and institutions, for example, and life to that which always inheres in forms even as it goes beyond them.* Though we might recognise and name something as law when the context makes it stand out – e.g., in a law court or in a legal document – we need to put that particular moment of recognition within the flux in which notions of life and notions of law unnoticeably and continually pass from one to another. This is the flux we might name as the everyday.

Till this point, my argument is that attention to everyday life (rather than life defined only as biological life) can help us to see that the boundaries between the instrumental and constitutive views of law – law as that which impinges from the outside, and law that not only constitutes the social world by its power to name but also draws from everyday concepts embedded in life – are neither stable nor impermeable. Many scholars have drawn attention to the fact that legal norms exist within the wider fields of normativity that structure everyday relations (Unger 1986). Thus, for instance, ideas of legal obligation draw from our more diffused understandings of what it is to promise (Cavell 1979); the standards of reasonableness that courts apply depend upon everyday understanding of what is reasonable, what is normal, and what is excessive. I want to go further and argue that it is not only particular normative concepts but also what is seen to constitute our understandings of life itself – life of the individual as lived in relation to others, life in a community – that inform the claims that people come to make on law. This is a somewhat different conception of life than biological life though it does not exclude biological life; rather, it represents the manner in which the natural and the social mutually absorb each other. As an example of such absorption, take Carolyn Walker Bynum's (1991) argument that what may appear to be 'bizarre' legal cases regarding the future preservation of bodies in courts of law, may be better understood if we related them to medieval Judeo-Christian concerns on the consequences of mutilating bodies or mixing body parts in the light of the certainty of resurrection. I would add that this notion of resurrection belongs to a history of the 'natural' in that it speaks to the way in which life, death and resurrection are constituted as 'natural' events within a form of life that might have now disappeared. Practices of law are then not necessarily found in spaces, objects and rules that can be identified unambiguously as belonging to the domain of law, such as courtrooms and legal documents. We may observe the force of the law in legal contracts but we might also track it in the everyday practices of promising – so, we can see how the affective force that particular legal concepts acquire may be traced to the notion of life, not only as a social construct or an entity to be managed by the State, but also in the insistence by inhabitants living in illegal shanty settlements that they have a moral standing to call upon the State.

I turn now to the third concept, that of a state of exception, since it is here that the relation between life and law stands out again and becomes visible.

Exception

One of the most important theoreticians on the state of exception, Giorgio Agamben (1998, 2005), argues that it is not only that sovereignty and exception are contiguous as established by Carl Schmitt (1985), but also that this contiguity is essential for understanding the relation between law and life. As Agamben sees it, law comes to deploy the notion of exception not simply as a matter of political expediency, but as a juridical figure as the means by which the living being as a legal subject is brought within the purview of law – both bound by the law and abandoned by it. In his earlier work on *homo sacer*, Agamben (1998) had proposed the Roman figure of man as one who could be killed but not sacrificed, to propose that such a figure made it possible to judicially recreate life as 'bare life' – mere biological life from which all signs of the social had been stripped. The later book on the state of exception allowed him to think of contemporary politics itself as a kind of necropolitics in which modern forms of sovereignty are about the taking of life without being held responsible for it. In this formulation, it is clear that law's relation to life is defined primarily by the capacity of the sovereign to take life arbitrarily; once the legal subject comes to be defined as homo sacer, neither can his death be assimilated to sacrificial death that would carry the potential to nourish the community, nor can the sovereign be held responsible for such deaths as, being the source of law, the sovereign has the right to declare what constitutes an exception. I will not rehearse here the criticisms of the mode of reasoning or the expansion of the idea of homo sacer to cover the wide variety of situations that Agamben brings under its purview (from the father's right to kill his son to the mechanised killings of the Nazi camps). What interests me is that when life comes under the purview of law in this formulation of the state of exception, it must do so after being stripped of its social dimensions, as 'bare life'. I concede that Agamben might be describing one face of sovereignty and that it provides a powerful way of thinking about some particularly grievous scenes of violence, though I regret the use of this trope for the widely dispersed examples he gives. Here, though, I wish to draw attention to another way of thinking about states of emergency and the relation between law and life for its potential to make visible an alternate tradition of conceptualising the notion of a rule and its suspension.

I have in mind the notion of *apaddharma* – or the rules to be followed in times of distress as propagated by Manu, the Hindu lawgiver. I am proposing the idea of apaddharma as an alternative theoretical formulation to that of Agamben, not as a culturalist argument to plead for the exceptionalism of India, though the issue of how certain figures of the past might continue to throw their shadow on the present even when the forms of life within which they were embedded have receded, poses theoretical challenges of the sort that many anthropologists struggle with.[3] It is not my intention to obscure the strong hierarchical elements in Manu, nor indeed am I unaware of the irony of evoking Manu in a lecture named after Ambedkar, but it seems to me that the ironist in Ambedkar might have appreciated the strange paths that intellectual trajectories can take.

As we know, Manu himself lived in times of *apad* or distress as foreign chiefs were establishing power over different regions in India when he formulated the laws by which everyday life was to be conducted.[4] The crucial question in the case of apaddharma is what kind of rule is to be followed during times of distress, such as a famine or a war, in which normal rules have been suspended (Davis 2006). Apad also seems to refer to an infringement so grave that the social order is itself put into question, as in cases of the murder of a Brahmin or a man sleeping with his preceptor's wife. Thus, the issues on which Manu records how one is to deal with suspension of normal rules are varied, but they seem to pertain to an imagination of what acts become permissible when biological life is threatened, on the one hand, and on the other hand, how the social order is to be restored when an act seriously violates the idea of *dharma*, not as caste-specific 'rules' but as violating the sense of life itself. An example of the former is the norms about the food that is permissible during famines, and that of the latter is the penance prescribed for major sins such as violating the bed of the *guru* (the spiritual preceptor).[5] Rules determining appropriate action during times of distress pertained primarily to the Brahmin and the king – the two central figures that Manu is interested in – and there is no question that most of the accommodations he permits re-inscribe the powers of these two figures. However, there are other concerns, such as that of naming the new castes resulting from intermixture of established castes, or determining what occupations might be pursued by various caste groups.

The particular verse that I find quite compelling for our discussion on the general reflection on rules is Verse 29, Chapter XI. According to G. Buhler's (1886) translation, it reads as follows: 'By the *Visve-devas*, by the *Sadhyas*, and by the great sages of the Brahmana (caste), who were afraid of perishing in times of distress, a substitute was made of the (principal) rule.'[6] We can get a sense of what a substitute rule means from the sequence of penances prescribed for someone who has committed the terrible sin of sleeping with his guru's wife or has committed incest, such as having intercourse with a sister. The sequence moves from the most severe penance leading to death of the offender, to the less severe ones prescribing temporary exile to the forest. While the general notion of dharma has received much attention in scholarly literature, the fact that the declaration of a rule is usually accompanied by a discussion of an alternative, or the exceptions under which the rule could be set aside or substituted by another, deserves more sustained discussion. The notion of a rule explicitly brought forth the notion of exception and formulation of a substitute, as if following the rule and setting it aside were joined together in imagination. Far from the sovereign being the one who could suspend the law through his power to declare an exception, the king himself was bound to use one of the substitute rules regarding his own conduct, as well as his obligations to his subjects when times of distress made it impossible to follow the normal rules by which such obligations were to be fulfilled. In the process of my fieldwork I would often find that if a rule was formulated – regardless of whether it was a priest pronouncing it or a local bureaucrat or a school principal – one common response of the person to whom the rule was to be applied was to ask how she or he could be freed from the orbit of that rule: *iska koi upay to batlaiye*. While we could literally translate this as 'please show me a way out,' that would miss the point that an appeal is being made to expert knowledge through which a substitute rule can be formulated. Thus, the issue that seems philosophically important is to ask what it is to obey a rule, and not simply, what is the content of the rule?[7] Manu's passage to the effect that the gods themselves sanction such 'substitute rules' shows that states of emergency in which the life of both the individual and the community is to be preserved, allow a new set of rules to be formulated rather than a simple suspension of laws that would lead to a state in which one is reduced to 'bare life'. It is the way that notions of life and law move in and out of each other that forms the texture of moral claims.

Moral Claims

Let me appeal to the most quotidian of examples to illustrate my point about citizenship as a moral claim that allows us to observe the traces of law in spaces that are not recognised as legal or juridical. The inhabitants in the cluster of shanties, which I will describe, are from the sprawling locality of NOIDA on the outskirts of Delhi. They are migrants from the states of Uttar Pradesh (UP) and Bihar, who came in different waves to these areas as new economic opportunities became available. The name NOIDA is an acronym for Naveen (New) Okhla Industrial Development Authority – it refers to a sprawling new township that traces its official birth to 17 April 1976, when it was set up as part of the National Capital Region during the National Emergency (1975–77). The administration was later taken over by the UP government as migration increased. According to the 2001 census, the current population of NOIDA is 290,000 and it is primarily composed of migrants from other cities as well as rural migrants. The official descriptions of the township boast of a high literacy rate (80 per cent), as well as the existence of major educational institutions and a hospital in every residential sector. Yet, nestling in between these affluent zones are the clusters of *jhuggi-jhopdi* colonies, some of whose residents have been living there for more than 40 years.[8]

As with many other squatter settlements, the rural poor, who came here first as a trickle in the late 1960s, and in waves since then, started by putting up shanties on unoccupied government land. The local expressions for such acts are *jagah gher lena* (to enclose a space), and the land itself is referred to as *kabze ki zameen* (land that was occupied). Although people did not have legal title to the land they occupied, mutual recognition within the community led to the notion that the land rightfully belonged to those who settled in the area, so that later migrants have to either buy or rent the space for putting up their shanties.[9] In administrative terms, such colonies are described as 'unauthorised colonies', but these colonies are always engaged in getting a recognised status from the local government. The state of affairs from the point of view of the residents might be described as that of a temporary permanence, since many residents have lived in these areas for close to 40 years but are still engaged in struggles to get some assurance of permanence.[10] In her astute analysis of urban governance in Mumbai, Julia Eckert (2006) calls attention to eclectic and pragmatic ways in which urban governance takes place, and calls such a form of governance, after Benda-Beckman (1992), 'unnamed law'. She argues that these unnamed laws do not refer to the specific basis of legitimacy but are produced in the interactions 'within regimes of governance'. I feel that stepping outside the overdetermined dualism of law and custom is a brilliant move on the part of Eckert, though I hope to extend her argument by showing that underlying these interactions are claims that derive from diffused notions about preserving life that bind residents of unrecognised slums and squatter colonies, on the one hand, and the State on the other. For the State, the recourse to juridical notions as embedded in such constitutional notions as right to life, becomes necessary to justify its actions especially when it sets aside the letter of the law in favour of other notions derived from the imperative to preserve the life of the individuals and the community.

Although always vulnerable to the vagaries of law and police action, the residents of the jhuggi settlement have acquired some legal protection. The decade of the 1980s saw various court decisions that held that the constitutional right to life was not limited to the right to not be deprived of life without due process – it included the obligation of the State to provide the means for pursuing livelihoods. In different class actions, the high courts in Mumbai, Delhi and Gujarat (among others) held that people who could show residence for a sufficiently long time in one place, as pavement dwellers or as jhuggi dwellers, could not be removed without provision of alternative housing. The law does not always speak with one voice – recently the courts have hedged some of the earlier decisions with various qualifications. The Nawab Khan case adjudicated by the Supreme Court in 1997 clearly stated that the State had the constitutional duty to provide shelter in order to make the right to life meaningful.[11] In addition to court judgments, various administrative decisions regarding city planning also impinged on various localities in different ways in metropolitan areas. As Roma Chatterji (2005) has noted, new administrative proclamations are simply added to earlier ones so that there is a maze of regulations, some of which might very well contradict each other. In NOIDA itself there have been whole clusters of shanties that have been demolished in the last 10 years or have been razed to the ground by unexplained fires. Escalating conflicts with property developers, or 'law-and-order' problems resulting in interventions by the local police who decided to clean up a cluster of jhuggis, resulted in many residents of such clusters having to flee to other places in the late 1990s. There are other cases, however, in which the jhuggi dwellers have been able to keep a tenuous hold over their dwellings. It is only by paying close attention to the manner in which the 'big' and 'small' processes are increasingly enmeshed that we can find a way to understanding some of the issues under discussion. Whereas once it was considered axiomatic that demands of theory required one to extract oneself from irregular details encountered at the so-called micro levels and to view vast landscapes panoramically, new forms of theorising have vastly complicated our understanding of scale.[12]

In the cluster of about 350 jhuggis in the area that is under consideration here, it was the negotiating skill of the local *pradhan* (caste leader) that helped in keeping local conflicts at bay and ensuring that residents could evade eviction or demolition of their jhuggis. The situation changed considerably after the death of this pradhan in 2006, both due to changes in State-level politics and because of a proliferation of new leaders in the locality. I will try to show that the strategies the pradhan used in collaboration with others, the alliances he built, and the particular vocabulary he used in describing these manoeuvres help us to understand not only how precarious the everyday life of jhuggi dwellers is, but also how everyday life itself provides the ground on which citizenship claims can be addressed to the law. At the same time, the forces unleashed after the death of the pradhan are evidence of the fragility of the strategies that are available to the poor, which might easily flip to reveal how contingent are claims to success in this kind of local environment. At one level, this story is indeed evidence of what de Certeau (1984) and James Scott (1985) see as the predominant feature of everyday life – viz., that it retraces the very marks left by the power of institutions in the mode of tactical resistance. There is, however, more to the story, as law and administrative procedures themselves come to make slow shifts in the face of some commitment to responding to the needs to preserve life – both biological life and the life of the community. Yet, the commitment is always precarious. Let me now return to the story of the pradhan, Nathu Ram.

The Local Tangle of Conflicts

Nathu Ram rose to a position of power in the locality sometime in the mid-1970s due to his ability, he said, to deal with outsiders, especially the agents of the State such as policemen. In this aspect, he was somewhat like the big men first made famous by Godelier and Strathern (1991), since he did not represent traditional authority, having displaced the earlier caste pradhan who was not able to deal with outside authorities. Though not a traditional caste pradhan, Nathu Ram used his dense kinship connections in the area to build support. He counted eight families of close relatives who lived within the same cluster of jhuggis and, as his power grew, he encouraged other more distant relatives to come and settle in an adjacent park on *kabza* (occupied) land.

Fast forward to the 1980s, when the residents of the area were embroiled in conflict with the neighbouring Gujjar community – the original residents of the area before it was claimed for industrial development.[13] For the Gujjars – whose fortunes over the years have changed radically as they too have taken advantage of the growth of industry in this area – the presence of a lower-caste cluster of jhuggis in the neighbourhood was seen as threatening their economic dominance. They feared that these jhuggi dwellers would 'corrupt' their young people.[14] Nathu Ram explained to me that most men in the jhuggis were performing the task of sweepers or working as load carriers for the local factories that had been coming up since the late 1970s. These were not jobs that the Gujjars would have performed, but as long-time settlers in this area, they did not want new settlements to come up. The Gujjars had clout with the police, so the police were all set to demolish the lower-caste cluster of jhuggis. In Nathu Ram's words, 'the bulldozers were literally on our threshold.' 'Someone' advised Nathu Ram that he should try to get a court order to stall the demolitions. The lack of specificity in Nathu Ram's account of who that someone was, or how he came to know him, is a typical feature of narratives among the urban poor I have encountered, and it indexes the fact of diffused forms of knowledge over which no one ever has full control but which, like a gambler's luck, can pay dividends.

Having gathered this bit of advice, Nathu Ram decided to go to the high court in the city of Allahabad, though he did not know anyone there. In his own account, he would go to the high court with a bag of roasted *chana* (chickpeas) and sit on the stairs munching them, hoping that someone would take notice of him. I should note that such a strategy for getting the attention of State officials, of doctors, of teachers, though not routine, is not uncommon.[15] As luck would have it, an activist lawyer saw him sitting there every day and asked him what he wanted. Nathu Ram explained his predicament and the lawyer agreed to file a petition for a stay order on the ground that the residents belonged to the Scheduled Caste category and were economically poor, and hence should not be deprived of their homes and their means of livelihood.[16] The lawyer, however, insisted that the jhuggi dwellers legally register themselves as a society under the UP Registration of Societies Act. The jhuggi residents thus acquired the legal status of a registered society, calling themselves the Harijan Workers Society for Social Struggle (Harijan Mazdur Sangharsh Sabha).[17] They were successful in obtaining a stay order from the court and used it in bargaining with the police. Simultaneously they tried to pursue the demand for alternative accommodation with various political parties, especially before elections, organising public meetings, holding demonstrations and submitting petitions to various political leaders. Despite promises made every five years during elections, no concrete results by way of getting alternative secure rights over housing came from these endeavours. After Nathu Ram's death, a variety of new leaders emerged, some from his own kinship group and others from different regional identities (e.g., one a migrant from Bihar and another from Madhya Pradesh who does not even live in the cluster). One can see that the intensity of party politics at the state level is now reflected in the locality, which has chapters of the major regional parties: the Bahujan Samaj Party, which explicitly identifies itself with the cause of the Dalits (an appellation that till recently the residents actively rejected in favour of the State-defined category of Scheduled Caste); the Lok Dal, that seeks to represent known middle castes such as the Jats; and the Samajwadi Party, which was dominant till 2007 but whose fortunes are now on the decline.

It would be evident from the above description that the matter of securing rights over their residence did not end for the jhuggi dwellers with obtaining the stay order. It is true that this protected them from demolition, but it did not ensure that they were provided alternative plots of land with permanent rights, which is their goal. Rather, the jhuggi dwellers have continued to find a variety of ways in which they can deepen their claims over housing. Just as the jhuggis are built incrementally – you first occupy a bit of land, you then put up thatched mud walls and a tin roof, and then as more money comes into the house and the family grows, you put up one cement wall, or you put a door or build a room on the roof – similarly, credentials for rights are built incrementally. The legal notion that you either have rights or you do not, would make no sense within these strategies of creating rights. As many people here say, you try first to get one foot in the obscure realms of the government, then the whole body can be inserted, referring to the popular folk tale in which a camel manages to displace the tent owner by incrementally occupying the tent. One way to track this phenomenon of creating incremental rights is to think of what dwelling, as distinct from building, entails in ethnographic terms. Perhaps we can shift our gaze from rules and regulations to actual material objects such as electricity meters, water taps and ration cards that become material embodiments of the rights to dwelling. Let me take up each of these objects in turn.

The Agency of Objects

As an unauthorised colony, the jhuggi cluster cannot claim either electricity or drinking water as a matter of civic rights. However, two opposite considerations have led the Water Board and the Electricity Board to grant some de facto rights to the residents in this regard. As far as the Water Board is concerned, the residents still do not have running water, but, because of the fear of cholera epidemics that plague Delhi and its adjoining areas every summer, there is a communal tap that gets potable water. At the height of summer when water supplies dwindle all over the city, residents are supplied with water tanks, which the pradhan claimed was a result of his political connections. This solved the problem of drinking water somewhat, but did not create any documents such as water bills that could be used as proof of residence.

The story of electricity is quite different. Unlike water, which can be treated as a public good because of health externalities, electricity is not considered a public good. As an unauthorised colony, the residents do not have any claims over electricity. Nevertheless, all households use electricity. I cannot put precise dates on when houses began to get electricity but the sequence of events is quite clear. Initially, some people began to draw electricity from the street pole, but no one remembers who were the first households to do so.[18] During the precarious period between 1985 and 1986 that I described earlier, the pradhan had suggested that if the residents were to apply for regular electricity connections and get electric meters installed, it could become proof of residence. At the same time various government agencies were propagating a drive to get people to pay for the water and the electricity that they used.[19] Thus, some houses were able to get electricity meters installed, and could show the bills they had accumulated. Other households hesitated because of the costs. As a result, the households are varied in the sources of electricity they use. Some continue to draw electricity from the electric poles in the street while others receive electricity legally and pay for it. Still others have arrived at a complex way of sharing arrangements. Since 2005, many households that use electricity have acquired TV sets or coolers for the summer and have accumulated large amounts in unpaid bills. Even in 2005, there was anxiety expressed by the pradhan that several people had not paid their electricity bills and that this might provide an excuse to the police to enter the settlement, and that might upset the fragile understanding that had been reached between the police and the residents to leave the latter alone.

Important as electricity and water are, perhaps the most important document for the poor is the ration card because it not only enables them to get various food items at subsidised rates, but also serves as an identity card for purposes of being able to claim entitlements over various government schemes for welfare. The ration cards are colour-coded. Red cards are issued to those who are below the poverty line, whose per capita income is less than one dollar a day. Next in importance are yellow cards given to those who are defined as vulnerable groups but are not below the poverty line. They are entitled to subsidised food items but at higher rates, while all other citizens can get white ration cards that entitle them to buy food items from designated ration shops at prices fixed by the government. The most important function of ration cards, though, is as identity cards, and they have to be shown for everything – from getting a child admitted in a neighbourhood school to establishing proof of residence.

The government undertakes periodic drives to verify the ration cards of all recipients in order to update the statistics on people living below the poverty line. In 2004, a survey was to be conducted in the area, and the pradhan persuaded everyone to contribute money towards regularising ration cards of all families. He is said to have arrived at an 'arrangement' (probably a euphemism for a bribe) with the local municipal office by which all earlier ration cards, including any forgeries, were to be turned in and fresh cards were to be issued. He thought he would be able to get everyone a ration card that was of the appropriate colour, but due to some confusion people ended up with either yellow or white cards. When I examined the cards, I found to my surprise that the date of issue is stamped on the bottom of the card while next to the name and the photograph of the person, the text in Hindi says, 'This is not recognised as a ration card' – *Yeh rashan card ke roop mein manya nahin hai.* Instead, it is a document that establishes a right (*pradhikaran patra*). What is more, the card also states that the period of validity of the card is three months. Yet, the record of transactions stamped on the card shows that people have been using it since 2004. Here, then, is an interesting paradox. The jhuggis are built on land that was 'occupied' as the term 'kabza' states – yet, this term comes to have legal recognition. Further, ration cards are issued that recognise the jhuggi dwellers as legal subjects while also undoing the claims of the State as being the upholder of law, since it issues a document that it itself proclaims to have no legal validity.

How is one to understand the fact that the State undoes its own legal standing in the most quotidian of manners? I claim that in setting aside the letter of the law in favour of a commitment to preserve life, the State is claiming its legitimacy by recourse to its ability to declare exceptions. Yet, there is a different notion of life that is operative here than what we find in Foucault's or Agamben's idea of bio-power and bare life respectively, as I argued earlier. 'Life' in this context is not only that which is managed by the State – for, in that case, people in the categories of illegal residents or migrants would simply fall on the side of 'letting die' in Foucault's (2003) terms. Nor do they fall into the category of those who represent bare life that can be taken at will – the idea of biological life is involved, but not to the complete exclusion of other aspects such as the recognition that life can only be lived in a community, as witnessed in the administrative actions to give the entire community ration cards, or access to potable water.

In Indian bureaucratic parlance, the kind of documents that are given for short durations are known as 'emergency measures'. This applies to passports and other temporary documents to establish rights of one kind or another for limited periods of time. But what is the notion of an emergency that is at play here? I have listened to the transcripts of my free-flowing interviews with the pradhan Nathu Ram several times, and I also studied the notes of various casual meetings with particular attention to the vocabulary he used. On one side, his language was replete with words that were like tracks left by his interactions with various State institutions that show how law impinged on the lives of the residents. Thus, there are words such as police, court, judge, police station, *hawaldar* (junior police officer), officer, bulldozer, Harijan society, registration (*panjikaran*), verification (*satyapan*). Along with these terms, though, there are others that have both legal and ritual meanings. Thus, *peshi* refers to both the state of possession by a hostile spirit and being summoned to court or to the office of a bureaucrat; *sunvai* pertains to a hearing in courts as well as the ritual of exorcism. In addition, such expressions as *kuch khilana pada* (something had to be fed) are used as an expression for bribes to officers as well as to hostile spirits; *zuban pe koi hasti aa gayi* (literally, an elephant came over my tongue) refers to how one might have become eloquent in court or in the presence of an officer, overcoming the normal nervousness when confronted with the law, as well as to ritual speech under possession.[20] Such mutual contamination of ritual and legal vocabulary tends to show that the manner in which one becomes a legal subject does not accord with the precise picture of how law imagines the making of such subjects. Such subject positions are sometimes haunted, sometimes animated by one's place within forms of life that certainly go deeper than what either the instrumentalist or the constitutive views of law suggest.

I am not making the case that the enormous coercive powers of law are completely tamed by other competing notions drawn from the flow of life, but I am suggesting that if we are to look at the everyday as the site on which we can track the movements of the State, of performance of citizenship, of constitutive powers of law, then the everyday cannot be treated as simply the secure site of routines and habits as Marcus (1995) suggests. Rather, it is the space on which we can see how, underlying these routines and habits, there is a struggle to bring about a newness in which we can track the workings of the law for better and for worse. The story till now has tended towards a limited success; let me now turn to the perils that the NOIDA residents have faced since the death of the pradhan.

I give a brief account of events in the last four years since the death of the pradhan, though I will have to reserve a more detailed discussion of the sprawling networks of people and affects for another occasion. New forms of politics have come to be inserted within the structure of anticipation that was created as the people here began to expect that they would not only eventually succeed in saving their places of residence from demolition, but would also be able to secure better housing from the State. After Nathu Ram's death, one of his nephews claimed the leadership of the welfare association he had founded, but despite the stay order obtained from the court, the promise of better housing was still unrealised. Meanwhile, the nephew's political career was cut short because of a criminal complaint filed against him by a rival group, resulting in his having to flee from the area to avoid arrest. In the last few years, the politics around housing has become a major issue in state-level politics, marked by bitter rivalries between the Samajwadi Party of Mulayam Singh Yadav and the Bahujan Samaj Party of Mayawati. It might be recalled that the pradhans of different settlements in NOIDA had begun to organise themselves in Nathu Ram's time by holding joint meetings and trying to negotiate the issue of alternative allotment of housing with various political parties, especially at the time of elections. By the time the state assembly elections of 2007 took place, the number of registered societies, each claiming to represent the residents of various shanty settlements in NOIDA, had risen to 23, each with alliances to local factions of different political parties.

The registered society formed by Nathu Ram (Harijan Workers Society for Social Struggle) had become defunct in 2001, having failed to meet certain procedural requirements. Nathu Ram's nephew (the one who was to abscond later) had helped in registering it under another name, Jhuggi Jhopdi Welfare Association, in 2001, and in 2006 its membership was renewed by the nephew's son (Vinod), who had now risen to a position of some power. Under the auspices of this society, a writ petition had been filed in court submitting the names of 1,440 jhuggi households as eligible for allotment of alternate housing. The high court found merit in the petition and ordered the NOIDA administration to provide alternative accommodations to these households on payment of Rs 62,000, to be paid in monthly instalments of Rs 120 per household. The lawyers of the society contested this decision on the grounds that, as a welfare state, India could not charge such exorbitant sums from the poor. There were other petitions filed on behalf of other registered societies claiming that their members had been left out of the list of those entitled to receive alternative housing.

In Chatterjee's rendering of the politics of the governed, we learn that political society was marked by the emergence of a new type of leadership as well as a new associational politics in the squatter colony he describes in Kolkata:

> The ICDS scheme is one example of how the residents of the squatter colony could organize to get themselves identified as a distinct population group that could receive the benefits of governmental programs. . . . Having set up the association, the residents now use this collective form to deal with other governmental agencies such as the railways, the police, or municipal authorities, with NGOs offering welfare or developmental services, and with political parties and leaders. (Chatterjee 2004: 56)

For my purposes, the expression 'the residents now use this collective form to deal with other governmental agencies' is a black box, since we are never told what this 'dealing with' means in terms of actual negotiations, and, hence, are left vague about the forms of power governmental instruments produce at the level of the community. I offer two extracts from interviews conducted with the local leaders in my field and one extract from political speeches made during a demonstration at the office of the NOIDA authority.

The first extract is from the interview with Vinod (Nathu Ram's nephew who had filed the successful writ petition) and the president of the welfare association I mentioned earlier.[21]

> VINOD: . . . so we asked K. K. Sharma from the NOIDA authority office that of the list of the 1,440 that was submitted to court – people are filling out the forms with verified documents – we have already had 350 forms filled, and sent by registered post, but we are not receiving the acknowledgements . . . he said that we will open a counter right here in the office that can be manned by you – you can collect all forms that people fill out everyday . . . the system of sending forms by registered post is to be discontinued.
>
> Q: You were saying that you gave a list of 1,440 members of your society

[meaning registered society] but that the number of claimants is larger?

VINOD: . . . till the survey of sector 9 and 10 is completed and verification of documents is completed, how can we definitively say how many people will make claims?

Q: You had once told [us] that there were 11 people to whom apartments were allocated in a different locality. What was that about?

VINOD: Not 11, 23 – that was Amar Singh [political leader from the Samajwadi Party] who authorised this allocation. But the names of the persons to whom this allocation was made were not in the original list.

SHIV KUMAR [an associate of Vinod]: Those were the victims of that Nihari atrocity [referring to an infamous serial child murder case from a village adjoining NOIDA].

VINOD, *cutting in*: There is a lot of politics – there are these 12 to 15 persons who are against our society . . .

SHIV, *interrupting*: But the SDM [subdivisional magistrate] has nullified their societies – we are the only ones recognised by law . . . but the public [*using the English word*] gets misled [*gumrah ho jati hai*].

The second citation is from an interview with an office-bearer of another registered society, affiliated to the Communist Party of India.

Q: . . . so this time, has the survey been conducted more seriously?

GANGARAM: Surveys were commenced many times but they were never completed . . . basically the *netalog* [leaders, big men] were asked to give the number of jhuggi owners – someone gave 1,440, someone gave 4,000, someone gave 8,000 . . .

Q: And this time?

GANGARAM: This time was more serious – at least surveyors came and put numbers on the jhuggis – videographs [*using word in English*] were done – at least they saw what the jhuggis look like.

The third extract is from a speech delivered during a demonstration at the office of the NOIDA authority.

SPEAKER [a local leader]: You will have to come to your senses! *Inqalab zindabad* – Long live the Revolution! Stop this performance [*tamasha*]! Stop this brokering! Stop exploiting us! Chairman, come to your senses!

[*Everyone is waiting for a more influential leader to arrive and address them. Meanwhile people waiting in the crowd get into conversation with each other.*]

ONE OF THE MEN: Here every day there is exploitation – sometimes in the name of survey for plots – another time for ration cards – the so-called leaders charge Rs 500 for filling forms – our demand is stop this brokering [*dalali*] – the officials are making money from the leaders and the leaders from the people.

[*Someone else addressing the assembled people exhorts everyone to sit – for women to settle on one side – slogans are raised intermittently but the leader does not arrive – the crowd begins to disperse after two hours.*]

A full linguistic analysis of the interviews and the public performances cannot be attempted here, but I note the following points. First, the vocabulary of 'registered society', 'corruption', 'dalali' (brokerage), *dharna, pradarshana* (demonstration), 'public', etc., is a political vocabulary honed out of actual engagement with processes of governmentality. Second, a local genealogy of events – stay order, writ petition, surveys, allotments, elections – creates a collective, though contested, memory that is locality-specific but that bears the traces of various court decisions on the rights of slum dwellers as well as regional political events.

We might summarise the situation in the jhuggis, which continues to be in a flux, as follows: The high court instructed the NOIDA authority to conduct an authoritative survey to submit a final list of jhuggi dwellers in all sectors of NOIDA with a view to providing them with alternative housing in 2008. Various registered societies sprang up and started to conduct their own surveys, often charging residents anything from Rs 500 to Rs 3,000 as a condition of their names being included in the authoritative list. After the electoral victory of the Bahujan Samaj Party in the assembly elections of 2007, the Dalit leader Mayawati was sworn in as chief minister of the state. While there was great hope that as a Dalit she would expedite the allotment of houses to the jhuggi dwellers who are predominantly from her own caste, what has happened is that more surveys have been ordered; several registered societies have been spawned as some have been derecognised as illegitimate by the administration; and residents of the cluster of households where I have been working have become so enraged by the various brokers who have emerged that they have held demonstrations against these brokers at the office of the NOIDA authority! As one resident of the area summarised the situation for me:

Every year we wait for Mayawati to make an announcement on her birthday in January to the effect that we have been given rights over our jhuggis or that all jhuggi dwellers have been given alternative plots. All that happens is that new surveys are announced, new documents have to be produced – the number of those who claim rights over jhuggis has gone up from 1,440 to 10,000 and will keep going up. Meanwhile, nothing is going to happen.

Nevertheless, I sense a cautious optimism in the simple fact that septic tanks are being installed by a number of households who have got together to make a collective arrangement; a new floor is added here or a room constructed there, though precariously perched on the unstable foundation of the house; walls are whitewashed, someone puts tiles on a square outside the jhuggi so that the space in front can be cleaned easily.

Concluding Observations

In following the struggles over housing among the poor, I hope to have shown that claims to citizenship are crafted not through or only through formal legal procedures. Instead, it is the actual labour put in by residents of such marginal places as the jhuggi-jhopdi settlements, a labour of learning how to deal with legal spaces of courts and police precincts as well as the labour in securing objects whose agency they can call on to establish incremental citizenship, that creates new forms in which citizenship can be actualised. One cannot but be moved by the manner in which an underlying allegiance to the idea of preserving life both at the level of the individual and that of the community comes to be expressed in the moments when the State is able to put aside its function to punish infringements of law, thus allowing claims of life to trump claims of law. It is also the case that new forms of politics open up the space for continuous surveillance through governmental tactics such as surveys or renewed procedures of verification of documents, though on a model that is almost a parody of Foucault's model of surveillance, since what it generates is the emergence of new forms of brokerage that drain people of their meagre resources. The very instruments of surveillance such as surveys and verification of documents provide an opportunity for brokers to emerge from within the community and become a new face of the State. Instead of a panoramic view of State and citizenship through the Hegelian lens of civil society or the Habermasian notion of public sphere,[22] the attention to the minutiae of everyday life allows us to bring into view the complex agencies at play here in the claim to citizenship.

Second Ambedkar Memorial Lecture, 23 August 2010, Ambedkar University Delhi.

Notes

[1] I am grateful to the residents of the jhuggi colony for sharing stories of their struggles and allowing my research assistants and me to participate in their activities. The staff at ISERDD, Delhi, has been exemplary in the research support they have given. I especially thank Purshottam Kumar for tracking the network of local leaders. This lecture is a revised and expanded version of a seminar first given at the Max Planck Institute, Halle, in 2008. My thanks to Julia Eckert, Pratiksha Baxi, Jennifer Culbert, Roma Chatterji, and Deepak Mehta for comments on earlier versions. I offer my gratitude to Vice Chancellor Shyam Menon, and the faculty and students of Ambedkar University, Delhi, for inviting me to deliver the second Ambedkar Memorial Lecture and for making the occasion truly memorable for me. I thank Pratap Bhanu Mehta for his astute comments as discussant.

[2] I arrive at this constellation of meanings of the term *haq* not by following its dictionary meanings according to which haq (a term found in Arabic, Persian, Hebrew, and Urdu) means both justice and truth, but through following its everyday use. While I cannot elaborate on the ethnography of its use here for reasons of space, the term was evoked primarily in the sense of 'standing' – as in having the standing to both give and receive. Thus, for instance, an elder sister might insist that she had acquired the haq to give gifts to a brother on his marriage, while parents might insist that a girl only has the haq to receive from her natal family, never to give. On the other hand such statements as 'I am only asking for my haq' evoke the notion of justice, while a police officer asking for a bribe by saying he is demanding his haq is extending the idea of standing, and not of justice. My argument, however, rests less on expanding on the discursive contexts of the term and more on showing the complex field of legal and political action through which notions of citizenship were actualised.

[3] To take a compelling example, '. . . while I complain of being able to glimpse no more than the shadow of the past, I may be insensitive to reality as it is taking shape at this very moment . . .' (Lèvi-Strauss 1974: 43).

[4] The other source for understanding the nature of the rule is the corpus of texts on sacrifice since this is a major concern in the interpretation of Vedic injunctions (*mimamsa*). The rules of interpretation formulated in these texts are also used to interpret legal rules.

[5] Since this form of sexual transgression is considered as grave as an incestuous relation with the mother, even though the guru's wife is not the biological mother but the wife of the person who fathers you into your place in the world, it nicely captures the notion of life as absorbing both the social and the natural and thus going beyond each in itself.

[6] The Sanskrit term that Buhler translates as 'substitute' is *pratinidhi*, which could also be translated as 'representative' – thus, the performance of an abbreviated ritual can 'represent' the more elaborate ritual.

[7] See Bruno Latour's (2010) masterful exposition of the manner in which such projects within the law as ripening the file, or binding the enunciation to the enunciator, as well as rhetorical techniques of detachment produce the effect of following a rule within the legal protocols he describes. My difference with Latour is in his understanding of law as strictly that which happens within administrative law, since it is here that, for him, facts can be made to disappear and the realm of pure law can be brought into view. A constitutive view of law would assume that law folds both into forms of governmentality and within subjects made through the interpenetration of the judicial and the governmental techniques, which then come to define legal subjects even when they are not present in court.

[8] '*Jhuggi-jhopdi* colony' is an administrative term referring to shanties located over land that has been occupied and over which no formal rights exist. This term is to be distinguished from official 'slums'.

[9] I want to emphasise that local histories of neighbourhoods in Delhi are varied. Some neighbourhoods came up because people were allocated land in exchange for participation in various government schemes. The most notorious example was that of allocation of house plots in the beautification-cum-sterilisation drive during the National Emergency of 1976 in Delhi. See Emma Tarlo (2003).

[10] In the case of Mumbai, the drive to clean slums, especially Dharavi, has led to fascinating local-level movements supported by NGOs, international donors and even state bureaucracies pressing for creation of permanent rights over land for slum dwellers. In part, this was due to the increasing value of land and the desire to convert occupied land parcels into commodities that would be securely transacted. However, market considerations are not the only ones that have led to struggles over housing for the poor. See Arjun Appadurai (2001) and Roma Chatterji (2005).

[11] *Ahmedabad Municipal Corporation v. Nawab Khan Ghulab Khan and Others* AIR 1997 SC 152. Significant cases with regard to the right to be provided alternative housing if one can show continuous dwelling by pavement dwellers and other vulnerable groups include *Olga Tellis v. Bombay Municipal Corporation* 1985 (3) SSC 545, which was adjudicated in the Bombay High Court and then went up to the Supreme Court in which Justice Chandrachud held that the destruction of a dwelling house is the destruction of all that one holds dear in life. Thus the court, while upholding the Bombay Municipal Corporation's act of clearing pavements of illegal occupiers, nevertheless held that they could only be evicted after they had been provided with alternative housing. This judgment was expanded in the 1990s in *Chameli Singh v. State of UP* and *Ahmedabad Municipal Corporation v. Nawab Khan Gulab Khan*. See the excellent summary of the cases by Jayna Kothari (2002).

[12] This is an important methodological point that I simply wish to flag here to block off the criticism that such examples of community-level politics do not help in telling the large story, as also to argue that spatial notions of State create the impression of the State as a container within which smaller communities are enclosed. Instead, my argument is that the presence of the State is also discerned in the texture of relations. See Thrift (1999), Das (2007) and, for the classic formulation on the significance of so-called small things, see Tarde (1999).

[13] Though classified as a 'backward' community now belonging to the administrative category of 'Other Backward Castes', historians identify several past kingdoms as Gujjar or Gurjara in origin.

[14] Observations based on interview with a local Gujjar leader in 2002, and frequent interactions with another upper-caste medical practitioner who does not have a formal degree in medicine but wields considerable influence due to his ability to give high-risk, high-interest loans to the jhuggi dwellers.

[15] I think that this form of supplication draws from the implicit idea of patron–client relations, which otherwise the migrant lower castes are vociferous in rejecting.

[16] As I noted earlier, the 1980s were a period of some landmark cases in which rights of pavement dwellers and hawkers to their place of habitation, even if illegally occupied, were strongly protected by various high courts of the country.

[17] The name of the society bears trace of the intervention of the upper-caste lawyer who might have suggested the name. Harijan was the term Gandhi used for untouchables, but later Dalit leaders rejected this appellation. Of the 23 or so

registered societies that are now active in the local politics of the area, none uses caste terms – preferring such titles as Jhuggi-Jhopdi Welfare Association, Society for Workers' Struggle, etc.

[18] It is important to mention that electricity has not been privatised in UP. Thus, the jhuggi dwellers interact with government officials over electricity claims and not with private companies. However, private arrangements, such as getting lines from street poles by paying a 'regular fee' to the local official or sharing the electricity provided to a neighbour, are common.

[19] Though electricity was privatised in adjoining Delhi, in the case of NOIDA the supply comes from a public sector undertaking.

[20] For a more detailed discussion of the use of such ritual-cum-legal vocabulary in exorcism rituals, see Das (2008).

[21] There were three of us when this interview was conducted. References to earlier conversations are not to any formal interviews but to conversations between Vinod, Purshottam and me during routine visits to the community.

[22] See, for instance, Bhargava and Reifeld (2005) for the variety of ways in which citizenship comes to be discussed through these overarching concepts, which, however, leave the lives of the poor outside the purview of these discussions.

References

Agamben, Giorgio. 1998. *Homo Sacer: Sovereign Power and Bare Life*, trans. D. Heller Roazen. Stanford: Stanford University Press.

———. 2005. *State of Exception*. London: University of Chicago Press.

Appadurai, Arjun. 2001. 'Deep Democracy: Urban Governmentality and the Horizon of Politics', *Environment and Urbanization*, 13(2): 23–43.

Arendt, Hannah. 1977. *On Revolution*. London: Penguin.

Benda-Beckman, Franz von. 1992. 'Changing Legal Pluralism in Indonesia', *Yuridica*, 8: 1–23.

Benjamin, Walter. 1978. 'Critique of Violence', in *Reflections: Essays, Aphorisms, Autobiographical Writing*. New York: Harcourt, Brace and World.

Bhargava, Rajeev, and Helmut Reifeld (eds). 2005. *Civil Society, Public Sphere, and Citizenship: Dialogues and Perceptions*. New Delhi: Sage.

Buhler, George. 1886. *The Laws of Manu* (*Sacred Books of the East*, vol. 25). Oxford: Clarendon Press.

Bynum, Carolyn Walker. 1991. *Fragmentation and Redemption: Essays on Gender and the Human Body in Medieval Religion*. Cambridge, MA: MIT Press.

Cavell, Stanley. 1979. *The Claim of Reason: Wittgenstein, Morality, Tragedy, Skepticism*. Cambridge, MA: Harvard University Press.

———. 1988. 'Declining Decline: Wittgenstein as a Philosopher of Culture', *Inquiry*, 31: 253–64.

Chatterjee, Partha. 2004. *The Politics of the Governed: Considerations on Political Society in Most of the World*. New York: Columbia University Press.

Chatterji, Roma. 2005. 'Plans, Habitation and Slum Development', *Contributions to Indian Sociology*, 39(2): 197–218.

Cohen, Lawrence. 2004. 'Operatability: Surgery and the Margins of the State', in Veena Das and Deborah Poole (eds), *Anthropology in the Margins of the State*, pp. 165–91. Santa Fe: SAR Press.

Das, Veena. 2007. *Life and Words: Violence and the Descent into the Ordinary*. Berkeley: University of California Press.

———. 2008. 'If This Be Magic . . .: Excursions into Contemporary Hindu Lives', in Hent de Vries (ed.), *Religion beyond a Concept*, pp. 259–83. New York: Fordham University Press.

Davis, Donald R. 2006. 'A Realist View of Hindu Law', *Ratio Juris*, 19(3): 287–313.

de Certeau, Michel. 1984. *The Practice of Everyday Life*. Berkeley: University of California Press.

Eckert, Julia. 2006. 'From Subjects to Citizens: Legalism from Below and the Homogenization of the Legal Sphere', *Journal of Legal Pluralism*, 53–54: 45–76.

Fassin, Didier. 2009. 'Les économies morales revisitées: Etude critique suivie de quelques propositions', *Annales: Histoire, Sciences Sociales*, 64(5).

———. 2010. 'Ethics of Survival: A Democratic Approach to the Politics of Life', *Humanity*, 1(1): 81–95.

Foucault, Michel. 2003. *Society Must Be Defended: Lectures at the College de France, 1975–1976*. London: Picador.

Godelier, Maurice, and Marilyn Strathern (eds). 1991. *Big Men and Great Men: Personifications of Power in Melanesia*. Cambridge: Cambridge University Press.

Kothari, Jayna. 2002. 'A Right to Housing?' Bangalore: Voices.

Latour, Bruno. 2010. *The Making of Law: An Ethnography of the Conseil d'Etat*. Cambridge: Polity Press.

Lèvi-Strauss, Claude. 1974. *Tristes Tropiques*. New York: Atheneum.

Marcus, George E. 1995. 'Mass Toxic Torts and the End of Everyday Life', in Austin Sarat and Thomas R. Kearns (eds), *Law in Everyday Life*, pp. 237–75. Michigan: University of Michigan Press.

Pitkin, Hanna F. 1998. *The Attack of the Blob: Hannah Arendt's Concept of the Social*. Chicago: University of Chicago Press.

Rabinow, Paul. 1992. 'Artificiality and Enlightenment: From Sociobiology to Biosociality', in Jonathan Cray (ed.), *Incorporations*, pp. 234–52. Cambridge, MA: MIT Press.

———. 2006. 'Biopower Today', *Biosocieties*, 1: 195–217.

Rose, Nikolas. 2007. *The Politics of Life Itself: Biomedicine, Power and Subjectivity*. Cambridge: Cambridge University Press.

Sarat, Austin, and Thomas R. Kearns. 1995. 'Editorial Introduction', in Austin Sarat and Thomas R. Kearns (eds), *Law in Everyday Life*, pp. 1–21. Michigan: University of Michigan Press.

Schmitt, Carl. 1985. *Political Theology: Four Chapters on the Concept of Sovereignty*, trans. George Schwab. Cambridge, MA: MIT Press.

Scott, James C. 1985. *Weapons of the Weak: Everyday Forms of Peasant Resistance*. New Haven: Yale University Press.

Tarde, G. 1999. *Les Lois Sociales*. Paris: Editions Decouvertè.

Tarlo, Emma. 2003. *Unsettling Memories: Narratives of the Emergency in Delhi*. Berkeley: University of California Press.

Thrift, Nigel J. 1999. 'It's the Little Things', in K. Dodds and D. Atkinson (eds), *Contemporary Geopolitics*, pp. 380–87. London: Routledge.

Unger, Roberto M. 1986. *The Critical Legal Studies Movement*. Cambridge, MA: Harvard University Press.

3

Discrimination and Justice

Beyond Affirmative Action

Deepak Nayyar

Vice Chancellor Shyam Menon, Professor Romila Thapar, Professor Salil Misra, distinguished guests, ladies and gentlemen, I consider it an honour and a privilege to be in your midst this evening, and I would like to thank Ambedkar University for their invitation to deliver the third Ambedkar Memorial Lecture, on what is his 120th birth anniversary.[1] I would also like to thank the Vice Chancellor for his warm and generous words of introduction. I am conscious of the fact that I follow in the footsteps of two distinguished scholars, Bhikhu Parekh and Veena Das. I can only hope that my endeavour conforms to the high standards set by them.

At the outset, I must confess to some hesitation and some diffidence. It is neither the podium nor the auditorium, for public lectures are so much a part of my life as an academic. It is the theme which is outside my usual domain. In fact, discourses on social justice are the preserve of philosophers, political theorists or sociologists, rather than of economists. But I was persuaded. For that, you can blame Professor Shyam Menon who moved from Physics to Education in a nimble, almost seamless, manner. It probably led him to believe that economists are, or should be, versatile enough. Of course, economists are narrow and boring beyond compare. I think he knows that but is too polite to say so. The decision, however, to take this plunge, was mine alone. It could be that fools rush in where angels fear to tread. It could be the attribute of economists who change the questions when they do not know the answers. But it is neither. I believe the time has come once again for economists to address questions in political economy and moral philosophy,[2] which are a part of our intellectual heritage, that have been forgotten in the narrow concerns of orthodox mainstream economics.

The object of my lecture this evening is to analyse discrimination and justice, in terms of theory and experience, to suggest that affirmative action is necessary but cannot be sufficient in the quest for social justice. The structure of the discussion is as follows. First, I will consider the origins of discrimination in historical perspective. Second, I will examine how discrimination leads to exclusion, and embedded injustice is an outcome of the process. Third, I will discuss the conception of justice as it has evolved, beginning in ancient India, through Enlightenment thinkers in Europe, to modern political thought in the contemporary world. Fourth, I will argue that the quest for social justice, which gathered momentum during the second half of the 20th century, is a relatively recent phenomenon even if discrimination and injustice are as old as humankind. Fifth, I will analyse the logic, the necessity and the limitations of affirmative action to highlight what else is needed. Sixth, I will endeavour to impart a dose of reality to the story through a tale of three countries, India, the United States and South Africa, even if the focus is on India. Seventh, in conclusion, I hope to draw some lessons from experience to contemplate the future.

Origins of Discrimination

Let me begin with the origins of discrimination. Societies are characterised by inequalities as a rule. Indeed, social stratification in one form or another is as old as humankind. It would be reasonable to ask a simple question. Was there discrimination at the very start of human social existence? If not, how did it begin? It is plausible to suggest, though impossible to prove, that the origins can be traced to the division of labour: in the household, in the community, in the world of work. It may also have been the outcome of conflict, whenever victors subjected the vanquished to subordinate roles and, then, discrimination. The classic example, perhaps, is the discrimination against women embedded in the division of labour in a household. Such gender bias has a wide range of manifestations, particularly in our society where women have no access to potters' wheels or farmers' ploughs, even if, ironically enough, this practice is juxtaposed with the worship of goddesses. People captured in battle, then enslaved, are another example. In sum, the division of labour and the outcomes of conflict shaped relationships in given historical contexts or conditions.

The divisions or thresholds that constituted the origins of discrimination were not defined once and for all. There was evolution and there was mutation. The forms of discrimination changed over time and differed across societies. Yet, the essential attributes of discrimination, whether its contours or its consequences, are similar in their manifestations of inequality and injustice in societies. It would seem that the divides between the privileged and the underprivileged, the exploiters and the exploited, the victors and the vanquished, or the fundamental divide between inclusion and exclusion, are two sides of the same coin. One cannot exist without the other. In fact, in any society, the inclusion of some necessitates the exclusion of others, if only as a point of reference. The lines that divide people differ across societies and change over time. But if such lines did not exist, they would be invented so that they could be drawn.

Discrimination and Exclusion

We can now turn to discrimination and exclusion. The term 'exclusion' has become a part of the lexicon of economists in recent years although it has been in the jargon of sociology and the vocabulary of politics for somewhat longer. The word 'exclusion' has multiple dimensions: social, economic and political. Exclusion is used not simply to describe a situation, but also to focus on a process which excludes individuals or groups from communities, livelihoods and rights, thus depriving them of freedoms that are constitutive of and instrumental in development, which is a source of well-being for people, ordinary people. The essential point is that stratification is almost inevitable in economies and societies which systematically integrate some and marginalise others, to distribute benefits of economic growth and social progress in ways that include some and exclude others. There is a strange irony in this process, which is captured almost perfectly in an epithet from Joan Robinson, one of my favourite economists, who taught at Cambridge. She once said, 'There is only one thing that is worse than being exploited by capitalists, and that is *not* being exploited by capitalists' (Edwards 2004: 12). Joan Robinson was a profoundly original mind but in this she was not. She probably borrowed from George Bernard Shaw who once said, 'There is only one thing that is worse than being talked about, and that is *not* being talked about.' Much the same can be said about markets in societies.[3]

Markets exclude people as consumers or buyers if they do not have any incomes, or sufficient incomes, which can be translated into purchasing power. This exclusion is attributable to their lack of income or *entitlements*. Such people are excluded from the consumption of goods and services which are sold in the market. Markets exclude people as producers or sellers if they have neither *assets* nor *capabilities*.[4] People experience such exclusion if they do not have assets, physical or financial, which can be used to yield an income in the form of rent, interest or profits. Even those without assets could enter the market as producers or sellers using their labour for a wage if they have some capabilities. Such capabilities are acquired through education, training or experience.

Markets exclude people both as consumers and producers, or as buyers and sellers, if they do not accept, or do not conform to, the values of a market system. The most obvious example of such exclusion is tribal populations or forest communities in market economies. But such exclusion may take other forms. There may be people who are unable or unwilling to sell their capabilities. For instance, a person may be unable or unwilling to charge fees as an astrologer or a musician because of a belief system that such talents cannot and should not be sold.

There is, of course, an interaction between exclusion from the market in the economic sphere and the non-economic dimensions of exclusion in the social, political and cultural spheres.[5] The social manifestations of exclusion can be powerful, for economic exclusion accentuates social exclusion. Economic exclusion from livelihoods often creates or accentuates a political exclusion from rights. Similarly, cultural exclusion such as that of immigrant groups, minority communities or ethnic groups interacts with economic exclusion from the market. Each dimension reinforces the other to produce a vicious circle of cumulative causation. The outcome is embedded discrimination.

This does not mean that exclusion is always bad and inclusion is always good. Coercive inclusion by markets, whether of child labour, tribal populations or immigrant workers, can be exploitative. The employment of women as wage labour on terms inferior to those of men provides another example. The basic point is that inclusion which is coercive, or on inferior terms, is not desirable. For similar reasons, exclusion is not always bad. To those who do not accept the values of the market system, any voluntary exclusion from market should be perfectly acceptable.

It is no surprise that there is a cumulative causation associated with exclusion, or inclusion, as a process. For those excluded, there is more and more discrimination, which creates vicious circles over time. For those included, there is more and more privilege, which creates virtuous circles over time. Discrimination, then, is embedded in relationships and processes that reinforce and strengthen it over time, which makes it difficult to curb, let alone reverse or eliminate. The divides that nurture stratification and foster discrimination differ across space and change over time. Yet, some are common enough everywhere in the world: race, caste, religion, gender, and ethnicity. It is worth noting that discrimination and exclusion are closely interwoven but could be different in their origins. Discrimination can be based on a common identity where the society breaks down the identity into a hierarchy. But exclusion, except for gender exclusion which is based on perceived natural differences, is created by society through different identities based on race, religion, caste, or ethnicity. Once introduced, however, exclusion and discrimination reinforce each other in societies.

Conceptions of Justice

The stage is set for us to consider conceptions of justice. It might be appropriate to begin with the classical distinction from ancient Indian jurisprudence, which offers a pre-modern conceptualisation of justice: *niti* and *nyaya*. In a literal sense, both stand for justice in classical Sanskrit. Niti is about what is right in terms of propriety, conduct and behaviour. Nyaya is about what is just, not as an abstraction but as a realised outcome. This conception has a point of reference in ancient India: *matsyanyaya*, justice in the world of fish, where, in times of drought, the big fish devour the small fish at will. This happens in two sets of conditions, either in bad times such as drought, or in chaotic times such as anarchy. The latter represents a situation of *arajya* associated with patent violations of human justice as nyaya. In terms of this characterisation of justice, Amartya Sen argues that the people who agitated for the abolition of slavery in the 18th and 19th centuries sought to eliminate intolerable injustice in the sense of nyaya rather than establish perfect justice in the sense of niti (Sen 2009). But I would differ from Amartya Sen in this interpretation. The reason is that nyaya is defined as justice not in the abstract but in a social context.[6] Matsyanyaya, or slavery, may have been contrary to the conception of nyaya as caricature or intolerable forms of injustice, but inequalities, or less-than-just situations, which were accepted as norms in society, may have been consistent with the conception of nyaya.

Enlightenment thinkers in Europe in the 18th and 19th centuries were encouraged by the political climate of change and the socio-economic transformation of the times. This led to a different, modern conception of justice. There were two basic, divergent lines of reasoning about justice in the radical intellectual tradition of that period: the contractarian approaches and the comparative approaches.[7] The contractarian approaches were initiated by Thomas Hobbes. They were developed further by John Locke, Jean-Jacques Rousseau and Immanuel Kant. The social contract was an ideal alternative to the chaos that might otherwise characterise a society. The most powerful and elegant exposition of this approach to justice can be found in the work of John Rawls, a leading political philosopher of our times (Rawls 1971, 2001). Other contemporary theorists, such as Ronald Dworkin and Robert Nozick, have taken a similar route. In terms of the jargon in the trade, Amartya Sen (2009) describes this approach as 'transcendental institutionalism' (see Dworkin 2000). But I think this approach can be explained in a simpler manner. It has two essential foundations: that of a just society as an idea, and that of institutions and rules as arrangements that deliver such a just society.

The comparative approaches owe their origins to the work of

Adam Smith, Jeremy Bentham, Karl Marx, and John Stuart Mill, all of whom were Enlightenment theorists concerned with social realisations resulting from actual institutions and actual behaviour. In my simplification of theories of justice, there are, once again, two essential ideas in this approach. The first seeks to focus on comparisons of situations as more just or less unjust. The second seeks to focus on realisations in terms of outcomes for people, whether they were just, unjust, more just, or less unjust. This realisation focus is the real point of departure for a number of contemporary theorists, including Sen.

Quest for Social Justice

From theories of justice, let me move to the quest for social justice. A prior question is: what is social justice? In what sense, if any, is it different from justice? The answer to this question is neither obvious nor clear. It is possible to speculate. It might refer to the distinction between the comparative and the contractarian approaches, to the distinction between justice that is contextualised in society and justice that is conceptualised in abstract principles of jurisprudence. It might also be that social justice is an ideal construct which creates a society, whose very being, as it were, ensures rights and opportunities for all people, irrespective of whether the state steps in to provide these rights and opportunities.

Be that as it may, discrimination in society is an obvious form of social injustice. The cognition of this reality goes back a very long time. However, the realisation that social justice is not an automatic outcome, on the contrary, it has to be discovered and established, is a more recent phenomenon. In fact, the quest for social justice which seeks to reduce, if not eliminate, discrimination is essentially a phenomenon that gathered momentum during the second half of the 20th century. It is motivated by a concern which arises from the observed reality that society does not provide rights and opportunities for a significant proportion of people who are subjected to discrimination in one form or another. This concern is attributable not so much to a sense of egalitarianism as it is to perceptions of injustice.

What were the factors underlying the quest for social justice? There were many. But I choose to highlight two that probably shaped and drove this quest: institutions and ideologies.

In institutions, I would focus on the nation state and political democracy. The emergence of the nation state was associated with the emergence of nationalism, which led to a slow but steady erosion of multiple identities that developed into a national identity. The spread of political democracy was associated with the idea of egalitarianism, which sought to reduce injustice even if it could not deliver justice, and to contest discrimination even if it did not seek equality. More often than not, the quest may have begun with a provision from above. Yet, in some places and at some times, it was pushed by claims from below. In retrospect it is clear that, taken together, the institutions of the nation state and political democracy played a critical role in this quest for social justice. So did ideologies.

In ideologies, I would focus on capitalism and communism. There can be little doubt that capitalism reduced, and sought to eliminate, pre-capitalist forms of discrimination embedded in feudalism, whether in the form of serfdom or bonded labour, but created new or different forms of discrimination or exclusion. Successive stages in the evolution of capitalism have been associated with exploitation, progress and dilution. It is possible to think of this sequence in terms of countries or of people. Consider countries in what is now described as the 'developing world': imperialism led to exploitation, nationalism was followed by some progress, and globalisation meant dilution if not regress. Consider people in industrial societies: early capitalism led to exploitation, which was corrected as political democracy introduced a role for the state in regulating the market, while the advent of social democracy as an ideology strengthened the quest for social justice, but it was followed by the rise of market fundamentalism and international capitalism in the age of globalisation, which diluted the same quest.[8]

Socialism or communism set out to reduce, if not eliminate, forms of discrimination that were characteristic of capitalism – capitalists and workers – or that persisted in capitalism – men and women. It made some of the transition from capitalism to socialism (from everybody according to their ability and to everybody according to their work), but none of the transition from socialism to communism (from everybody according to their ability and to everybody according to their need). In fact, socialism may have reduced some old forms of discrimination, but it also created new forms of privilege and exclusion. This was experienced by citizens and understood by scholars of the erstwhile Soviet Union. It was carried over easily, in different manifestations and in accentuated form, into post-transition Russia. The Cultural Revolution in China did not create, as Mao Zedong had hoped, a new socialist man. Indeed, just a decade later, Deng Xiaoping's modernisations ushered in what was described as market socialism, which developed some attributes of unbridled capitalism over time. In fact, among the socialist countries with communist governments, Cuba seems to be the solitary exception, where discrimination based not only on gender but also on race was eliminated; Cuba is possibly the only society that created equality of opportunity in those domains even if it had failings in most other spheres. In retrospect, it would seem that communism did succeed in bringing about a substantial reduction in gender discrimination by creating equal opportunities. But why it failed elsewhere remains an open question.

Affirmative Action

The quest for social justice needs some form of affirmative action. In situations where exclusion takes the form of discrimination against identifiable groups defined or identified by race, caste, religion, gender, or ethnicity, social legislation is necessary. But it may not be sufficient, because it is difficult to implement and to enforce a law of equal opportunities wherever discrimination is embedded in history. That leads me into the logic of affirmative action. In situations where discrimination and exclusion have a history, affirmative action, or positive discrimination, in favour of the underprivileged or the excluded is necessary as a corrective to compensate for embedded discrimination. The term 'affirmative action' refers to a set of policies and practices that are used to create equal opportunity and maximum diversity. These target primarily workplaces and educational institutions while using race, caste, gender, or ethnicity as factors that must be taken into account when employment or admissions-related decisions are made. The object is to redress perceived disadvantages attributable to overt institutional, or involuntary, discrimination.

But we must recognise that remedial action does not always provide a sustainable solution. Affirmative action is almost always conceived of, when it begins life, as a transitional remedy that would end once there are equal opportunities for all citizens. In other words, even if affirmative action is both necessary and desirable, it cannot continue in perpetuity. Indeed, I believe affirmative action is a success wherever and whenever it makes itself dispensable. But this may not, and often does not, happen. The reason is simple. Discrimination is often embedded in beliefs and ideologies. Affirmative action cannot always combat these beliefs or ideologies, let alone change the initial conditions which created discrimination in the past. In the ultimate analysis, the economic, social and political empowerment of the excluded is essential. Affirmative action seeks to provide from above, but this must be transformed into a claim from below. For that to happen, political democracy is an imperative. However, it is necessary but not sufficient. This is borne out by experience – consider, for example, the oldest and the largest democracies of the world, the United States and India. Yet, there is a strong correlation between the idea of justice and the practice of democracy.

In contemporary political philosophy, democracy is best seen as government by discussion, given the central role of public reasoning supported by freedom of the press and intervention of civil society. There is a critical role in this process for government as a catalyst if not leader, through mediation and intervention, which has to be performed because in the ultimate analysis, governments are accountable to people. This is obvious in democratic regimes, although even in authoritarian regimes governments are ultimately accountable to their people. The idea of government by discussion is essentially about the importance of voice in political democracy.[9] The problem is that democracy, while conducive and necessary, is not sufficient to actually produce development and deliver social justice.

Development and justice may or may not be provided from above by benevolent governments, but must be claimed from below by people as citizens from governments that are accountable. The empowerment of people then is an integral part of any process of change that leads to social justice, to development. A political democracy, even if it is slow, provides a sure path for two reasons. It increases political consciousness among voters to judge political parties for their performance. At the same time, it increases participation in political processes when it leads to mobilisation on some issues. This highlights the significance of Amartya Sen's conception of development as freedom.[10] Expanding freedoms for people at large constitute development, but the same expanding freedoms which empower people are instruments that drive the process of change in development. Of course, elites in democracies, or those who rule, are not easily persuaded. Indeed, many governments might have a strong preference for silent people.[11] And, come election time, such governments would, if they could, change the people rather than allow a change in government! It is clear that democracy, while essential, cannot suffice to ensure affirmative action for social justice. And it should be no surprise that the task cannot be performed by governments alone.

There is a fundamental role for society. For people who have been subjected to discrimination, the transition from the creation of opportunities to the realisation of opportunities requires two essentials. First, there must be a social consciousness among those included, that is, the privileged. Second, there must be a rights consciousness among the excluded, that is, those discriminated against. Yet, there are persistent difficulties and stubborn obstacles. For one, there is resistance on the part of those privileged, those who are included. Why? The answer is simple. It is about ceding the social, economic and political space which they occupy. This is particularly important in societies where people are poor and opportunities are scarce. There are vested interests on the one hand, and there are embedded prejudices on the other. These are both very difficult to fight, let alone remove. What is needed, then, is social consciousness on the part of individuals and collective action on the part of communities. Another difficulty is resentment on the part of those who are discriminated against, who are excluded. People who have long been subjected to discrimination in society sometimes see affirmative action as a process that reinforces notions of exclusion. In their perception, identities are seen as labels, or as symbols of exclusion. In such situations, the struggle against social injustice through affirmative action becomes far more complex and difficult.

A Tale of Three Countries

There are three countries in the contemporary world that are characterised by a history of embedded discrimination and social injustice, which have sought to address the problem through affirmative action beginning in the second half of the 20th century: India, the United States and South Africa. Their problems are similar in terms of consequences even if they are different in terms of origins.

Surprisingly enough, India was the first to introduce affirmative action, soon after independence, beginning 1950. The object was to address problems of discrimination and injustice which were embedded in history. For centuries, indeed millennia, society discriminated against a significant proportion of its indigenous population on the basis of a social hierarchy created by the *varnashrama dharma*,[12] which provided the foundations of a complex caste system. The outcome was social injustice experienced by a significant proportion of the population, which is now estimated at about one-fourth of the total population.

The US introduced affirmative action beginning with civil rights legislation in the mid-1960s, and not since the Civil War which ended slavery in 1865. The discrimination it sought to address was not embedded in the pre-colonial past. It began life as an outcome of early colonialism in the 18th century. The European migrant population began with discrimination against the indigenous people. But it was not long before the native population of American Indians was almost decimated. And, even now, the few who remain live in abject poverty in remote reservations with almost no integration into society. The same European migrant population imported labour from Africa to work on plantations as slaves. Slavery came to an end in 1865, but the black population continued to experience discrimination and injustice for a century thereafter. This population of African Americans is now estimated at about 10 per cent of the total population.

South Africa was the last to introduce affirmative action among the three countries, following liberation in 1994. The discrimination it attempted to redress was not embedded in its pre-colonial history. It was an outcome of colonialism, as in the United States, albeit of a somewhat different kind and somewhat later, during the 19th century. A small migrant population of white settlers from Europe practised discrimination against the native African population. However, the indigenous people were not eliminated, but were turned into labour for mines and plantations. At the same time, indentured labour, which constituted a new form of slavery, was imported mostly from India to work on the mines and plantations. In addition, a small number of people were brought in from India as traders, to create a middle class that did not exist before. The black and the brown populations were discriminated against by the white population, although there was a hierarchy in this triangular structure of discrimination. The African population is now estimated at more than 80 per cent, while people of Indian origin are about 7 per cent of the total population of South Africa. It should be obvious that the nature and scale of the problem are very different as compared with the other two countries, because more than four-fifths of the population has been subjected to discrimination for at least 150 years.

What can we learn from the experience of affirmative action in these three countries? It is only natural that my focus is on India. But I would also like to consider, even if briefly, the US and South Africa as points of reference if not comparison.

India

Embedded discrimination and social injustice provided the rationale for affirmative action in independent India. The Republic of India introduced affirmative action as part of the Constitution that was adopted in 1950. It is worth noting that Dr Ambedkar played a lead role, as architect and author, in drawing up that Constitution.[13] In considering the Indian experience, it is necessary to explain the logic of the model, recognise the successes, analyse the failures, and note the dilemmas that persist.

The model is simple enough. Its conception and design were based on two essential attributes. The first was *affirmative action* in favour of Scheduled Castes and Scheduled Tribes, as discrimination against these social groups was embedded in history, so that caste and tribe were the defining basis of the policy. The second was *proportional reservation*, quotas roughly in conformity with the proportion of these groups in the total population – which was 15 per cent for Scheduled Castes and 7.5 per cent for Scheduled Tribes at that time – in government employment and in higher education. These reservations were introduced when the Constitution was adopted in 1950. The same reservations were renewed from time to time, most recently in 2010. Such reservations were extended to Other Backward Classes (OBCs) in 1991 for employment in the government sector, and in 2006 for places in higher education. The proportion in both sectors was specified as 27.5 per cent of the total, to keep overall reservation to Scheduled Castes, Scheduled Tribes and OBCs within 50 per cent, as per the Supreme Court ruling in this regard. There is draft legislation, pending consideration for quite some time, which proposes that 33 per cent of seats in the national Parliament and in state legislatures be reserved for women. Such reservation for women was, in fact, introduced in panchayats in 1993. It is worth noting that affirmative action in each of these spheres, in the form of proportional reservations, is a legal right under the Constitution.[14] Therefore, in India, affirmative action is a matter of right.[15]

Given the legacy of embedded discrimination, the experience of the past 60 years suggests that affirmative action did succeed, even if the success was modest. It would seem, at least *prima facie*, that the objectives of reservations have been met in so far as the quotas have been filled. There is proportional representation of Scheduled Castes and Scheduled Tribes in state legislatures and in the national Parliament (the Lok Sabha), just as there is proportional reservation for Dalits and tribals in employment in the government and in the public sector, particularly at lower levels. Clearly, there is inclusion for some, and there can be little doubt that the situation would have been worse, distinctly worse, without such affirmative action. Success therefore lies in the counterfactual. But that has another dimension. In my view, outcomes could and should have been better.

At the same time, it is clear that there were failures. Outcomes of reservations in higher education were not quite as good as in government employment. The situation would have been much worse without affirmative action, but could have been far better if such intervention had been more effective and more purposive. Even after six decades of reservations, the quotas for Scheduled Castes and Scheduled Tribes in higher education remain under-fulfilled by large margins. The stipulated quotas are simply not met, either because a sufficient number do not make the threshold in terms of much reduced minimum eligibility criteria, or because admission processes circumvent the stipulation by stealth or design. The dropout rates are high, while the completion rates are low among students from Scheduled Castes and Scheduled Tribes who do obtain admission through reservations in higher education. The reason is clear. Their school education has not been good enough to prepare them for higher education. And most higher education institutions, with a few exceptions, do not make any serious attempt at remedial teaching. There are some exceptions, as a few institutions make the effort, often supported by committed individuals. But most such students who come into the higher education system through reservations are first-generation learners and are not on a par with the average student who enters the world of work. Yet, reservations exist only at the point of entry. However, creating a hierarchy of reservations, at every level, is no solution. It could turn out to be worse than the problem, if performance is substandard. What is more, it does not address the real issue. In fact, it would be no exaggeration to state that the benefits of reservations have accrued mostly to the better off, the more educated, among Dalits and tribals. Those included through affirmative action in the first instance are, in a sense, co-opted into the system. Thereafter, privilege is reproduced in the form of pre-emptive access for the next generation, as also the next, which continues in perpetuity. The outcome is that a small subset of people from groups that were subjected to discrimination have privileged access through affirmative action, whereas most people from the same groups are left out, marginalised or excluded. We have simply created what the Supreme Court describes as a 'creamy layer'. But exclusion persists for a large number, who constitute a substantial proportion of those for whom affirmative action is needed and of those for whom affirmative action was introduced in the first place.[16]

It is no surprise that dilemmas persist. There is patronage for those included rather than equal opportunities for all. There is co-option of those included rather than an empowerment – economic, social or political – of all people who are subjected to discrimination and injustice. There is exclusion on a massive scale. More than 60 years after affirmative action was introduced, an overwhelmingly large proportion of Dalits and tribals remain excluded from higher education and from government employment because they have little, if any, access to social opportunities, most of which come from school education. It would seem that the real failures, as also the persistent dilemmas, are attributable to the limited spread of education in society, which is the only sustainable means of providing social opportunities for ordinary people, particularly those excluded on account of embedded discrimination. Such exclusion begins with school education and cannot ever end for those denied access because there is a path dependence in the process. It needs to be said that this exclusion is not based on caste alone. It is based on gender, religion, location, and, most importantly perhaps, income. Hence, there cannot be any caste-based solution to the problem of economic inequality (Teltumbde 2009). What is more, addressing the problem of disparities between groups cannot resolve the problem of inequality among individuals in economy and society.[17] This compounds difficulties for affirmative action in higher education, where the experience has been mixed if not disappointing, and possibly not on a par with outcomes of affirmative action in other spheres.

The United States

It is interesting to consider the US as a point of reference for a brief comparison. The origins of consciousness about social justice can be traced to the end of the Civil War in 1865. The 13th Amendment to the US Constitution made slavery illegal. And the Civil Rights Act of 1866 guaranteed every citizen the same right to make and to enforce contracts. But the real quest for social justice in the US began almost 100 years later.[18] The civil rights movement, in the early 1960s, strongly protested against discrimination and segregation of African Americans in the southern United States because such discrimination was seen as unjust, unacceptable and intolerable. The efforts and the struggle of this movement ended segregation through legal change. The 14th Amendment to the Constitution guarantees equal protection under the law. The Civil Rights Act of 1964 forbids racial discrimination in public accommodations and stipulates that there is to be no discrimination on the basis of race and sex in employment. The 15th Amendment to the Constitution followed soon thereafter, with the Voting Rights Act of 1965 forbidding racial discrimination in access to voting.

Interestingly enough, the US began affirmative action almost in the same mode as India. But it was not long before reverse discrimination surfaced as a problem. The famous example is the Alan Bakke case of 1978.[19] The Supreme Court of the United States outlawed inflexible quota systems in all affirmative action programmes but upheld the legality of affirmative action. Strict quotas no longer exist. Discretionary diversity policies are present. Equality of opportunity laws are in force. In a more recent case in 2003, the Supreme Court upheld the University of Michigan Law School admissions policy, ruling that race can be one of the factors considered by colleges when selecting their students if it improves diversity. It is clear that affirmative action in the US is a matter of policy, which provides a sharp contrast with India where it is a matter of right.[20]

It would seem that, for almost a century after slavery was outlawed in 1865, progress on redressing discrimination in the US was little, just as it was slow, but it gathered momentum in the early 1960s after the success of the civil rights movement. In the 50 years since then, there have been some clearly discernible successes. The idea of equal opportunities, which was created in law to start with, slowly turned into a degree of social consciousness in the sphere of higher education and in the world of work.

The attitudes of the elite to social mobility among those discriminated against in the past changed from hostile to permissive without becoming enthusiastic. Most importantly, perhaps, the sanctity of glass ceilings eroded slowly over time in politics, in corporates, in professions, in academia, and in media. Of course, there are still not enough African Americans, or women, in leadership positions in any sphere, as significant asymmetries persist. Yet, the election of President Obama represents the shattering of one such glass ceiling.

It would be too much of a digression to enter into a discussion on the factors underlying this progress in the US. Even so, it is worth noting some factors that could have been important in the process of change. The legal framework and legal institutions made a significant contribution. The common schooling system, which created equality of opportunity in school education, made an enormous difference. The spread of education in society and levels of income in the economy were supportive of, rather than resistant to, the associated social change. And the task was more feasible than elsewhere, as only 10 per cent of the total population had been subjected to discrimination.

South Africa

South Africa is a very different story. The apartheid regime institutionalised discrimination. It was characterised by extreme repression embodied in a division of labour that locked the African population into poverty. The vicious circle of cumulative causation stretched beyond income poverty and living conditions. There was little in terms of access to education and healthcare. For large numbers of black people, the reality came close to disguised slavery. Given this context, where more than 80 per cent of the population was subjected to acute discrimination, affirmative action was bound to be difficult and challenging. In theory, the process began in the late 1970s, with some loosening of the apartheid regime, when there was a small attempt at providing equal opportunities in terms of equal protection in the law for all employees. As the liberation struggle gathered momentum and the regime came under increasing pressure from outside, black advancement of sorts was introduced during the late 1980s; non-white residents obtained legitimate status, mixed marriages were legalised, white educational institutions began to accept non-white students. But most of this was symbolic. Little of it was substantive. There was no arrangement for sharing political power.

In effect, affirmative action started after liberation, when the African National Congress captured political power. There were two key principles enunciated by the newly elected government: disadvantaged groups would see improvements in their quality of life, and past discrimination had to be redressed. Hence, the social focus of the legislative effort in the Economic Equity Act of 1994 was on the black African population. The Employment Equity Act of 1998 went further. It extended beyond the government and stipulated that private sector firms must make their workforce demographically more representative: 75 per cent black and 50 per cent female. In addition, under the doctrine of Black Economic Empowerment, white-owned firms are urged to transfer portions of their equity to black people, without which such firms will not be eligible for government contracts. Government employment, of course, is based on strict race and gender quotas. Since then, there has been some progress. But this progress is modest. Contemporary South Africa is sometimes described as a 'cappuccino' society, which is mostly black at the bottom and has a thin layer of white at the top interspersed with a sprinkling of chocolate. It is obvious that affirmative action is necessary but cannot be sufficient. The time has come for the African National Congress to move from the phase of reconciliation to a period of social change. The real answer to past discrimination and social injustice in South Africa lies in education and land, because a very large proportion of the African people still do not have access to education, and those who live in the rural sector have almost no rights in land.

Conclusions

In conclusion, rather than sum up, it would be appropriate to reflect on the future. In doing so, I would like to start with some prior observations. This is followed by an attempt to outline some contours of the journey and some essentials with regard to the destination.

There are three critical propositions that are prior. First, we must learn from the experience of the past 60 years. What went wrong and why? It would serve no purpose to wish away the problem like an ostrich that hides its head in the sand. Second, we must evolve a longer-term perspective about our time horizon for what we set out to do. It cannot be more of the same in perpetuity. Third, we need to recognise that words cannot be a substitute for substance. The time has come to shift from palliatives and correctives, often the soft option, to effective action and sustainable solutions.

The journey to a less unjust, or a more just, society in India must follow some basic contours. First, equal opportunities in school education are an imperative. We know that access is unequal, completion rates are uneven, and dropouts are asymmetrical. The only way to address this issue in the long term is to provide access and create equal opportunities at school. Second, it is necessary to recognise that discrimination, hence exclusion, is multidimensional. We cannot turn a blind eye to that reality. In India, discrimination is not only about caste. It is just as much about religion, about gender, about ethnicity, and, ultimately, about income. Hence, there is a need to construct some composite index of deprivation, for which income could be a proxy, but only a proxy. Third, it is essential to accept the idea that affirmative action must be limited to first-generation learners or first-time entrants. And, even with this correction, reservations cannot suffice. The time has come for an Equal Opportunities Commission to ensure implementation and to adjudicate conflicting claims. Last, but not least, we need to think of a world beyond affirmative action. Whatever we do must unite rather than divide people in the quest for social justice. Therefore, policies that seek to address embedded discrimination must integrate rather than separate people in society. After all, we are a society plagued by so many divides that our quest for inclusion or social justice should not accentuate those divides. This is not an illusion. It is real, for it is about ceding economic, social and political space. And, in societies where opportunities are scarce, there is bound to be resistance. It would be easier if we create more opportunities. School education and higher education provide the obvious examples.

In thinking about the destination, some reality checks are both necessary and desirable. First, equality is an ideal. It is an abstraction or a construct that exists in our mind. Second, justice is a utopia, which is much like the perfection of a just society in the contractarian approaches. The essential objectives that any humane society can aspire to are less abstract and more concrete: progressively reduce and eliminate discrimination, progressively reduce and eliminate social injustice. It is possible to make societies less unjust, or more just, by providing capabilities, opportunities and rights to people who are subjected to discrimination and injustice. But we would be deluding ourselves if we believed, even for a moment, that we will create egalitarian, let alone equal, societies. Inequality will reproduce itself in society. Even so, a better world is possible if social injustice can be progressively reduced and ultimately eliminated. For that, equal opportunity is an imperative, so that every person has access to economic and social opportunities for a better life.

Third Ambedkar Memorial Lecture, 14 April 2011, Ambedkar University Delhi.

Notes

[1] I am indebted to Romila Thapar for helpful discussion and constructive suggestions. I would also like to thank André Béteille for valuable comments and conversations. Jonas Shaende provided useful assistance in my search for information on the United States and South Africa.

[2] See, for example, Smith (1984). It is ironical that the same Adam Smith is invoked as its guru by orthodox mainstream economics.

[3] For a more detailed discussion on markets and exclusion, see Nayyar (2003).

[4] I use the word 'capabilities' to characterise the mix of natural talents, skills acquired through training, learning from experience, and abilities or expertise based on education embodied in a person that enable him or her to use these capabilities as a producer or worker for which there is not only a price but also a demand in the market. It follows that even persons with capabilities may be excluded from employment if there is no demand for their capabilities in the market. It is essential to note that the same word, 'capabilities', has been used in a very different sense by Amartya Sen, who argues that the well-being of a person depends on what the person succeeds in *doing* with the commodities (and their characteristics) at his command. For example: food can provide nutrition to a healthy person but not to a person with a parasitic disease; or, a bicycle can provide transportation to an able-bodied person but not to a disabled person. Thus, for Sen (1985), *capabilities* characterise the combination of functionings a person can achieve given his personal features (conversion of characteristics into functionings) and his command over commodities (*entitlements*).

[5] This interaction is considered further in Nayyar (2003). See also Nayyar (1998).

[6] Consider the example of India, where the concepts of niti and nyaya originated. The social context was characterised by distinctions based on varna and jati, in which there was a hierarchy with the Brahman at the top and the Shudra at the bottom. These social norms were embedded in the conception and understanding of nyaya.

[7] For a detailed discussion on theories of justice, as also on different approaches to justice, see Sen (2009).

[8] In his seminal book, Karl Polanyi (1944) analysed what he characterised as the 'Great Transformation' in Europe in the 19th and 20th centuries. In doing so, he described a double movement: the first, from a pre-capitalist system to market-driven industrialisation in the 19th century; the second (which he termed the 'Great Transformation'), from the predominance of the market model to a more inclusive world in which the state played a corrective, regulatory role. This transformation, which began in the early 20th century, was completed by the mid-20th century. But it did not last long. There was a resurgence of the market model in the late 1970s. Hence, in the early 21st century, before the financial crisis surfaced in late 2008 and led to the Great Recession, the situation in developing countries was similar to that in pre-transformation Europe, while the situation in industrialised countries was such that the creation of equal opportunities in the quest for social justice was almost forgotten.

[9] This idea is set out with remarkable clarity by Nelson Mandela in his auto-biography, where he describes how impressed and influenced he was as a young boy seeing the democratic nature of the proceedings of local meetings that were held in the Regent's house in the village of Mqhekezweni: 'Everyone who wanted to speak did so. It was democracy in its purest form. There may have been a hierarchy of importance among the speakers, but everyone was heard, chief and subject, warrior and medicine man, shopkeeper and farmer, landowner and

labourer, the foundation of self-government that all men were free to voice their opinions and equal in their value as citizens' (Mandela 1994: 21).

[10] For a lucid exposition of the idea, see Sen (1999).

[11] It is ironical that former prime minister Clement Attlee, who played a leading role in the creation of a welfare state in Britain and was deeply committed to the idea of social justice, made the following statement in a speech at the Oxford Union in June 1957: 'Democracy means government by discussion, but it is only effective if you can stop people talking' (Sen 2009: 332). This remark by Attlee, even if uttered in jest, captures the sentiments of the many governments besieged by protests from citizens.

[12] Varnashrama dharma is regarded as the central principle of traditional Hindu practices. There are four varnas: Brahmanas, Kshatriyas, Vaishyas, and Shudras, and four *ashramas* (stages of life): *brahmacharya* (learning and self-discipline); *grihastha* (householder); *vanaprastha* (withdrawal); and *sanyasa* (renunciation). Characteristic duties and obligations are associated with each of the varnas and ashramas.

[13] Ambedkar wrote at length about these issues. For some of his essential writings on the subject, see Ambedkar (2004).

[14] Article 330 and Article 332 of the Constitution of India, which provide for reservations in the Lok Sabha and the state legislatures, respectively, are clearly mandatory provisions that create a legal right.

[15] This is widely believed and accepted. But it could be a subject of debate in a legal sense. Article 16, which sets out fundamental rights, is an enabling provision, while Article 335, which provides for the state to introduce reservations as a matter of policy, is somewhat ambiguous in its mix of what is mandatory and what is enabling.

[16] For a lucid and perceptive discussion on this issue, see Teltumbde (2009). He argues that reservations have created more inequality within castes which are meant to be beneficiaries than there might have been between them and other castes. Indeed, he suggests that the entire Dalit population be divided into two categories of families: those that have availed of reservations and those that have not benefited from reservations so far. On this basis, he suggests a simple solution to the problem of reproduced privilege. The latter group which has not derived any benefit from affirmative action should have prioritised access to reservations, whereas families that have had access to reservations earlier would be eligible only if some places remain thereafter.

[17] For a discussion on this issue, see Béteille (2003).

[18] President John Kennedy first used the term 'affirmative action' in 1961 in his Executive Order 10925, which stated that federal contractors must 'take affirmative action to ensure that applicants are employed, and that employees are treated during employment, without regard to their race, creed, colour or national origin'. See https://www.eeoc.gov/eeoc/history/35th/thelaw/eo-10925. html (accessed on 20 July 2018). In 1967, President Lyndon Johnson extended protection of the affirmative action requirements to women.

[19] Alan Bakke, a white male, had been rejected as an applicant for admission two years in a row by the medical school at the University of California, Davis, that had accepted less qualified black applicants as the school had a separate admissions policy for minorities and reserved 16 out of 100 places for minority students. For a lucid discussion on reverse discrimination, see Dworkin (1985). In his analysis, Dworkin makes a distinction between the 'right to treatment as an equal', which is primary, and the 'right to equal treatment', which is secondary. In

terms of this analysis, Alan Bakke was denied his right to treatment as an equal.
[20] For a lucid analysis of the distinction between equality as a right and equality as a policy, see Béteille (1987).

References

Ambedkar, B. R. 2004. *Essential Writings of Ambedkar*, ed. Valerian Rodrigues. New Delhi: Oxford University Press.

Béteille, André. 1987. 'Equality as a Right and as a Policy', *LSE Quarterly*, 1(1): 75–98.

————. 2003. *Equality and Universality: Essays in Social and Political Theory*. New Delhi: Oxford University Press.

Dworkin, Ronald. 1985. *A Matter of Principle*. Cambridge, MA: Harvard University Press.

————. 2000. *Sovereign Virtue: The Theory and Practice of Equality*. Cambridge, MA: Harvard University Press.

Edwards, Michael. 2004. *Future Positive: International Co-operation in the 21st Century*. London: Earthscan.

Mandela, Nelson. 1994. *Long Walk to Freedom*. Boston and London: Little, Brown & Co.

Nayyar, Deepak. 1998. 'Economic Development and Political Democracy: Interaction of Economics and Politics in Independent India', *Economic and Political Weekly*, 33(49): 3121–31.

————. 2003. 'The Political Economy of Exclusion and Inclusion: Democracy, Markets and People', in Amitava Krishna Dutt and Jaime Ros (eds), *Development Economics and Structuralist Macroeconomics*, pp. 94–104. Cheltenham: Edward Elgar.

Polanyi, Karl. 1944. *The Great Transformation*. New York: Farrar and Rinehart.

Rawls, John. 1971. *A Theory of Justice*. Cambridge, MA: Harvard University Press.

————. 2001. *Justice as Fairness: A Restatement*. New York: Columbia University Press.

Sen, Amartya. 1985. *Commodities and Capabilities*. Amsterdam: North-Holland.

————. 1999. *Development as Freedom*. New York: Alfred E. Knopf.

————. 2009. *The Idea of Justice*. London: Allen Lane.

Smith, Adam. 1984 [1759]. *The Theory of Moral Sentiments*, eds. D. D. Raphael and A. L. Macfie. Indianapolis: Liberty Fund.

Teltumbde, Anand. 2009. 'Reservations within Reservations: A Solution', *Economic and Political Weekly*, 44(41–42): 16–18.

4

Theories of Oppression and Another Dialogue of Cultures

Ashis Nandy

Every generation likes to believe that it is living in momentous times,[1] witnessing the death of one world and the birth of another, negotiating what pre-war Bengali writers used to grandly call *yugasandhikshana*, the moment when two epochs meet. This generation of Indians too believes that it is seeing such changes and even participating in them. Perhaps they are. However, I shall argue here that, along with transitions in society and politics to which they like to stand witness, there are transitions in cultures of knowledge and states of awareness of which they may be gloriously innocent. And they perhaps try to protect that innocence. The categories we deploy to construe our world images are parts of our innermost self and to disown them is to disown parts of ourselves and jeopardise our self-esteem. Even when we struggle to shed these categories, they survive like phantom limbs do in some amputees. Or perhaps they survive the way one of Freud's three universal fantasies, the one about immortality, does. When you imagine yourself dead, you are still there, fully alive, looking at yourself as dead.

Yet, with the passage of time, the emancipatory ideas of one generation are always hollowed out through overuse and misuse, and become for the next generation poisoned gifts, sanctioning new forms of violence and oppression. Human beings, given long enough time, adequate opportunities and a culture of impunity, can turn any theory of liberation into its reverse.

Such poisoned gifts continue to play a key role in public life and in academic social sciences. Few talk of social Darwinism these days, but many cannot give up its sanitised versions in a whole range of social-evolutionary epithets. The ideas of developed and underdeveloped, advanced and backward, progressive and conservative, modern and traditional, historical and ahistorical, are all infected with the crude Darwinism that came to us not only through thinkers like Herbert Spencer (1820–1903), at one time a well-known name in the Indian academe, but also through some of the more distinguished Left-Hegelians talking incessantly of historical stages and historical compulsions, stages of economic growth and development.

Elsewhere I have shown how evolutionary principles began to be applied to even the human life cycle and early education and how, by the late 18th century, childhood had lost its intrinsic sanctity and the child had become, almost by definition, an inferior, underdeveloped version of the adult, who had to be guided, sternly and coercively, towards productive adulthood and 'normal', 'healthy' citizenship (see Nandy 1987). Later, the metaphor of life cycle was applied to entire societies and civilisations so successfully that even a humanist like Albert Schweitzer could not resist saying, 'The African is my brother, but a younger brother.'[2] I supply here a rough sketch of the overall environment in which the social sciences grew and how our theories of violence and oppression carry the burden of their origins.

I

Let me start at the beginning. By the 19th century, the Enlightenment values had already made deep inroads into the middle-class cultures of Europe and had begun to shape the continent's intellectual climate. Human beings were no longer the toys of fate or the playthings of gods. At the same time, simple domination, exploitation and the marauding style of colonialism, which Spain and Portugal pioneered in South America in 17th and 18th centuries, were no longer acceptable. Self-interest had become more legitimate with the entry of industrial capitalism on the scene, but one had to give weighty reasons for one's greed and violence; Christianisation of the pagans and the absence of soul in the American Indians and Africans were not enough. To kill, rape or rob, you had to invoke more secular causes like nationalism and sciences like biology, eugenics and anthropology. It was a bit like the English who, even when they pick pockets, George Bernard Shaw once said, do so on principle.

In this ambience, Europe spawned a whole range of social and political theories, which included a number of brand-new theories of secular salvation. Along with new disciplines like sociology and political science and strands of radical thought – from anarchism to Christian socialism to communism – these theories of secular salvation reshaped existing social knowledge not only in the West but also entered the colonised societies through new educational initiatives and universities. Gradually, the likes of Jeremy Bentham (1748–1832), Robert Owen (1771–1858), John Austin

(1790–1859), James Mill (1773–1836), John Stuart Mill (1806–1873), Mikhail Bakunin (1814–1876), Karl Marx (1818–1883), John Ruskin (1819–1900), Herbert Spencer (1820–1903), William Morris (1834–1896), William James (1842–1910), Pyotr Kropotkin (1842–1921), Sigmund Freud (1856–1939), and Thorstein Veblen (1857–1929) entered important pockets of urban middle-class awareness as lasting influences in the world being brought within civilisation.

It was the high noon of modern colonialism. There was, in Europe and in the two newly white continents, a heady mix of the self-righteous certitudes of the Protestant ethics confidently driving industrial capitalism to new heights and the self-confidence of the explorers and the circumnavigators of the earth who discovered for Europe new worlds, old civilisations, and old civilisations that by common consent could be turned into new worlds. It was a time when well-intentioned, important thinkers in the Northern Hemisphere could not but think of the good of the entire world as their *noblesse oblige*. Dutifully, many of them proposed universal theories of oppression and human liberation. Unfortunately, almost all of them knew nothing about the non-European world. Fortunately, this did not cramp their style.

If you force me to name this culture of the social sciences, I shall call it a regime of narcissism. (Despite my efforts, it is becoming in some of my recent writings a nosological term, a diagnostic category.) A common feature of these human sciences was their eroticised investment in themselves and in the cultural zone where they were born and the extent to which they struggled to confine non-European knowledge systems within hermeneutically sealed academic vaults, open to only anthropologists and historians. For the rest of the knowledge industry, these alien knowledge systems became either ethnic curios, things we collect when we travel on a small budget to other countries to widen our minds, or unknown but feared bacterial strains that might infect the newfound scientific purity of social thought and practices or force our favourite grand theories to rethink their categories and epistemologies.

I do not want to spend time on this part of the story though. Thanks to a number of scholars, it is better known today. I want to speak about how, when some of the pioneers in the social sciences were claiming modestly that their theories and methods were timeless and trans-territorial, their diverse and competing ventures began to show some common results.

First, it became a general tendency in scholarly circles to translate geographical space into chronological time – to see distant countries outside Europe and North America not as culturally, ecologically and socially different, as their forefathers did, but as an earlier stage of history, as in fact an earlier phase of the history of Europe. While the earlier generations in Europe had seen China and India as ancient civilisations that were exotic, rich, intriguing, and unique, now they began to see these countries as having impressive if feudal pasts, but trapped, in recent centuries, in decadent, dissolute, primitive social and religious practices and waiting to be engineered into something more contemporary by the young, vigorous, advanced European civilisation.[3] Colonialism had become a pedagogical exercise.[4]

Second, in a related development, there emerged after the first flush of enthusiasm for social Darwinism, subtler social-evolutionary theories of history, modernisation, state formation, nation building, and, later, education, child rearing and economic development. Whatever else these theories did or did not, they began, with immense enthusiasm and efficiency, to steamroll, flatten and secularise the diverse visions of a desirable society in African and Asian societies into a single monolithic vision. And this new shared vision increasingly began to look like contemporary West Europe and North America.

Today, this process has reached its apogee. One billion Chinese and one billion Indians seem to have internalised the project and eagerly bought into this utopia. Mimicking Oscar Wilde, one might say that the good Chinese and the good Indian, if they have lived a virtuous life, have now started going not to heaven but to New York.

Third, gradually, over the last 150 years, the marginalised and dominated of the world, too, have been acquiring an increasingly homogenised look in scholarly work, irrespective of their social location and cultural features. Ethnographic accounts of them, of course, vary in details, but they tend not to vary in political-economic and ethical thrusts. In public imagination and in policy circles, the situation has been worse. Sometimes to underscore the depth of the suffering of a community, all dignity is sucked out of the community's culture and lifestyle. The assumption is that the more gruesome the detail, the more serious is the criticism of the oppression. After a point, descriptions lifted from one part of the world in the 19th century are almost indistinguishable from descriptions from another part of the world in the 20th century. Indeed, this commonality cuts across the political and ideological boundaries of the theories deployed to interpret the plight of the victims.

Ethnographers may not agree, but whether they are Dalits of India in the 21st century or the working class huddling in the gin alleys of industrialising Britain, be they the fishing communities in southern India resisting the encroachment of trawlers today or the Maoris fighting colonisation in New Zealand, the victims of structural or institutionalised violence and exploitation have gradually acquired the same look. The victims have been prised out of their cultural context to be given a new two-dimensional identity – they are poor and they are oppressed. The theories that speak for them and want to have a monopoly on their welfare are usually aggressively global. They have no time or patience for the lifestyles of individual communities, which in any case they – the theories – consider secondary.

Fourth, while the oppressed and the poor remain a social category, a potentially revolutionary formation or a rebellious mob, and as such have agency only potentially – that is, after adequate conscientisation or old-fashioned mobilisation – the oppressors have agency here and now, on the basis of the historical role they have played as innovative entrepreneurs, as a social sector having better scientific and technical knowledge and, above all, as self-aware citizens, liberated intellectuals, vanguard of the proletariat, or simply as awakened, informed citizenry who have already brought about nothing less than a successful bourgeois revolution.

More recently, the legitimation of this agency has become subtler and more difficult to combat. Dominance is increasingly dependent on categories, not on institutional forces. In knowledge societies, dominance does not look like dominance if one can partition off one's professional self and subject it to the existing knowledge hierarchy, while ranting all the while against social hierarchy. George Bernard Shaw's aphorism that all professions are a conspiracy against the laity may have become stale, but the idea of 'disabling professions' of Ivan Illich has acquired a sharper edge (Illich 1987; see also Illich 1974).

Fifth, the psychological climate I am trying to capture was founded on what was seen as the triumph of reason. The Enlightenment had the whole of the 18th century to seep into the European and North American societies. The social theories that 19th-century Europe and North America spawned during the transition from the culture of slavery to the culture of colonialism broke with traditions that drew their values from multiple sources, such as transcendental or divine injunctions, compassion, empathy, aesthetics, and reason. The new theories drew their values almost exclusively from reason. The psychoanalytically minded might say that rationalisation or intellectualisation became now the preferred ego-defence.

Despite the dangers of marginalising compassion and empathy as sources of values, the emphasis on reason as the primary or only source of values can have some virtues. I can imagine that in societies that had maintained cultural continuities over centuries, reason must have appeared to many a new, liberating and healthy vantage ground for social criticism. Understandably, African and Asian intellectuals and social reformers took to the change like fish to water. In India, the powerful Brahmanic tradition found the change especially attractive. More so in Bengal, where the British Empire was founded and the colonial capital was located.

In Bengal, the obsession with epistemic issues – some might call it logic-chopping – of the dominant school of philosophy, Navya Nyaya, could easily adapt to the demands of the new enchantment with reason, to blunt the powerful social criticisms and egalitarian movements that had surfaced in medieval times. The Brahmanic literati of the region kept itself busy for more than a century doing so.[5] Navya Nyaya might have originated at Mithila, but the Bengali upper castes had made it their own. Enlightenment, I dare say, began its career in India on the wrong foot; almost by default, it established a powerful, social alliance with the existing social stratarchy. So did the colonial political economy. Medievalism, following the European usage, became a dirty word in India, too, even though it was arguably the golden age of India's cultural and social creativity.[6]

Alas, the violence of the 20th century has quite conclusively shown that reason in both of its popular forms – as instrumental reason and as scientific rationality – can be an excellent sanction for genocide and dominance. Indeed, by using Rudolph J. Rummel's data on genocide, one can easily show that at least 20 times as many people have been liquidated in the name of reason and science in the last century than in the name of religious fanaticism (Rummel 1994).[7]

Sixth, as new dichotomies were set up in the 19th century to describe the journey from the past to the future, say, from tradition to modernity or underdevelopment to development, one end of the dichotomies was pluralised, not the other. This perhaps was nothing terribly new or strange. At the beginning of *Anna Karenina*, Leo Tolstoy says: 'Happy families are all alike; every unhappy family is unhappy in its own way.' And in the modern clinical disciplines, we know, one can be ill in myriad ways but healthy in usually one way. In psychiatry, psychoanalysis and clinical psychology, one can be insane in a variety of interesting ways and sane within a much smaller, more boring range of options.

However, in political and social knowledge and in applied philosophy, such asymmetry can have serious implications. If we have a rich phenomenology of underdevelopment but sparse work on varieties of development, or if we have a wide range of work on threats to national security but only a unitary concept of national security, it obviously does something to our public imagination. A few have worked hard to correct these asymmetries, mostly without any noticeable impact. Ideas have their own lifespans that are tough to curtail or extend. In the last five decades

I have seen how transient and fragile have been attempts to pluralise the concept of development. I have seen concepts like rural development, micro-development, alternative development, eco-development, ethno-development, indigenous development, inclusive development, and sustainable development enter the social sciences with much fanfare and, then, ingloriously fall by the wayside.

Only one development has survived: Development with a capital D. More recently, in a country claiming to be the birthplace of Gandhi, the definition of national security has steadily become narrower as the threats to national security have multiplied and become richer in descriptive content, limiting the range of our public imagination and our policy options. No wonder our first response to all terrorism has become statist counter-terrorism.

II

I do not dismiss the efforts or the sacrifices of those studying or fighting human suffering and exploitation and making sense of them. I myself work predominantly on the nastier side of life. But I do believe that we have hollowed out the lives and lifestyles of those who live under regimes of dominance and exploitation.

I am not concerned here with those who have used social knowledge to justify slavery, colonialism, imperial wars, child labour, indentured labour, and genocide. I am concerned with the minds of those who deploy the dominant theories of oppression and human liberation. I am disturbed that Frederick Engels justified the colonial conquest of Algeria by France because, he felt, 'The conquest of Algeria is an important and fortunate fact for the progress of civilisation' (quoted in Tabb 1983: 161). I am disappointed that Karl Marx, who crossed the boundary of his ideology to congratulate Abraham Lincoln when he abolished slavery, never extended the same favour to the countries in the Southern Hemisphere. When it came to India he argued that British colonialism, however exploitative and gory, would still manage to pull this unwilling country, screaming and kicking, into the modern world. His 'brainchild', the noted economist Joan Robinson, who lovingly brought up two generations of Indian students on Marx's ideas of radical politics and economics, put it more bluntly. The only thing worse than being colonised, she used to insist, was not being colonised.

I believe that most dominant theories of oppression and human liberation bequeathed to us have drawn legitimacy from three sources: the Baconian idea of scientific rationality, the social-evolutionary ideas of historical compulsions and historical stages, and the Left-Hegelian idea of state. The three together have been the core myths of our times, which refuse to die even at the beginning of the 21st century. Together the triad have fashioned a dangerous political-psychological contradiction that frames our intellectual life and defines our ideas of the progressive, the radical, and the developed or advanced: on the one hand, there has been an expansion of democratic awareness; on the other, there is a new technocracy claiming intellectual and political leadership on the grounds that it understands the technicalities of exploitation and dominance better than the actual victims and has, therefore, the right to be the voice of the people. The targeted beneficiaries have become the new laity, either as disposable, lowly foot soldiers of reform or the cannon fodder of revolution, or as passive spectators of their own liberation.

The well-educated, urban middle classes in this part of the world, who like to fight the structures of oppression around them, have been brought up on these ideas. They resented the ruthlessness of the colonial state and the reality of exploitation, but not the categories and the world view that sanctioned the ruthlessness and the exploitation. They have borrowed their categories from the imperium of knowledge, to contain the deficit in their self-esteem, and have ended up fighting imperialism from within its own world view.

This is as true of those we call the Right as of those we call the Left. Vinayak Damodar Savarkar (1883–1966), freedom fighter and the father of Hindu nationalism, hated Mohandas Karamchand Gandhi for his lack of scholarship, unscientific mind and, of all things, absence of familiarity with modern European political theory (Keer 1954: 530).[8] It never struck Savarkar that others may have thought Gandhi a path-breaking politician for exactly the same reasons – because he was an outsider unimpressed by the authority of university-based knowledge systems, especially modern science, and European concepts of statecraft and radical politics. (If you read Savarkar with genuine empathy and not like a police sub-inspector writing a first information report, you will find that, except for a few peripheral concepts here and there, there is almost nothing Indian about his ideas of state, nation and nationality. They are charmingly antique, borrowed from 19th-century Europe. In his writings, his hostility to the Muslims overlies his savage criticism of the Hindus as a non-martial, non-masculine, unorganised, fractious people who will only be a true nationality in the future. And you do not have to be an empathetic reader to discover Savarkar's not-so-secret admiration for Muslims and Christians for being more martial and for being better human material for running a modern state. This ambivalence towards the Muslims and the Christians persists in most texts of the Rashtriya Swayamsevak Sangh too.) Savarkar *did* believe that the Europeans had earned the right to read the Vedas and the Upanishads, not the Indians. Indians, he felt, were at a historical stage when they should read, as Shudras, only western textbooks of science and technology (Savarkar 1984: 5).

Conformity can never be as dangerous as tamed, defanged, predictable dissent, for such dissent allows dominance to turn into hegemony. At the same time, being transparent and predictable to the powers regnant, such dissent allows itself to be monitored, scrutinised, co-opted, and efficiently managed, with minimal use of force. It can even become an ornament and a testimonial to a system and an endorsement of its democratic credentials. What we are trying to do to the dispossessed and the marginalised in our midst – to the tribals, the Dalits and the predominantly artisan Atishudras who include a large proportion of Muslims – is exactly what the western intellectual establishment has sought to do to us. This is the core psychodynamics of intellectual imperialism in our times.[9]

I propose that one of the first tasks of social knowledge in India today is to return agency to the communities at the receiving end of the system. We can do so only if we take seriously the various cultural modes of self-expression of these communities. Democracy can be, I admit, a slow-moving, inept, obtuse tool in the case of small communities. But it still remains a powerful enabling device for those not pushed to the margin of desperation. I believe that those we call the oppressed and the poor can take care of themselves in a truly open system. I am suggesting that it is in our self-interest that we shed this imperial obligation as representatives of the coming knowledge society, as pace-setters in a globalised political economy or as vanguards of the proletariat. (This plea is also directed at those who stand on the other side of the ideological barrier, the ultra-Hindus who populate the ranks of the Hindu nationalists and have now fragmented into small urban sects of censorship freaks, united by the arrogant belief that their gods and goddesses cannot protect them; they have to protect the gods and goddesses. Naturally they are even more protective towards the Dalits and the Adivasis, whom they see as vulnerable and naïve, forever susceptible to the seductive charms of a whole range of conspirators, from evangelists to Maoists.) It is necessary to shed this baggage for our own psychological health and ethical well-being. When we grant dignity to others, we grant dignity to ourselves, however preachy this might sound.

To grant this dignity to those to whom we are not used to granting it, we must learn to enter the cultural space they occupy. Education need not be only pedagogy or teaching; it also includes proactive learning. The ability to learn is biologically given and is not even species-specific. In this instance, it means opening a dialogue with the oppressed and cornered cultures in India first, and then – only then – with other countries and civilisations we have to treat as our equals. Such an internal dialogue will give us an opportunity to learn by expanding our moral horizon and allow us to transcend the narrow cosmopolitanism foisted on us by the 19th-century European ideas of civilisation and Kultur. What I am saying is not well-packaged ethnocentrism. It is an admission that when oppression is community based, resistance has to be so, too.

Dialogue of civilisations and cultures has become a fashionable and ubiquitous intellectual pastime these days. These dialogues have tried to bring into conversation peoples, countries and communities in conflict when normal statecraft fails to make them talk to each other. But what about dialogue among cultures within the same nation-state, when they cannot talk to each other because they live within a nation-state as different 'countries'? I think the Dalit and the tribal communities of India now constitute two formations of cultures about which most other Indians know little and believe that they need to know nothing. A dialogue with them should be able to humanise our polity and make it a richer, more informed democracy.

All dialogues have to cross borders – cultural, political and, above all, psychological. Usually these borders are thought of as international or civilisational borders. When we cross these borders, we are supposed to get a new, deeper, more empathetic understanding of other ways of looking at the world and at ourselves. There is an implicit assumption in this proposal, particularly when it involves crossing the borders within us: Others are never entirely strangers. They are also templates of the temptations and possibilities within us. We are what we are because we are shaped by the seductive pulls of these templates. A dialogue breaks stereotypes more easily than it erases these partly alien fragments of our self, operating as anti-selves and rejected selves. Both our creativity and destructiveness depend upon how we grapple with these inner vectors. It is thus that a dialogue sharpens and widens our awareness of what we are and what we are capable of. Only when we are in dialogue can we claim to have opened India to the other India where the Dalits and the tribals live.

Sixty years after formal decolonisation, small sections of the post-World War II democracies are at last showing some signs of offering resistance to the obscenity of speaking on behalf of the oppressed and the exploited. Some of the victims, too, are now obstinately refusing to fit into the model of a one-dimensional life as the 'the poor and the exploited', perpetually dependent on experts and ideologues who have become their voices and guides to a better future. These victims are claiming the right to imagine and write their own future.

Pity and sympathy, after a point, can be degrading and vulgar. Instead of shedding copious tears for the poverty and the exploitation of the Dalits and Adivasis, the time has come to celebrate their self-affirmation and the enormous diversity of cultural, ecological, artistic, technological, and intellectual riches they, as communities, have nurtured over the millennia. I refuse to believe that in these communities grandparents do not tell stories to their grandchildren and mothers do not sing lullabies to their babies. I refuse to believe that, outside the reach of sloganeering and propaganda, they do not have mythic heroes and myths of origin, their own and that of the world. There are impressive ethnographic works on the healing traditions, technological knowledge and agronomic practices of some of these communities. Now there is even some interest in their distinctive cuisines, and there has been some serious interest in their artistic traditions. All this can be a reasonable vantage ground to launch a search for different world views and different visions of the future. I am tempted to adopt the plea of the Zapatistas that one of their finest thinkers, Gustavo Esteva, articulates: the challenge today is nothing less than 'to host the otherness of others' (Esteva 1996: 249). We have been terribly busy all these years hosting the sameness of others.

Dialogue of cultures can acquire new depth if it engages communities and cultures at the receiving end of the system and reaffirms their right to intellectual – yes, intellectual, not only social – dignity. The oppressed do have their own, often implicit, theories of oppression and have no obligation to be guided by our ideas of the scientific, the rational and the dignified. They have every right to be historically, economically and politically incorrect.

Fourth Ambedkar Memorial Lecture, 14 April 2012, Ambedkar University Delhi.

Notes
1. This is a revised text of the Ambedkar Memorial Lecture delivered at the India International Centre on 14 April 2012, under the auspices of Ambedkar University Delhi. I thank Partha Chatterjee who, as the discussant for the lecture, raised important issues, which I have been able to handle only cursorily in this version of the lecture.
2. As quoted in the *Observer*, 23 October 1955; Schweitzer is later supposed to have repudiated this statement, saying, 'the time for speaking of older and younger brothers has passed.'
3. Actually, 'feudalism', one of the few technical terms in the discipline of history,

itself became a handy, elastic term for the character assassination of any cultural product or social order that was non-European and unpopular among the new converts to modernity. I might even pre-empt my critics by calling this argument of mine uncompromisingly feudal.

⁴ I am currently reading a manuscript in which four young academics, talking of Australia, a former colonial society that has refused to confront the full implications of that past, say, 'Bentham's ideas were especially popular in Australian educational practices, even more so than in Britain, with their focus on categorisation and ordering students according to their progress' (Garbutt et al. 2011: 16).

⁵ I am aware of the creative and critical use of the traditions of Navya Nyaya by scholars such as Bimal Krishna Matilal in recent times. But that use can have its own hazards, as Matilal's own work shows. If one pushes the compatibility between Indian neo-logical thought and the Enlightenment values and European modernity too far, the former becomes perfectly superfluous for those not specialising in the history of Indian philosophy. At the same time, it certifies the Enlightenment values and European modernity as new markers of an old stratarchy. That is exactly what happened, first in undivided Bengal and then in West Bengal. It is probably the one state in India where, despite a 34-year-long, uninterrupted rule by a Marxist regime, a Dalit or an Adivasi probably cannot enter even the imagination of Bengalis as a future chief minister of the state. In fact, the Leninist theoretical apparatus itself has dutifully endorsed the political and intellectual style associated with the Bengali *bhadralok* (upper social class, usually belonging to the three upper castes). Bengal can only take pride that it produced the subcontinent's first minister of law, Jogendranath Mandal (1904–1968), who, like India's first minister of law, Bhimrao Ambedkar, was a Hindu Dalit. But he had to go to Pakistan to be so. He took his oath of office a few days before Ambedkar did.

⁶ Both Rabindranath Tagore (1861–1941) and Mohandas Karamchand Gandhi (1869–1948) believed that the clues to India's cultural unity lay not in the Vedas and the Upanishads but in the multi-religious, cross-cultural, vernacular traditions of the medieval saints, mystics, poets, composers, itinerant philosophers, and social reformers. But that is not the official position either of the Indian state or of a majority of India's historians and social scientists.

⁷ See also http://www.hawaii.edu/powerkills/welcome.html (accessed on 25 June 2018).

⁸ For a more detailed discussion of this part of the story, see Nandy (2009).

⁹ See in this context the brilliant work of Nagaraj (2010).

References

Esteva, Gustavo. 1996. 'Hosting the Otherness of the Other: The Case of the Green Revolution', in Frédérique Apffel-Marglin and Stephen A. Marglin (eds), *Decolonizing Knowledge: From Development to Dialogue*, pp. 249–78. Oxford: Clarendon Press.

Garbutt, Rob, Erika Kerruish, Baden Offord, Kirste Pavlovic, and Adele Wessell. 2011. 'The Necessary Other: Inside Enlightenment Australia'. Unpublished manuscript.

Illich, Ivan. 1974. *Medical Nemesis*. London: Calder and Marion Boyars.

———. 1987. *Ideas in Progress: Disabling Professions*. London: Marion Boyars.

Keer, Dhananjay. 1954. *Veer Savarkar*. Bombay: Popular Prakashan.

Nagaraj, D. R. 2010. *The Flaming Feet and Other Essays: The Dalit Movement in India*. Ranikhet: Permanent Black.

Nandy, Ashis. 1987. 'Reconstructing Childhood: A Critique of the Ideology of Adulthood', in

Traditions, Tyranny, and Utopias, pp. 56–76. New Delhi: Oxford University Press.

————. 2009. 'The Demonic and the Seductive in Religious Nationalism: Vinayak Damodar Savarkar and the Rites of Exorcism in Secularizing South Asia', Heidelberg Papers in South Asian and Comparative Politics, Working Paper no. 44, University of Heidelberg, http://doi.org/10.11588/heidok.00009086 (accessed on 26 June 2018).

Rummel, Rudolph J. 1994. *Death by Government: Genocide and Mass Murder in the Twentieth Century*. Rutgers, NJ: Transaction Publishers.

Savarkar, V. D. 1984. *Echoes from Andaman*. Bombay: Veer Savarkar Prakashan.

Tabb, Bill. 1983. 'Marx versus Marxism', in Ward Churchill (ed.), *Marxism and Native Americans*, pp. 159–74. Boston: South End Press.

5

Restoring 'Title Deeds to Humanity'
Lawless Law, Living Death, and the Insurgent Reason of Babasaheb Ambedkar

Upendra Baxi

Apologies are owed for delaying this conversation, which was due to a cerebral stroke I suffered last March and from which I am slowly and painfully recovering. This would also excuse, I hope, the occasional alcoholic slur in my speech which is not out of my penchant for gibberish that some would say marks my talks, but rather owes itself to the near destruction of the motor functions of the left side of the brain. I thank you all in advance for your indulgent reception and I thank in particular Vice Chancellor Shyam Menon for his initial invitation and his patience for nearly a year for this occasion. His colleague Dr Rukmini Sen and her colleagues also helped with every detail of this event.

Ambedkar University Delhi is a relatively new university, but it has taken giant strides in curricular, pedagogic and evaluative roles. Its fine faculty, painstakingly assembled by Vice Chancellor Menon, has already made a splendid contribution. And its student body is disciplined, motivated, and committed to some fine values of university education and research. The officials and all karamcharis of the university deserve a special mention for their arduous start-up operations for a new university. Knowing a little bit about the travails of universities in India, it is a pleasant task to thank this congenial collectivity. I do not know how far what I call the Critical Ambedkar Studies Movement (CASM, hereafter) has been advanced by the university, but I have no doubt that it will eventually live up to the great name it proudly bears. There has been ferment in Ambedkar studies, especially since the publication by the Maharashtra government of his collected works and the birth centenary celebrations that followed. The University Grants Commission has endowed universities, chairs and centres for social inclusion, and the Indian Council of Social Science Research has not lagged far behind in assisting specialist research and seminars in

Ambedkarite thought. Independent scholars in universities have to their credit some fine studies on Ambedkar's thought and action. And judges and lawpersons have accorded Dr Ambedkar his due through their daily constitutional work, as well as on the occasion of the Golden Jubilee and 60 years of Indian constitutionalism.

Whether all these put together amount to the CASM is the question. Certainly, what I described in my Ambedkar oration (via Jacques Lacan) is true even today as I finalise this lecture for the present volume after five years: 'the murmur of anonymous persecutors' still haunts his thought and action; so do the persistent Brahmanical 'schizoid-paranoid' thought formations. How notions of globalisation are thus 'Sanskritised' also remains an important question.

I look forward with keen anticipation to our conversation, already singularly blest by the inestimable presence of Professor (Dr) Gopal Guru as 'discussant'. I look forward keenly to the day when he will deliver the Ambedkar oration, an event where my co-presence may scarcely merit a footnote attention!

Some Concerns

In this conversation, I promote further the CASM rather than follow my distinguished predecessors in the Ambedkar Memorial Lecture series. I believe that we need a *movement* based on a *critical* study of Ambedkar's life and work. The time is long past for any hagiographic narrative, although we must continue to celebrate his luminous presence amidst us and protest against any party-political appropriation of his name (see Baxi 2016a).[1] We need to revisit the silences as well as antinomies in Ambedkarite thought and action, while pursuing the rather solitary task of taking Babasaheb Ambedkar seriously as the 'Aristotle of the Atishudras' (as I fondly name him) (Baxi 1995).[2]

I engage here his imageries of 'lawless law' and 'living death'. Further, while both M. K. Gandhi and B. R. Ambedkar remain exponents of what I name as 'insurgent reason', I engage Ambedkar's practices in particular, given the fact that the recent academic and political rediscovery of Gandhi's *Hind Swaraj* scarcely relates to an equally germinal text of Ambedkar: *What Congress and Gandhi Have Done to the Untouchables* (Ambedkar 1945).[3]

Towards the end of *What Congress and Gandhi Have Done to the Untouchables*, Ambedkar poses a poignant question: '. . . can it be said that Mr Gandhi has recovered the title deeds to humanity which the Untouchables have lost' (Ambedkar 1945: 281). In law, title deeds relate mainly to lawful transfers of property. The right to property inheres in the power to transfer, and one of the central incidents of that right (besides the right to possess, use and enjoy) is the power to alienate it through a market transaction.

But the way in which Babasaheb deploys the legal phrase is extraordinary. It inverts altogether a term of art in the law concerning private property rights. The property here (in the sense of attributes) is *dignity*, which forbids the reduction of human beings to chattel or things which may be owned; rather, it demands equal regard for the recognition of, and respect for, all those born as humans (see Guru 2009). The title deeds are ontological (being and being called 'human') and can be neither bought nor sold in the market overtly. Their confiscation by power cannot but be a sustained act of violence, in which the State and civil society vanguards must be, and remain, complicit.

Ambedkar suggests that the Untouchables were denied their title deeds to humanity by being condemned to *'merely living'*, and not being allowed acts of *'living worthily'* (Ambedkar 1945: 295). Indeed, Ambedkar presciently flays 'Gandhism' as a 'call . . . back to nature . . . back to *nakedness*' (*ibid.*; emphasis added). Astonishing, indeed, remains Ambedkar's anticipation of the voice of Giorgio Agamben, who draws a distinction between 'bare life' – 'naked life' in the original Italian edition – and the way in which life is lived (Agamben 1998: 180). In any event, restoration of the title deeds to humanity means for the Untouchables 'their emancipation from [the] thraldom of the Hindus', which they can secure by *'political power, and by nothing else'* (Ambedkar 1945: 281; emphasis added). While this assertion may sit well with Hannah Arendt's *new* politics, does it do equally well in Agamben's *anti-politics politics*?

Ambedkar speaks to us about collective unfreedom, and therefore of oppression, in ways distinct from his contemporaries and successors, especially the new modern political philosophers. In contrast to his contemporaries, Ambedkar addressed the problem of swaraj by not confining it to decolonisation (here he broadly agreed with the Gandhian notion of swaraj as not just freedom but *just* freedom). Instead, he maintained that independent India should, above all, tackle the problem of violent social exclusion, with the Untouchables serving as the paradigm. Not surprisingly, the given model of constitutional liberalism and the normative device of fundamental rights – as a solvent of the problem of violent social exclusion – were found to be inadequate by Ambedkar. However, many of his successors – the new modern political philosophers – are not in agreement among themselves on what collective unfreedom may signify and, in particular, if this is a problem of sheer 'negative liberty' of individuals rather than groups subjected to oppression.[4]

More theoretical gestures and concerns, thus, also remain impaled, questions that CASM ought to pursue. First, how may conferment of power (and *nothing else*) ever rectify millennial harms and injustices? This is a problem of what has been called intergenerational or historic injustice. The ethical and legal question is: how does one socially learn to 'take responsibility for the past'?[5] Do the poignant descriptions of the confiscation of the title deeds of humanity from the Untouchables in Babasaheb's writings provide us with any silhouette of a theory of justice across generations?[6] Second, did Babasaheb have a notion of justice that addressed affirmative action? Is *intragenerational* justice to be considered an integral aspect of *intergenerational* justice?[7]

Third, what did Babasaheb have to say about individuals and groups other than Untouchables, such as Muslims, indigenous peoples or sexual minorities? A fourth and related question: how does the corpus of Ambedkar deal with the now insistent claim of 'reasonable pluralism', advanced notably by John Rawls?[8] Fifth, what role, as an instrumentality of social control and change, does religion (as compared to the law) play in Ambedkar's life and thought? The lifelong interlocution of ritual features of Hinduism, and struggles against exclusion, culminated in an embittered renunciation of Hinduism as a faith and the embrace of the Dhamma, finally and formally marked in a mass conversion to Buddhism. Does this mark merely the rejection of an inegalitarian religion encouraging exclusion, or is it indicative of disenchantment with, and distancing from, constitutional legality?

Finally, how does one read and extend Ambedkar's theory of inclusion (and representation) to dignitarian considerations for some non-human animal persons and objects in natural nature? How does one adapt Ambedkarite thought patterns to the accelerating Anthropocene?

My acts of reading of Ambedkar's *Collected Works* (and related fragments) do not yet allow me to suggest an approach to such questions. Yet, it must be said that Dr Ambedkar speaks to us much beyond the conventional languages of contemporary human rights and salient ways of theorising 'justice'.

'Living Death'

The principal indictment of Gandhi by Ambedkar is that the former narrates 'caste'-based discrimination as at best an *anachronism* but not an *evil* (Ambedkar 1945: 308; emphasis added). This is a major point of departure, animated by a specific theory of evil which is more than the absence of good.

Writing almost contemporaneously with Hannah Arendt,

Ambedkar reflects her dilemma: as we all know, Arendt moves ambivalently betwixt her description of *radical evil* (states of affairs that we may neither understand fully nor fully punish) and the thesis of the 'banality of evil'. I suggest a need for installing a CASM-type understanding, enabling acts of reading both Ambedkar and Arendt and also Agamben. They, in a deep affinity, speak to us about the production and reproduction of conditions of 'living death' – which is, at the same time, both a radical as well as a quotidian evil.

If for Agamben 'living death' remains the production of the quotidian performance of the State as a 'lethal machine' (1998: 117), Ambedkar speaks to the idea of the Hindu civilisation itself as such a lethal machine. Both accomplish the narratives of production/reproduction of *pre-social bodies* as 'walking corpses', 'living dead' and 'mummy-men', 'faceless persons', and the 'shadows' (Agamben 1999: 54–55). If for Giorgio Agamben, it is the (concentration) camp which furnishes some horrific insignia for the nomos of modern (European) law, for Ambedkar it is the *samskara*s (purificatory/liberatory practices) of Hindu culture and civilisation codified by Manu (or their DNA, as it were) that continue to define the law as an iteration of foundational violence.

Further, the presentation of the caste system as productive of conditions of 'living death' invites a comparison with Agamben's paradigmatic case of a *homo sacer* – a being whose killing constitutes neither a crime nor any form of sacrifice (see Norris 2005: 4, 21–22n15). Ambedkar would have surely endorsed Agamben's deep and provocative disagreement with Michel Foucault, who importantly developed the notion of biopower/biopolitics as distinctively 'modern' phenomena or the state of affairs, as an aspect of European 'modernity'.

Instead of luxuriating in the narrative differentials between Foucault and Agamben (to be sure, an important postmodernist vocation), let us open ourselves to Ambedkar's anguished voice:

> The system of Untouchability is a gold mine to the Hindus. In it the 240 millions of Hindus have 60 millions of Untouchables to serve as their retinue to enable the Hindus to maintain pomp and ceremony and to cultivate a feeling of pride and dignity befitting a master class, which cannot be fostered and sustained unless beneath it there is a servile class to look down upon. In it the 240 millions of Hindus have 60 millions of Untouchables to be used as forced labour. . . . In it the 240 millions of Hindus have 60 millions of Untouchables to do the dirty work of scavengers and sweepers. . . . In it the 240 millions of Hindus have 60 millions of Untouchables who can be kept to lower jobs and

prevented from entering into competition for higher jobs which are preserved for the Hindus. In it 240 millions of Hindus have 60 millions of Untouchables who can be used as shock-absorbers in slumps and deadweight in booms, for in slumps it is the Untouchable who is fired first and the Hindu is fired last and in booms the Hindu is employed first and the Untouchable is employed last. (Ambedkar 1945: 196)

Regardless of how one may today further re-edit the minutiae of this description, it is clear that six-plus decades of Indian constitutionalism have done little to abate the conditions of 'living death'; indeed, and sadly, it remains even possible to maintain that these have been further aggravated. The 'eternal scavenger' continues to coexist *literally* amidst us even today. Should you have the least bit of doubt as to this, please note the vicissitudes of the law abolishing manual scavenging passed as recently as 2013!

Lawless Law

Far from being an 'oxymoron' – or even a 'Baxi'-moron – Ambedkar vivifies this imagery for us. Pending further textual elaboration, I summarily speak to at least five types of lawlessness of law.

First, Ambedkar presents, as lawless law, any order of normativity that prescribes and perpetuates conditions of living death for the Atishudras, or the 'wretched of the earth', or the worst-off humans. The *Dharmasastra* and *Arthasastra* traditions perpetuate violent social exclusion and so do traditions of Hindu 'living law', in open defiance of the Constitution of India. Ambedkar's category may be extended to any legal order that inaugurates and perpetuates violent social exclusion.

Whether his critique of *the* law may be extended to *a* law remains an open question. Most modern, all postmodern, criticisms of law often focus on the *lawlessness of law*; these do not recognise Ambedkar, or Hinduism as concerns untouchability, as inaugural on this score. Aside from this historical fallacy, the expression 'lawless law' as extended in particular to *a* law puzzles a positivist lawperson (for whom positive law is the law laid down as such by the sovereign or the State) and mystifies a natural lawperson (for whom the source or the foundation of the law is transhuman, whether divine or human will or reason, or nature).

Second, in an essay entitled 'Their Wishes Are Laws Unto Us' (Ambedkar 1989b), Babasaheb reads dharma also as providing standards of critical morality by which customs and practices of violent discrimination against the Untouchables may be adjudged. Ambedkar insightfully archives these forms of *adharmic* conduct and practices[9] (equally in the registers of social practices and hermeneutic conduct) as generating constitutive formations of 'lawless law'. He emphatically suggests that the *chaturvarna* did not originate with Manu,[10] and indeed flays forms of the degenerate installations of a category of 'those who are outside Chaturvarna'; Manu's feat of adharmic interpolation fortifies, and fructifies, an encyclopaedic variety of forms of 'lawless law'.

Third, for Ambedkar, lawless law exemplifies the *micro-fascism* of the local acts/performatives of unspeakable hostile discrimination reinforcing caste apartheid practices (for example, drawing water from a single village well, entering public spaces ordained and exclusively reserved by, and for, the upper castes) as well as practices of embodiment, like wearing a shirt or sprouting a moustache (as illustrated by Ambedkar). Today, the question for us is just this: how may CASM contrast and combat the micro-fascism of the local with the macro-normativity of Indian constitutionalism with its hyper-goals such as outlawry of discrimination based on the grounds of untouchability (Article 17), assorted politics of 'reservation' in state-based educational institutions, and employment as well as legislative reservations?

Fourth, the formations of lawless law name some unending and limitless potential for grave and sinister forms of injustice:

> The worst of it is that all this injustice and persecution can be perpetrated within the limits of the law. A Hindu may well say that he may not employ an Untouchable, that he will not sell him anything, that he will evict him from his land, that he will not allow him to take his cattle across his field, without offending the law in *the slightest degree*. . . . The law *does not care with what motive he does it*. The law does not *see what injury it causes to the Untouchable*. The police may *misuse* his *power and his authority*. He may deliberately falsify the record by taking down something which has not been stated or by taking down something which is quite different from what has been stated. He may disclose evidence to the side in which he is interested. He may refuse to arrest. He may do a hundred and one things to *spoil the case*. All this he can do *without the slightest fear of being brought to book*. The loopholes of law are many, and he *knows them well*. The magistrate [is vested with] *an enormous amount of discretion. He is free to use it*. The decision of a case depends upon the witnesses who can give evidence. But the decision . . . depends upon whether the witnesses are *reliable or not*. It is open to the magistrate to believe one side and disbelieve the other side. He may be quite arbitrary in believing one side, *but it is his discretion, and no one can interfere with it. There are innumerable cases in which this discretion has been exercised . . . to the prejudice of*

the Untouchables. However truthful the witnesses of the Untouchables, the magistrates have taken a *common line* by saying 'I disbelieve the witnesses', and *no body has questioned that discretion.* What sentence to inflict is also a matter of discretion with the magistrate. . . . An appeal is a way of getting redress. But this may be blocked by a magistrate by refusing to give an appealable sentence.

> *Such are the forces which are arrayed against the struggling Untouchables. There is simply no way to overcome them because there is no legal way of punishing a whole society which is organized to set aside the law.*
> (Ambedkar 1989a: 270–71; emphases added)

This crucial passage needs to be read repeatedly. 'Let the law take its own course' is a phrase made familiar in each era. However, the law never does take its own course; rather, in a merciless fiction, it tries to show that the actual injuries and injustices never really occurred. In reading the law, Ambedkar asks us to bear the social realities in mind. These are characterised by discrimination and prejudice, which set the context of the law's operation. The law, in the course of its operation, would not take into account caste motives, but the injury caused to the Untouchable is also made socially invisible in the legal process. It is not merely the loopholes in the law and the uses of the magistrates' discretion which make the law's remedies illusory, but the 'whole society' that is set against the law. Here the structure of impunity is made fully legible: it can only be reversed when the institutions of the State set themselves apart from the majority in civil society. This need for separation explains Ambedkar's insistence on providing the fundamental right against untouchability in Article 17 and on making it a constitutional offence, which further suspends constitutional federalism (via Article 35) and imposes on the Parliament alone the power and duty to make penal laws in this regard.[11]

In this extremely important passage, Ambedkar emerges as a foremost critic of governance discretion. What is clearly wrong is institutional discretion when used systematically to perpetuate violent social exclusion. Ambedkar was too good a lawyer to argue against discretion as such or to subscribe to the general thesis that the abuse of power is a ground against its conferral. He is instead interested in showing what we today know as 'institutional bias', of the police and magistracy against the Untouchables, and in arguing that such a bias must be *questioned all the way.* Only such questioning endows social agendas and movements with the power to practise the reversal of perspectives, which is essential to justice.

Fifth, Ambedkar presciently directs us to understanding the imagery of lawlessness of law as a *sphere and a theatre constitutive of biopolitics*. This descriptor was not fully available to Babasaheb; yet he remains its foremost and early exemplar. Ambedkar would have endorsed fully Jean Baudrillard's (1993) imagery of sovereign power as comprising the powers of administering biological and social death.

Leaving aside here Ambedkar's critique of Gandhi's adroit uses of fasting unto death as acts of biopower militating against the emancipation of India's Untouchables, his historic summons – 'educate, organise, agitate' – for India's postcolonial Dalit subjects moved towards biophilic imageries of Indian constitutional futures. He believed somehow that the forms of postcolonial Indian constitutionalism may still mitigate bit by bit what Hannah Arendt (1992: 252) described as the 'terrifying, unsayable and unimaginable banality of evil'.[12]

Demosprudence

In so doing, Ambedkar speaks to us monumentally not so much about Indian *jurisprudence* as about new forms and grammars of Indian *demosprudence*. The distinction is recent, and as is usual, of American origins (Guinier 2007; see also Ray 2011).[13] However, Ambedkar invented demosprudence even before the term was invented; he was too good a lawyer not to know the distinction between the two. He knew the need for the development of jurisprudence in India – that is, principles which will inform the conduct of governance and in general, and lead to (here to use a Foucauldian expression) the 'immense criticizability of things' (Foucault 2003: 6).

Ambedkar the activist–social reformer practised demosprudence when he converted some basic needs into rights, but as a constitution maker he was careful not to convert all such needs into rights, as we can see from the chapter concerning the directive principles;[14] likewise, in crafting representative democracy for a free India, he deliberately refrained from sculpting the principles and practice of referendum.[15]

The tension between the institutions of representative governance – and, looked at closely, between those of direct democracy – is neatly reflected in Ambedkar, the constitution maker and Ambedkar, the social activist. At the same time, it is also his message that we eternally combat abuse of governance discretion; that is, for each new type of jurisprudence we erect a new demosprudence. Demosprudence is the new jurisprudence. This is the principal message of Dr Ambedkar's lifework.

This carries a postmodern implication: the demos whose manifestation we may wish to carry in the halls of justice and legislative chambers is the one we chose to construct as such. While this message has important implications, Ambedkar was no postmodernist: his was the battle against the essential discrimination against the Untouchables who were ascribed a permanently servile status – a fixed identity from which there was no exit. How we carry his fight, still unfortunately very necessary in the 21st century, is the important, and some would say the only, question before us. Can the alternative fashioning of solidarity amongst all victims of discrimination and humiliation provide a total answer?

Fifth Ambedkar Memorial Lecture, 5 March 2014, Ambedkar University Delhi.

Notes

[1] Already, the importance of CASM stands recognised though not named as such. For an early study of Dalit literature, see Guru (1997). See also Guru (1998), Rodrigues (2002) and Rege (2008).

Sharmila Rege (2008: 20) distinguishes 'critical memory' from 'nostalgia': the former is '[a]rticulation of the present crisis through linking it to moments of the time past' while the latter is 'selective and conservative in that it does not link the past to the crises of the present'. Rege's is an important contribution towards recoiling from hagiographic Ambedkar narratives. She emphasises exploration of the 'Ambedkarite counter public' and 'the passionate politics that constitutes it' as it 'brings emotional reflexivity into the analyses of dalit assertion by allowing a mapping of the relation between representations of Ambedkar and the generation of subversive counter emotions. If gratitude and loyalty to Ambedkar and his ideology emerge as the predominant cementing emotions; moral outrage and anger against the leadership coopted by the state play an important role in holding back cynicism or resignation – emotions that otherwise demobilise the popular masses' (*ibid.*).

Refer also to Anand Teltumbde, who inveighs against Ambedkarites, saying that it is not just a matter of expediency but even in theory, one may not describe Ambedkar's thinking as 'Ambedkarism'. Ambedkar did not 'leave behind any [such] systematic body of thought' as 'he did not believe in one. He does leave for us his vision, his goals and a role model to follow' (Teltumbde 2013: 11).

[2] As to the comparison with Aristotle, see Choudhury (2011).

[3] Much as I would like to, I do not here cite from Ambedkar's *Annihilation of Caste*, a classic text now republished with critical annotations and a sort of foreword, 'The Doctor and the Saint', by Arundhati Roy. See Ambedkar (2013). Though the thematic overlap between *What Congress and Gandhi Have Done to the Untouchables* and *Annihilation of Caste* is considerable, the latter focuses more on 'social reform' than on the clinical consideration of untouchability given in the former.

[4] For a recent discussion, see Grant (2013). See also Cohen (1983), Young (1990), Tuomela (2000), and Kramer (2003).

[5] See especially Thompson (2000); see also Thompson (2001, 2002, 2008, 2009); Thaler (2012).

[6] See the valuable discussion in Barry (1989).

[7] To give an example, Ambedkar as a constitutional architect made a distinction between legislative reservations – which were to be renewed, if necessary, every 10 years by an amendment to the Constitution – and educational and employment reservations for the Scheduled Castes and Scheduled Tribes, the

educationally backward, as well as for other backward classes, which may from time to time be determined by the states and the federal government. Was this arrangement animated by any notions of intergenerational justice? And, was there any difference between his thinking on the subject during the independence struggle and while making the Constitution?

[8] See Rawls (1995); see also Rawls (1997, 2001, 2008). Refer also to Freyenhagen (2011).

[9] Adharmic, i.e., not in accordance with or prohibited by dharma.

[10] Chaturvarna: the fourfold social ensemble of Brahmana, Kshatriya, Vaishya, and Shudra.

[11] Articles 23 and 24 prohibit child labour, trafficking in human beings and *begar* (forced labour), while other practices of agrestic serfdom also attract Article 35. Thus, the Parliament alone is declared constitutionally responsible for combating this plight.

[12] Ambedkar remains rather un-perplexed by the problems of 'bearing witness', or the lacuna of testimony, to invoke the Agambenian shorthand here. See Arendt (1966).

[13] I have tried to demonstrate the relevance of this notion as integral to the Indian constitutional jurisprudence (Baxi 2016b; see also Baxi 2017).

[14] This modifies somewhat the position reflected in Baxi (1995).

[15] See the discussion on the amending article in the Constituent Assembly debates. Ambedkar's early position regarding referendum by the Depressed Classes for the Scheduled Caste reservations was more complex (see Keer 1950).

References

Agamben, Giorgio. 1998. *Homo Sacer: Sovereign Power and Bare Life*, trans. Daniel Heller-Roazen. Stanford: Stanford University Press.

———. 1999. *Remnants of Auschwitz: The Witness and the Archive*, trans. Daniel Heller-Roazen. New York: Zone Books.

Ambedkar, B. R. 1945. *What Congress and Gandhi Have Done to the Untouchables*. Bombay: Thacker & Co. Reprinted in *Dr. Babasaheb Ambedkar: Writings and Speeches*, vol. 9. Bombay: Education Department, Government of Maharashtra.

———. 1989a. 'Held at Bay', in *Dr. Babasaheb Ambedkar: Writings and Speeches*, vol. 5, pp. 259–71. Bombay: Education Department, Government of Maharashtra.

———. 1989b. 'Their Wishes Are Laws unto Us', in *Dr. Babasaheb Ambedkar: Writings and Speeches*, vol. 5, pp. 272–86. Bombay: Education Department, Government of Maharashtra.

———. 2013. *Annihilation of Caste*, ed. S. Anand. New Delhi: Navayana.

Arendt, Hannah. 1966. *The Origins of Totalitarianism*. San Diego: Harcourt.

———. 1992. *Eichmann in Jerusalem: A Report on the Banality of Evil*. London: Penguin.

Barry, Brian. 1989. *Theories of Justice: A Treatise on Social Justice*, vol. 1, pp. 179–254. Berkeley: University of California Press.

Baudrillard, Jean. 1993. *Symbolic Exchange and Death*, trans. Iain Hamilton Grant. London: Sage.

Baxi, Upendra. 1995. 'Justice as Emancipation: The Legacy of Babasaheb Ambedkar', in Upendra Baxi and Bhikhu Parekh (eds), *Crisis and Change in Contemporary India*, pp. 122–49. New Delhi: Sage.

———. 2016a. 'How Not to Recall an Icon', *Indian Express*, 18 April. http://indianexpress.com/article/opinion/columns/how-not-to-recall-ambedkar-2758030/ (accessed on 8 June 2018).

———. 2016b. 'Demosprudence and Socially Responsible/Response-able Criticism: The NJAC Decision and Beyond', *NUJS Law Review*, 9(3–4): 153–72.

————. 2017. 'Farewell to Adjudicatory Leadership? Some Thoughts on Dr Anuj Bhuwania's "Courting the People: Public Interest Litigation in Post-Emergency India" – In Memoriam: Justice Prafulchandra Natwarlal Bhagwati', *NLUD Student Law Journal*, 4: 1–19.

Choudhury, Soumyabrata. 2011. 'Ambedkar contra Aristotle: On a Possible Contention about Who Is Capable of Politics'. Unpublished manuscript.

Cohen, G. A. 1983. 'The Structure of Proletarian Unfreedom', *Philosophy & Public Affairs*, 12(1): 3–33.

Foucault, Michel. 2003. *Society Must Be Defended*. New York: Picador.

Freyenhagen, Fabian. 2011. 'Taking Reasonable Pluralism Seriously: An Internal Critique of Political Liberalism', *Politics, Philosophy & Economics*, 10(3): 323–42.

Grant, Claire. 2013. 'Freedom and Oppression', *Politics, Philosophy & Economics*, 12(4): 413–25.

Guinier, Lani. 2007. 'The Supreme Court 2007: Foreword – Demosprudence through Dissent', *Harvard Law Review*, 22(4): 138.

Guru, Gopal. 1997. *Dalit Cultural Movement and Dialectics of Dalit Politics in Maharashtra*. Mumbai: Vikas Adhyayan Kendra.

————. 1998. 'Understanding Ambedkar's Construction of National Movement', *Economic and Political Weekly*, 33(4): 156–57.

———— (ed.). 2009. *Humiliation: Claims and Context*. New Delhi: Oxford University Press.

Keer, Dhananjay. 1950. *Dr Ambedkar: Life and Mission*. Bombay: Popular Prakashan.

Kramer, M. H. 2003. *The Quality of Freedom*. Oxford: Oxford University Press.

Norris, Andrew. 2005. 'Introduction: Giorgio Agamben and the Politics of the Living Dead', in Andrew Norris (ed.), *Politics, Metaphysics, and Death: Essays on Agamben's Homo Sacer*, pp. 1–30. Durham, NC: Duke University Press.

Rawls, John. 1995. 'Political Liberalism: Reply to Habermas', *Journal of Philosophy*, 92(3): 132–80.

————. 1997. *The Law of Peoples*. Cambridge, MA: Harvard University Press.

————. 2001. *Justice as Fairness: A Restatement*, ed. Erin I. Kelly. Cambridge, MA: Harvard University Press.

————. 2008. *Lectures on the History of Political Philosophy*, ed. Samuel Freeman. Cambridge, MA: Harvard University Press.

Ray, Brian. 2011. 'Demosprudence in Comparative Perspective', *Stanford Journal of International Law*, 47: 111–73.

Rege, Sharmila. 2008. 'Interrogating the Thesis of "Irrational Deification"', *Economic and Political Weekly*, 43(7): 16–20.

Rodrigues, Valerian. 2002. *The Essential Writings of B. R. Ambedkar*. New Delhi: Oxford University Press.

Teltumbde, Anand. 2013. 'Ambedkarites against Ambedkar', *Economic and Political Weekly*, 48(19): 10–11.

Thaler, M. 2012. 'Just Pretending: Political Apologies for Historical Injustice and Vice's Tribute to Virtue', *Critical Review of International Social and Political Philosophy*, 15(3): 259–78.

Thompson, Janna. 2000. 'Injustice and the Removal of Aboriginal Children', *Australian Journal of Professional and Applied Ethics*, 2(1): 2–13.

————. 2001. 'Historical Injustice and Reparation: Justifying Claims of Descendants', *Ethics*, 112(1): 114–35.

————. 2002. *Taking Responsibility for the Past: Reparation and Historical Injustice*. Cambridge: Polity Press.

————. 2008. 'Apology, Justice and Respect: A Critical Defense of Political Apology', in M. Gibney (ed.), *The Age of Apology: Facing Up to the Past*, pp. 13–30. Philadelphia: University of Philadelphia Press.

————. 2009. *Intergenerational Justice: Rights and Responsibilities in an Intergenerational Polity*. Abingdon: Routledge.
Tuomela, R. 2000. *Cooperation: A Philosophical Study*. Dordrecht: Kluwer Academic Publishers.
Young, Iris Marion. 1990. *Justice and the Politics of Difference*. Princeton: Princeton University Press.

6
Leading India

Gopalkrishna Gandhi

I am grateful to Ambedkar University Delhi, and to its Vice Chancellor Professor Shyam Menon, for inviting me to speak in this series of lectures commemorating Babasaheb Dr B. R. Ambedkar.

Nearly six decades after he passed away, Dr B. R. Ambedkar remains more alive, more invoked, more honoured than any political leader, dead or living, in India's political imagination. The name that comes closest to his in terms of an undiminished and, in fact, a growing posthumous following is that of Shaheed Bhagat Singh. Their images are iconised on hoardings, posters, calendars.

Custom decrees that portraits of Gandhi hang on official walls; protocol places those of the president of India there. But Ambedkar adorns those walls because none dare leave him out. Not anymore. This is the tribute realism pays to history. This is the correction time carries out on its own defaults.

It is, however, in the unbounded commons of India that his image reigns, not by official leave or institutional facilitation, but by the granite strength of popular will. Cyber cafes, computer training one-roomers, taxi and auto stands, shoe repair and cycle repair stalls, and countless hundreds of our country's improvised livelihood corners display his portrait proudly, as that of an inspiring forebear, with no sentiment other than a sense of belonging. But we must note, self-chastisingly, that the overwhelming number of such non-official sites where Ambedkar is commemorated by means of photographs or busts and statues, are powered by Dalit India. The India of the so-called higher castes stands by, cautiously if courteously distant, acknowledging him half-heartedly, even absent-mindedly. This is no loss to Ambedkar's contribution; it is a great loss to India's collective ownership of his legacy. We are great, we Indians, at squandering what we have and chasing after what we do not.

Dalit organisations have had to act as trustees, conservers and disseminators of the Ambedkar legacy. If they did not function as the agency for the dissemination of his word, the interpretation of his thoughts, the application of his ideas to contemporary situations, who would – Manu's India, Gandhi's, Nehru's India, or that of the RSS? In the process, we see two responses to Ambedkar – self-depriving neglect by the upper strata on the one hand and, on the other, something Babasaheb would, I believe, have been uncomfortable with. In Shakespeare's words, it is the 'gilding of refined gold, painting the lily, smoothing the ice, the throwing of a perfume on the violet' of the transformational man's transformational life and work.

Nothing in political allegiance can be as injurious, both to the hero and the hero worshipper, as the placing of a halo of attributed perfection over the hero's head. That inhibits, as Anand Teltumbde has recently shown in an incisive article (Teltumbde 2013), access into the hero's mind which can, like all minds, be as fallible as it can be formidable. Hero worship anoints the worshipper, rather than the worshipped. Political India uses Ambedkar's legacy self-servingly. He is placated, commemorated, by crass co-opters, used, misused, exploited to settle scores, gain absolute and differential advantage in influence, control, power, and, above all, in leadership contestations.

Leadership deficits are sought to be filled by the surpluses of Ambedkar's charisma, values and vision. Ideational vacuities are made up for by the clarity of his writings; deficiencies in political understanding, historical associations and cognitive interpretations are routinely made up for by recourse to quoting Ambedkar. An Ambedkar head-quote can indemnify a piece of writing against mediocrity. An Ambedkar mid-course quote can mitigate tedium, while an Ambedkar final quote can prevent its intellectual demise. His intellect is tunnelled, like the mines of Bellary or Chhattisgarh, opportunistically, impudently and self-aggrandisingly, by political Mafiosi.

Here his leadership of India shares something with another iconic figure, Periyar E. V. Ramasamy Naicker (1879–1973), whose revolutionary leadership of the Dravidian movement generated an ideological dividend of such richness and versatility as to provide intellectual life support to the two Dravidian parties in Tamil Nadu. Both keep drawing nourishment from the Periyar legacy without making any ideological value additions to it. He provides the rationale; they add the rhetoric.

The nationwide celebration of Ambedkar may be summarised thus: (*a*) the state hails him out of a sense of respectful obligation and intelligent 'play-safe'-ness; (*b*) millions of Dalits adore him with passionate commitment as their emancipator; (*c*) great and salutary exceptions apart, political organisations, Dalit and non-Dalit alike, link themselves to his legacy out of sheer opportunism.

   This historically narrow, intellectually stunted and politically gross limiting of Ambedkar is, however, not a new phenomenon. In a very crucial way, this happened in his lifetime as well. Whether acting on Gandhi's instinct, Nehru's democratic temper or sheer intellectual compulsion, the Indian National Congress did the right thing in encouraging Ambedkar to head the Drafting Committee of the Constituent Assembly and to join the Nehru cabinet as minister for law and justice. But it is a thousand pities that the same Congress could not see its way to backing him in his first electoral contest in 1952.

   As we all know, when the time came for India to identify its first president and first vice president, Dr Rajendra Prasad, as quondam president of the Constituent Assembly, was regarded as the natural choice for the first president of the Republic. I believe the Congress, which was wise enough to have utilised Dr Ambedkar's intellect for the drafting of the Constitution, should have seen him as the unanimous choice for India's first vice president. A great politico-psychological leap would have ensued in India's political maturation had that happened, for it would not only have placed Dr Ambedkar in the direct line of succession to the office of head of state, but would have given India's political leadership an altogether new and vital impetus.

   No one has any say in the laws of mortality. Dr Ambedkar was to die in 1956. But had he been vice president from 1952 onwards and lived into and beyond 1957, India could have had Dr Ambedkar as president and Dr Sarvepalli Radhakrishnan as vice president,[1] a sight for the gods and for us humans, perhaps in reverse order.

Leading India

   Leading and leadership in political India was, during the movement for freedom, about commitment, about sacrifice, about placing the nation above one's self. The country saw, in unprecedented profusion, leadership examples which would have generated discussion on the question Plato raises in the *Republic* regarding the qualities that distinguish a leader. Carlyle's *On Heroes, Hero-Worship and the Heroic in History* (1841), where he discusses leadership attributes in terms of skills and acquired prowess, including the human physique, we can be sure, was widely discussed while analysing our leaders. What has now come to be known as 'the trait theory of leadership', as against the Galtonian positing of

heredity and bloodline inheritance as decisive factors (Galton 1869), must
have been the subject of speculation in the 19th and early 20th centuries,
with the leaders of 1857, subaltern heroes like Mangal Pandey, and self-
honed charismatic men like Vivekananda, Aurobindo, Tilak, Gandhi,
Narayana Guru, Ayyankali, the bravehearts of the Chittagong Armoury
raid, and Ambedkar himself, spectacularly refuting the heredity principle,
the role of 'blue blood' or of leadership genes. History being created by the
intervention of great men and women with powerful personal attributes
must have seemed a real-time incontrovertibility in tune with the 'trait
theory' of leadership. 'Do the times produce the person or do persons make
the times?' must have been a subject for conclusion-less if luxurious enquiry.

Hero worship, an old trait handed down to us by the legacy of epic
literature, legends and mythologies, was anathema to Ambedkar. He said
in an address delivered in 1943: 'You must know that your man is really
great before you start worshipping him.' And he added:

> This unfortunately, is not an easy task. For these days, with the Press in
> hand, it is easy to manufacture great men. Carlyle used a happy phrase
> when he described the great men of history as so many Bank Notes. Like
> Bank Notes they represent gold. What we have to see is that they are not
> forged notes. (Ambedkar 1979: 230)

In the 'manufacturing of great men', in the making of leaders and
leadership, the real and the fake, the true and the forged, the genuine and
the counterfeit, arise together. It requires an Ambedkar-style winnowing
of the chaff from the grain to tell one from the other. That he himself was
whole wheat grain, no one doubted then, no one doubts now. He himself
doubted it not at all.

Ambedkar showed a remarkable degree of patience with mediocrity
and worse in the Constituent Assembly. Prejudice was clearly at work
against him, even in that august assembly. And so he gave it back, very
often, and very rightly, in hard kind. There was Prasad, a meticulous
and hard-working president of the assembly, overseeing its work. There
was Nehru, young and lucent, casting a spell on its proceedings by the
loftiness of his vision. But it was Ambedkar who was the assembly's mind,
not just working from its helm but actually being the helm. And he had
to go against his colleagues' dominant traits, which, for instance, in the
case of Pandit Kamalapati Tripathi, made that gentleman from Varanasi
say, addressing the chair during the discussion on India's official name, in
chaste Hindi, 'Sir, I am enamoured of the historic name: "Bharat".... The
gods have been remembering the name of this country in the heavens. . . .
The gods have a keen desire to be born in the sacred land of Bharat.' The

pandit then invoked the benediction of Sri Rama. He referred to Rama 'twanging the chord of the bow' which, he said, 'sent echoes through the Himalayas, the seas and the heavens'. At this point, Dr Ambedkar had to rise. 'Is all this necessary, Sir?' he asked the chair. Tripathiji tried justifying his invocations. Dr Ambedkar responded tersely, 'There is a lot of work to be done' (Government of India 2009: 5650).

He was leading India from the helm, saving the day from debasement at the hands of blind dogma, stale conditioning and atavistic recoil. But, most importantly, he was leading all of India, not some segment of it, some shard, some splinter of it. He could, like Pandit Kamalapati Tripathi, allow his own subliminal mind to get the better of his larger picture, but no, he was holding fast to that larger picture. There was a rage in Ambedkar. But it was a rage over which he had total control, not the other way around. It was, in a sense, almost a calm rage. Those two attributes – calm and rage – are great connectors. His rage linked him to the enraged in our midst. His calm connected him to those – 'intellectuals', one might term them – who responded to his impassioned dispassion.

It is important now to let Ambedkar be accessed as the helmsman that he was, for the whole of India, and not just for that section of its population whose immiserations he sought very pointedly to remove. It is important that if none patronises, marginalises or diminishes him out of bias, none praises him for fear of a sectarian backlash either. He is too great to be anybody's bête noire, too big to be anybody's totem. His leadership is too pervasive to be an ideological vogue. He compels engagement – serious but not uncritical; appreciative but not cultist. Those who enshrine Gandhi do him greater disservice than those who pillory him, for enshriners put a lid on all thought vents, while traducers only lower the slats. That must not happen with Ambedkar.

India's height contrasts with its abysses, its accomplishments of the mind and spirit are annulled by its depravities. I, for one, am appalled by Katherine Mayo's *Mother India* (1927) for its conceit but am shaken by its uncomfortable truths. Let us not delude ourselves into imagining that the freedom struggle was free of narrownesses, latent prejudice and active bias. It was not. The Grand Old Party contained in it then, as it does now, all the biodiversity of Indian politics, including communal bacteria. Cliques existed then in the Congress as they do now, but, difficult as it is to visualise this, pre-independence cliques cliqued at a higher clique level than they do now. And, by and large, leadership visions were at their broadest then, in terms of regional inclusion and social embrace. For the leaders, the nation came above politics, politics above party. And something of that vision had to permeate the rank and file.

Today, there are many parties on the scene. But, with great and redemptive exceptions, particularly in India's Left, leading India now is about first leading a community, then a faction within the party, then a conglomerate of factions within that party, then the party with fault lines sharp and ready to tear, and then, if at all and very optionally, a vision that is all-India. Leading India politically today is about adhering to those regressed wedges of belonging. It is about being known, being, in a sense, anointed and made recognisable within those wedges in the vocabulary of known parameters and only thereafter, if at all, about being understood intellectually, being interiorised in terms of ideas, being made a thought partner.

It would be lyrically gratifying but intellectually self-indulgent to expand on the Wordsworth quote: 'Whither is fled the visionary gleam? Where is it now, the glory and the dream?' (Wordsworth 1884: 23). I must resist that temptation and proceed rationally with the theme under discussion.

It is not that we, as a people, are unfamiliar with reason and reasoning that require decoding, disassembling and deconstruction; we are not. We have a tradition of ratiocinative disputation, as Professor Amartya Sen has tried to explain to us (Sen 2006). But, we are more comfortable, more easy, more at home with capsular coda. We are happier with aphorisms than with exegeses, with formulae rather than with formulations, with broad-brush colours than with nuances. We prefer that which is mnemonically accessible, acoustically mimetic and visually replicable over what seems to require intellectual hosting.

It is not that Indians are intellectually inert or psychoanalytically passive. But broadly speaking, there is a trait in us that makes us better disciples than analytics, better followers than equals, and better imbibers than reflecting listeners. This trait advantages the laryngally dominating over the intellectually suasive. This trait does not contradict and in fact complements another trait, a twin trait which makes factions of the disciples, cliques of the followers, schismatics of the adherents, each trying to win the leader's favour, nod or pat.

In this latency, as in everything generic about India, there are great and redemptive exceptions. We have one in Gautama Buddha, no less. He had disciples, but he was aware of the perils of discipleship, which is why, one may assume, he taught his disciples not to adopt even his teachings uncritically.

The Buddha certainly knew the unquestioning traits of his people, which included uncritical worship of preceptors, gurus, leaders. To consciously impart the trait of questioning, including self-questioning, to such a society was no ordinary task. And even though in his own case this teaching meant that he was subjecting himself to critical analysis and possible rejection, he maintained his position firmly.

The Political 'Helm'

Was the helm that the Buddha occupied a philosophic or a political helm? In so far as he forsook a present and future public office to extend his inherited political obligations to a willed engagement with the wider and deeper field of the human condition, the Buddha occupied, in my view, a political helm. In so doing, he was upsetting many social and political conditionings, leading to the setting up of a Sangha which, in intricacy and intent and also, alas, in future splintering and self-debilitation, rivalled any political organisation. The Buddha, anticipating the egalitarian movements and theories of the future, dismantled notions of inherited hierarchy.

Leading India, rather more than leading any other part of the world, is therefore about belonging to its peoplehood without exculpating the drawbacks and the debasements that blotch its copybook. Leading India, if it is to be honest and not self-seeking, has to be an exercise in challenging those who are misleading India. This, ipso facto, means that leading India is about risking widespread opposition, unpopularity and now, increasingly, violent intolerance. Leading India is, therefore, no occupancy of a cushioned helm. Leading India is about creating a helm in terms of a pivot from where the leader can command attention, without that helm being a destination.

Leading India politically is about being at the helm in India and about how that helm is viewed by India. There are certain venues for this helm that are easily identified in our *pauranik* (mythological) and *aitihasik* (historical) traditions. One is the fabled chariot, another is the very historical elephant howdah. Others include the horseback, with the heroic horse rider firmly and dramatically in the saddle in the style of Chhatrapati Shivaji, Maharana Pratap and Rani Lakshmibai of Jhansi.

This is a stance which came effortlessly to Jawaharlal Nehru when he chose to arrive on horseback for parleys in 1946 with the Cabinet Mission at the Viceregal Lodge in Shimla, when others arrived in motor cars or in hand-pulled rickshaws. Equestrian statues are about being at the helm. The more flared the stallion's nostrils, the more distended its neck veins and the more horizontal its flying tail, the greater the helmsman's or helmswoman's stature is supposed to be.

The ramparts of a fort, the flagstaff and, of course, the throne make for great helms, as do, in miniaturised form, royal insignia in the shape of textuality and animation. The wordings of land grants and the state-minted coin with the regnal image embossed on it have made the helm mobile, kinetic, puissant, carrying the leader's legend into active public currency. When resorted to by upstarts and putatives, these coins were exercises in hilarious futility but, in serious instances, they were anything but frivolous. Ashoka, as ingenious a communicator as he was inspirational a leader, devised his own accoutrement in his great edicts, making it clear that the leader was leading visibly, from heights of public command and depths of personal belief. He created, in effect, a bandwidth of communication with his subjects, the pillar and rock edicts in their differentiated format serving as the Mauryan equivalent of a G2 and a G3 spectrum.

An extraordinary symbol of helmsmanship, as literal as it is mind-churningly metaphorical, is the ingeniously raised central pillar in the Divan-e-Khas at Akbar's Fatehpur Sikri, with a circular platform for Akbar to sit on and meet with representatives of different religions and discuss their faiths, which, with Akbar, was as shrewd a political move as it may have been a philosophical one.

Leading India, politically, philosophically and intelligently, was never more imaginatively facilitated by state architecture than in that nugget of carved policy by Akbar, at least not until decades later when Shah Jahan repeated the triumph of symbolic architecture by thinking of the great ramparts of the Lal Qila in Delhi. From this promontory he could see and be seen by his subjects on their way to and back from their prayers at the Jama-e-Masjid and the venues of worship for other faith traditions in the vicinity. Leadership is about plinth, about a differential in persuasive height. But the elevation has to be on hard rock, on terra firma, not clayey loam if it is not to implode. The incorporation of the Lal Qila's leadership plinth in the political landscape of India by Subhas Bose in his aborted imagination, and by Nehru in his physically realised and lyrical somnambulism, is a gift in faith from helmsmanship to the unpredictabilities of leading India. Modern symbols of political helmsmanship in India include, in a bizarre reversion, the old chariot.

Buses and trucks, creaking in their aluminium bodies and reeking of diesel, have been re-tinkered with to carry the Chosen One standing under a canopy of tinsel and marigold, to play-act heroism. The 1990 Jan Chetna Yatra of Mr L. K. Advani, which coincided or synchronised with the telecasting of Ramanand Sagar's 78-episode *Ramayana*, with chariots, arrows and ballistic missiles, was greatly embarrassed when the bus-*rath* (chariot) got stuck under the Koilwar bridge on its way from Patna to Ara. The TV serial advertised as 'the world's greatest mythological serial' was frank enough to subtitle this with the 'Limca Book of Records'. Buses getting stuck, and impeding passengers' journeys, is no strange thing, but this leader-carrying rath, in its mock-up edition, getting stuck, threw mock helmsmanship at the unforgiving feet of truth and created a record of its own kind, Limca or not.

India's modern helm-symbols include the national emblem and the national flag, both deriving from Ashoka and, while giving to the Indian nation-state an impersonal palladium, also daubing the prime ministerial forehead with the legitimising unction of moral authority. The Nehru–Radhakrishnan descriptions of these two symbols of state are colophonic, and cannot but make any leader who is sworn into office self-chastisingly mindful of his or her responsibilities.

Following the ancient coin model, the currency note which bears a particularly banal representation of the Father of the Nation, pre-emptively, I suspect, to keep other claimants and counter-claimants out, is another signet of helmsmanship. Helmsmanship is as visual, as tactile as currency. And it is as liable to devaluation.

The Counter-'Helm'

For each 'helm' which valorises and platforms the established leader, there is a counter-helm which does the opposite from the other end of helmsmanship. This is the helm which interrogates and can excoriate the official helm, thereby leading India, not from the vantage of power but from the pivot of influence. This is the influence of refutation, of rebellion, of revolt. Here the helm is not the throne but the counter-throne – in the shape of the agitated street corner, the eloquent dock and the heroic gallows. From these sites, the counter-helm is massively unsettling for the helm, which it decries, destabilises and demolishes.

Faiz Ahmed Faiz's stirring *nazm* 'Hum Dekhenge' can be called the anthem of the counter-helm.[2] It has these peerless lines: *Sab taaj uchhaale jaaenge, sab takht giraae jaaenge ... hum dekhenge, laazim hai ki hum bhi dekhenge*. (All crowns will be thrown off, all thrones will be overturned ... we will see, we too shall see.)

The counter-helm upturns the traditional helm. It shows up the conventional helm, the seat of power, temporal or ecclesiastical or, indeed, social, in terms of oppression, of *zulum* (cruelty). That is when the counter-helmsman challenges the establishment by labelling it evil and promising redemption. Gandhi said famously, after the Jallianwala Bagh massacre, 'co-operation in any shape or form with this satanic government is sinful' (quoted in Hardgrave and Kochanek 2008: 47).

Among the sites of the counter-helm is an intangible one, disappearing after it has done its subversive magic. Though not made of physical materials, it is very real. This is the pivot in a procession of protest, the sharpened point at its lead, where the procession's dialectical tension, its dramatic appeal and its deconstructionist arsenal get concentrated. At the head of his 1913 satyagrahic march in South Africa and then at his 1931 march to Dandi, Gandhi was at that processional counter-helm. Both marches were huge successes, bringing about huge changes in public thinking, self-esteem and priorities, and leading government to make strategic moves. Three decades later, after the march in South Africa, Subhas Bose's 'Dilli Chalo!' call on 25 August 1943, essentially a grand plan for a march on to Delhi, was classical counter-helming, but fated, like his political career, to end prematurely.

In 1946, undivided Bengal saw the Tebhaga Movement led by the Kisan Sabha of the Communist Party, for equity in crop sharing. As many as 70 peasants were killed in police firing, but the imagination of the country was stirred as never before. Post-independence, Kerala and the Andhra region of Madras saw many movements based on the land rights of *kisan*s (farmers). But the most significant leading of Indian opinion came in 1974, when Jayaprakash Narayan at the age of 72, spearheading a formidable movement, led a silent procession in Patna. The procession was lathi-charged and he received brutal blows. The effect of that on the national mood was electric. This counter-helm point was a turning point in the Bihar movement and consequently in the politics of the Indira Gandhi era.

Leading India at that point, as no one else did, J.P. declared: 'After 27 years of freedom, people of this country are wracked by hunger, rising prices, corruption . . . oppressed by every kind of injustice. . . . it is a Total Revolution we want, nothing less!'[3] The words have a strangely contemporary ring to them. All we have to do is substitute 27 years by 67 years, and we have today's counter-helm. The counter-helm is the pedestal that seeks to turn disadvantage into advantage, both in the person of the counter helmsman or helmswoman and as a cause, the cause of the disadvantaged, as one who cuts a path where there was none, a path which is both a way and a world in itself, a way to new awareness, new understanding, a new belief by which to better our inner and outer world.

Leading India by Advantage

It would be instructive to see how one major 'advantage', the advantage of birth, becomes an ingredient in leading India. Galton might not be amused but I call this principle 'ascent by descent'. Whether one likes that phrase or not, approves of that or not, heredity and leadership in India and in what used to be called the subcontinent of India are literally joined at birth. However, it is not limited to the sense of 'family leadership' alone, as heredity can be about the family of people as a collectivity. The term 'family' is modular. There is one's immediate family, in terms of the *khaandaan* (clan) one is born into. Then there is the larger family of the caste and community one belongs to, and then the federation of those communities within a country and so on. Heredity, therefore, is an extendable term and in that larger sense, India has had the most amazing community leaders.

Since no one wills his or her own birth, it follows that those who are born into political families are innocent, at birth, of political aims or ambitions even as a baby born into a royal household is blissfully unaware of the merits of monarchy verses a republican order, or as one born into an agricultural family cannot have a clue about the advantages or disadvantages of Bt brinjals over organic ones.

Those born into political families take birth in and grow into a fait accompli. Politics is, for them, a pre-established and ineluctable destination. Now, this is not a new phenomenon. This was the case during the freedom struggle in India and what are now Pakistan and Bangladesh. We find many father–son, brother–brother, husband–wife, and, less frequently, father–daughter teams in the political theatres of the subcontinent of India. And so the children of leaders become *chhota* (small) leaders in themselves, from the start.

The Mahatma is regarded as one who did not 'project' his biological descendants onto the political screen. In the struggle in South Africa, however, Gandhi's eldest son, Harilal Gandhi, played not just an important political role but also a vital leadership one. He was, in fact, his father's alter ego. Harilal was called 'Chhota Gandhi' and was a valued leader, going to jail with and without his father and earning his respect. If Harilal Gandhi had not been enervated by personal setbacks, many of them of his own making, he could well have evolved into one of Gandhi's front-ranking colleagues, sharing his political helm.

Harilal Gandhi is the classic anti-hero, anti-leader who only validates his opposite number. But, compared to some of the leaders of today, what a refreshing contrast he provides! He destroyed himself, not others. He borrowed and squandered money on his indulgences, but not one paisa of public money was spent on Harilal Gandhi.

Symbiosis marked the great pre-independence pairings, as did synergy. No one thought of such team-ups then as being monopolist. On the other hand, they were regarded as natural, felicitous. The Motilal Nehru–Jawaharlal Nehru example is, of course, the best known. Countless others have followed. In India, home and work have not been so strictly demarcated and the families of politicians invariably get hurled or hurtle into the world of campaigns, agitations, manifestos, elections. In the main, politics does not leave the families of political leaders alone. It envelops them. One might even say it traps them.

The families of political leaders get willy-nilly drawn into political ways of thought, political ways of behaviour, a political vocabulary (often at the cost of other forms of study and learning), political activity, then on to political leadership and the yo-yo of political adversity, political opportunity, success, popularity, un-success, unpopularity, even obloquy, and, alas, more often than is acceptable, tragically, in the snapping of everything by a violent death. Yo-yos swing, yo-yos snap. Entering a political legacy is therefore not necessarily the same as walking to a golden throne. It is often like falling into a snake-pit. Biological inheritors of a political legacy have to come to terms with the pluses and minuses of that legacy, its sweets and bitters, its crowns and its crosses. That legacy can be a privilege, it can be a punishment. It can, often, be both.

Leading India has, therefore, two seemingly contradictory originations: first, predetermination or pre-design by caste, community, kinship, and family expectations and obligations; second, the chance throw of Fate's fatal dice on the other. The same matrix of kinship operates powerfully in both. This is the standard pattern.

But, that said, leadership of the really alchemic kind, leadership that has been truly transformational and has left an extraordinary impress on Time, has come from beyond the confines of kinship. And I must, there, own allegiance to the 'trait theory' which validates the leadership examples of the Mahatma, Dr Ambedkar, Shaheed Bhagat Singh, Netaji Subhas Chandra Bose, Sardar Patel, and a host of pre-independence national leaders, with the same being said, in more recent times, of the Loknayak Jayaprakash Narayan.

Leading India by Disadvantage

Democratic processes in India are responding with different degrees of immediacy and efficacy to the rages and agonies of the people. The result: the rise of what is called the politics of street power, of the public square, of the *khula maidaan* (open ground). This politics is neither strange to us, nor is it undemocratic, because it is essentially non-violent. But it is coercive in that it is at cross-purposes with the conventional processes of democratic remedy.

The far more serious result of the slow and inadequate response of democratic procedures is the rise of organised armed violence as an alternative. No violent movement or initiative is a one-shot affair. It is like a *shikaar* (hunt), which never stops with one kill. No bullet has only the name of one user or one target engraved on it.

Violence feeds on itself, evolving from a tool with an objective to a cult with none other than its own nameless, faceless, soulless gratification. Convention has decried violence. It has fallen to the violence, a victim. But it is yet to call violence's bluff convincingly by showing itself to be a better harbinger of change than violence. And so, 'leading India by disadvantage' is now less a democratic phenomenon than a violent one.

Leading India: Today and Tomorrow

Wherever else they may or may not be applicable, philosophical approaches, ranging from Plato's *Republic* to Plutarch's *Lives*, to the question of what qualities distinguish an individual as a leader are still of academic interest in India. India has had leaders, great ones and petty ones.

Anything unusual in that? Have not all societies and nations had those?

Yes, except that India's great leaders have been truly millennial, starting from the Buddha. Great leading is a desideratum in India. And that greatness has meant farsightedness. Anything narrow, shortsighted or fractured might helm India awhile; it cannot and does not lead it. Stagnation ensues; stillness does. Listlessness and the doldrums result.

We need to be aware that we are now at a cusp in India, when a narrow-eyed, pinch-hearted and stuntingly bigoted ideology is claiming our trust. And a dictatorial creed, cruising on the fallacious self-definition of nationalistic strength and patriotic virility, is poising itself for power over this diverse nation. What makes this claim towards the leadership of India sinister is the underlying appeal to glorify one individual above normal scales of human potential, into a political giantism of unprecedented proportions.

The helm, underserved by those it gave of its hospitality over the last decade, is now up for grabs by a skein of ethnic prejudices passing deceptively for a nationalist ideology. Hindutva may or may not be the short term for Hindu-*mata-tvam* (or Hindu identity); it certainly is a shortcut to human credulousness. The lack of vision, of far sight, and of what Radhakrishnan invoked when he said Indian statesmanship should *dirghampasyatu ma hrasvam* (look far ahead, be not shortsighted), is sought to be made up for by this shortcut. Have no vision, give PowerPoint demos from our epics, *purana*s, *itihasa*s, with the current hero playing all the epic heroes at once.

Leading India by stoking subliminal prejudices, creating new bogeys, mixing ancient biases with new and imagined insecurities, superimposing, on new manifestos, old testaments with rings that stir subconscious memories of mythic wrongs and legendary vistas, is to seek a shortcut intravenously, into popular endorsement. It is also to revive, after a long exile, fear as a tool of leadership. Machiavelli might well gloat that his theory 'Better to be feared than loved' seems to imbue the political creed of a claimant to the prime ministership of India.

The facts of the matter, as a legal order might say, are that:

Political leadership in India is in difficulty.

Its credibility is at stake.

And so it is resorting to dangerous short-termism, sinister shortcuts.

Leading India is now about survival, rather than service, placing faction above party, party above politics, and politics above nation. Leading India is now about desperation. The desperate is dangerous.

The grip of money and, therefore, of moneyed manipulation over politics, adds an edge that cuts to this desperation. The pre-independence leading of India was about ideals; it was about, literally, leading the way, showing a new and a bigger road, away from the older and narrow ones. It was about correcting India where the leaders thought it needed correcting. The post-independence leading of India is not about ideals but, dropping the 'i', it is about deals, cutting deals with the status quo, with existing prejudices, existing polarities, fault lines, which is why the fledgling challenge thrown to the mainstream parties by the Aam Aadmi Party holds interest and promise, if it also holds anxieties of even this initiative being gobbled up by the known patterns of political leadership.

Being hugely well informed and discerning, the public knows there still are some noble exceptions – both in terms of persons and political formations – to this general reputation for desperation and recklessness in its political leadership. But those exceptions are insignificant in numbers.

Not surprisingly, therefore, non-political leadership is beginning to look attractive. At a remote school on the Kerala–Tamil Nadu border, to my question, 'What do you want to be?', came the reply: 'A footballer like Messi' and 'a bird watcher like Salim Ali'. Not one child mentioned politics as an avocation or a single political leader as an exemplar.

Leaders of NGOs and non-elected constitutional authorities are held in a level of regard that is much higher than that of politics and politicians. One hears regularly, 'I have faith in the judicial system.' Not in a long time has one heard: 'I have faith in our political leaders.'

Legislative bodies remain the most reliable vessels for the expression of public opinion, public grievances, public expectations, and, of course, for the modification of existing laws where modifications are needed and the enactment of new ones called for by our times. Those bodies cannot afford any further drop in public estimation.

The great challenge before the political leadership today is the retrieval of its credibility, of leading, from *leaderbaazi* (a pretence of leadership). But the greater need is the rediscovery of a leading that is not about politics or even governance and statecraft, but about the human condition in India. We need the leadership of social philosophers, ecological philosophers, philosophers of science, thinkers who may themselves be activists or generate activity, like Bertrand Russell, Ernst Schumacher, Wangari Maathai, Chandiprasad Bhatt, and Sunderlal Bahuguna. We need leaders who can walk out of palaces, parliaments and pontiff seats, and speak for the plundered forests, decimated mines, scooped-out rocks, ravaged water bodies, polluted river basins, neglected monuments, ruined craft traditions, threatened tribal life systems, our wildlife, and our ageing populations.

We need leaders, and our womankind, especially the girl child so often and so tragically facing the most bizarre exploitation, neither of these have constituencies. But they are about the most precious things on our earth.

Leading India has to be about leading India, not one chunk of it, howsoever large. Leading India has to be about making it just, not giving it an air-pumped illusion of becoming a superpower. Leading India has to be about speaking bitter truths about what are we doing or rather not doing about the tonnes of garbage that we know we generate and the nuclear waste we know nothing about. And around which garbage, often within inches of which, thousands of human beings live, cook, wash, sleep, and, being human, procreate, give birth and die. It is on these that politicians, in the business of leading India, descend like vectors at election time, laden with cash and hooch, to buy their votes. Babasaheb had spoken of how this India may well explode and blow up our constitutional edifice. Why and how that has not happened yet defies my understanding.

Leading India has to be about leading and not misleading India.

Sixth Ambedkar Memorial Lecture, 14 April 2014, Ambedkar University Delhi.

Notes

[1] Dr Sarvepalli Radhakrishnan (1888–1975) was a philosopher who was the first vice president (1952–62) as well as the second president of India (1962–67).
[2] Nazm is an important genre of Urdu poetry.
[3] This speech by Jayaprakash Narayan was in Hindi. Professor Bimal Prasad has rendered the above passage as follows: 'After 27 years of that freedom the

people are groaning. Hunger, soaring prices and corruption stalks everywhere. The people are crushed under all sorts of injustice. . . . this is a movement for total revolution' (Narayan 2009: 286–94).

References

Ambedkar, B. R. 1979. 'Ranade, Gandhi and Jinnah', in *Dr. Babasaheb Ambedkar: Writings and Speeches*, vol. 1. Bombay: Education Department, Government of Maharashtra.

Carlyle, Thomas. 1841. *On Heroes, Hero-Worship and the Heroic in History*. London: James Fraser.

Galton, Francis. 1869. *Hereditary Genius*. London: Macmillan.

Government of India. 2009. *Constituent Assembly Debates*, vol. IX. New Delhi: Lok Sabha Secretariat.

Hardgrave Jr, Robert L., and Stanley A. Kochanek. 2008. *India: Government and Politics in a Developing Nation*. Boston: Thomson Wadsworth.

Mayo, Katherine. 1927. *Mother India*. New York: Cornwall Press. https://archive.org/details/motherindia035442mbp (accessed on 19 May 2018).

Narayan, Jayaprakash. 2009. 'Towards Total Revolution, Patna, 5 June 1974', in Bimal Prasad (ed.), *Jayaprakash Narayan Selected Works*, vol. 10, pp. 286–94. New Delhi: Nehru Memorial Museum & Library and Manohar.

Sen, Amartya. 2006. *The Argumentative Indian: Writings on Indian History, Culture, and Identity*. London: Penguin.

Teltumbde, Anand. 2013. 'Ambedkarites against Ambedkar', *Economic and Political Weekly*, 48(19): 10–11.

Wordsworth, William. 1884. *Ode: Intimations of Immortality: From Recollections of Early Childhood*. Boston: D. Lothrop and Company.

7

Is Unbridled Capitalism a Threat to Constitutional Democracy in India?

Aruna Roy
(with the MKSS collective)

As we all know, thinking is not dependent on literacy, and our mental vocabulary is not restricted by the ability to read or write. Collective thinking and writing give us the space to acknowledge the wisdom of the people whose experience is the basis of this talk and this piece. All writings and speeches – including articles, memorial lectures, convocation addresses, and speeches accredited to individuals working in the Mazdoor Kisan Shakti Sangathan (MKSS) – owe their ideas, ideology and theoretical assumptions to the MKSS collective and to a larger citizenry of articulate and thinking people.

An Explanation

I work with people strongly embedded in the oral tradition. The written word is unfamiliar. Whether lyrics, poetry, song, or politics, whether expressed in anger or in peace, with wisdom or bigotry, it is housed in the oral tradition. But to only speak, which is all I did in the beginning, has led to some degree of chaos. Reproductions of transcripts have been problematic. The time constraint, the ambience, the surly or engaging look of a listener can make one stumble and go off the strict logical build-up that a written script requires. The written script has a life of its own. Written words travel bereft of the support of mime and ambience. That is why we speak as well as write: two scripts on the same theme.

Provocative as the title of this paper may sound, it reflects a live predicament. A question such as this would not have been framed three decades ago in India. However, we live in the era of 'liberalisation of the economy' – perhaps more aptly referred to as neoliberal globalisation, where international capital and its movement in and out of the country determine many aspects of policy. There has been a steadily growing concern about the manipulation of democratic institutions and instruments that might enhance inequality and justify autocratic state action – all in the name of development and growth. The polity is shrouded by a functioning electoral process, lulling the mind into comfort. But the foundation on which the nation was built and its guiding principles enshrined in the Indian Constitution are being systematically eroded. They are even dismissed as being out of date and irrelevant. Growth rates in gross domestic product (GDP) are presented to the country as the only defining principle of 'development', with scant attention to the distribution of that growth, and almost no attention to the costs of such 'growth' for people or the environment. The capitalist system has a very selective bottom line. India's Gini coefficient is 33.6 on a curve where 0 constitutes the highest level of equality of distribution.[1]

There is, in fact, a strong and obvious tension between the growth of individual and corporate wealth and issues of equity. Consequently, the architecture of the Indian Constitution, designed to ensure that growth occurs evenly and with justice, is now seen as an impediment to high growth rates and to 'progress' as it is defined in the neoliberal paradigm. It is understood that the GDP depends on the efforts of the private sector to begin and expand economic enterprise, and therefore the profit motive of the private sector is to be given priority in order for the country to 'progress'. There is no clear definition of 'development' or 'progress'; no statement of intent given to the people. The focus is no longer on issues of equity.

Capitalism likes to project a symbiotic relationship with democracy. However, as we are witnessing in India, it cannot brook any opposition. Therefore, a situation emerges in which democracy itself needs to be converted into a marketplace where money and capital will decide policies and only those with money will have voice.

National liberation is hollowed out by seeking to limit the concept of independence to the flag and a national anthem. The Constitution and those who invoke its principles are inconvenient because they remind us that independence promised much more to the people.

Undermining Constitutional Guarantees

[T]he Swaraj wherein there were no fundamental rights guaranteed for the Depressed Classes, would not be a Swaraj to them. It would be a new slavery for them. – B. R. Ambedkar (quoted in Keer 1971: 42)

Lively deliberations about the Constitution began in the Constituent Assembly. For every 'argumentative Indian', the Constitution has been a subject of discussion and debate. But current policies have brought these contestations into sharper focus, with the immediate fallout nudging an indifferent citizenry to understand the implications of tampering with basic constitutional rights. Ideological perspectives may have kept changing with the times but the sanctity of free speech, expression and democratic space was never undermined, except during the dark phase of the Emergency. But now positions are taken to ridicule rather than debate, in which dissent and opposite points of view are sought to be obliterated.

Ours is a Constitution built by people who understood struggle. It was drafted by political leaders who spent their lives fighting against exploitation and oppression from powers both within and outside the country. As a result, they were careful to ensure that the voices of the marginalised were amplified; that plurality was protected; and that those fighting for equality and justice would be supported by the Constitution and the state.

In the era of neoliberal globalisation, with GDP as *the* indicator of performance and success, constitutional values are being brushed aside as outdated, irrelevant, and an impediment to the objectives of 'economic growth'. Nothing could be a bigger mistake. All of us would do well to take stock, and examine what we stand to lose as individuals, as a people, and as a nation, when in the name of 'opening up' the economy to investment, there are disguised and direct attacks on the citizens' fundamental rights to equality, liberty and fraternity through executive and legislative measures. In fact, what professed nationalists should realise is that this formulation is the biggest threat to the idea of India. When the sanctity of the Constitution is undermined by ignoring its spirit, it affects the Constitution itself in a fundamental way, and the fine balance that holds us together could begin to fall apart. The ordinance on land and the substantial cuts in social sector budgets have been bad enough. Now, even the rhetoric of inclusive growth has gone. There is middle-class outrage against 'subsidies' to the poor. But the subsidies to the rich, tax reductions and waivers are passed over without a murmur. There is talk against crony capitalism and yet, Adani is given a $1 billion (Rs 6,200 crore) loan by the State Bank of India.[2] In such a scenario, it is even more important to reinforce the centrality of a Constitution created to safeguard the interests of a nation fractured in its social fabric by discrimination and inequalities, which are perpetuated by feudal and colonial power. The Indian Constitution remains an extraordinary document that embodied an unusual consensus.

These constitutional values were an outcome of the collective consciousness of a complex, organic national movement that sought independence from an external exploitative power. It sought to build a society that would guarantee an equal sense of justice and opportunity. In

appointing Dr Ambedkar as the chair of the Drafting Committee of the
Constituent Assembly, there was an implicit understanding that a society
built on an exploitative and pervasive caste structure could only be recast
if the alternative was shaped by and with people who had experienced the
nature of oppression unique to Indian society. Today we have ruling elites
who have no experience of struggle in their personal or political lives. It
is reflected in their insensitivity to those who present a different point of
view. Having cornered the larger share of resources for themselves, they
believe that economic growth is the path to progress. How can they not
– considering they have been the beneficiaries of an unbridled capitalist
'growth' machine?

A poor woman says in a Bharatiyar (Subramania Bharati) poem
that she wants her bowl of gruel in order to stay alive, but much more
important for her is the right to say that she wants the gruel. Free speech
without equality finds easy approval only when self-interest is not hurt.
For the rich who have easy access to power, free speech is often seen as an
impediment – especially when it amplifies voices that hurt their financial
and other interests. The investment sector and big business have succeeded
in using propaganda to sanctify growth. Such propaganda generates a false
picture that anything that is an impediment to their plan(the state included)
is seen and described as anti-development, anti-progress and finally as anti-
national. Such is the case of Priya Pillai being deplaned as she was leaving
to testify in the UK against a UK-based company and its anti-people, anti-
environment policies in India.[3] The collateral victim is the Constitution
and its guarantees. There are many voices of professional groups, from
the global South and North, questioning the grand success of a pillaging
capitalist universe, but the corporate-monopolist control over the media,
in most cases, prevents their message from reaching the ordinary citizen.

The monopoly – influencing thought through a combination of
technology and capital – over our minds and ways of thinking is perhaps
ultimately the most threatening. We all read and were worried about Big
Brother in George Orwell's 1949 masterpiece *Nineteen Eighty-Four*. At
least the controls were visible externally. Now we have an insidious system
that seduces people into a false comfort zone while reducing basic rights.
The apple dangles forever just a few inches from one's reach. Pushing us
on to take that one more loan, till the dream and finances crash! In the
past, there was a counterpoint which pointed out the pitfalls of a system
that ignored distribution and encouraged inequality. Today, capitalism is
not allowed to face an adversary, and the poor have few friends.

Capital investment comes with the motive of seeking profit,
and justice demands prior information on what its impact may be on

equality. In India, equality is a new space for millions of people who lived crushed under discrimination and poverty for millennia. Constitutional guarantees have been the tenuous link to justice. It is a fragile space that post-independence India has managed to construct, with creativity, sweat and tears. Capitalism finds itself confronting those who have now tasted and cherish freedom with equality. The usual lure of money has a point beyond which it does not play. The coterie where money and the power of the state collude is obvious and visible. Nowhere more so than in rural India, where niceties are done away with. When money power does not succeed, having an acquiescent state becomes imperative and state violence becomes a necessary byproduct.

The present political system works with capitalist structures and the means of the business world. It uses every trick of business management from sales strategy to monopoly controls. It is no longer a secret for people who know that a 'brand' can be built equally for toothpaste and for political candidates – including the prime minister and chief ministers. This is a build-up used eventually to either propagate or dismantle an idea, or a structure. Words and acts perpetrated against constitutional principles may possibly be part of an attempt to dismantle these principles that are so fundamental to democracy and are enshrined in the Constitution. This is why any attempt to move from guaranteed and legislated basic principles of equality – humanity and fairness – must be viewed with deep concern.

The 'educated elite' may be shocked but are careful not to upset the economic apple cart. It is in the nature of the propaganda machine to slowly build up from a single voice to many, gaining courage from being abusive or unconstitutional. All attempts at equality are whittled down while giving credence to irrational arguments.

Can the Indian Constitution withstand the brute force which is an accompaniment of the capitalist enterprise? Can a set of ideas enshrined in law offer enough support to the many people and communities who need its protection the most? At first glance it would seem to be an unequal and impossible task. However, when we understand the impact of vast numbers of people facing increasing hardship and difficulty, it is clear that there will be many significant battles ahead. People understand what is happening and who is benefitting from it. Sixty years of democracy have also given them the experience of organising and coming together to legally demand what is their due. This is why there are many battles today around laws; some of these laws are demanded and protected by ordinary people while other laws are resolutely opposed by them. In December 2014, more than 20,000 people from across India representing a large cross-section of voices assembled at Jantar Mantar under the banner of 'Abki baar humaara adhikaar' (This time it's our right). These were diverse communities and people who have been displaced economically and politically through a process of development that leaves them bereft of the right to life itself. They were representatives: a single voice at Jantar Mantar spoke for thousands who could not travel to Delhi from their villages. They were able to make the Mahatma Gandhi National Rural Employment Guarantee Act (MGNREGA) non-negotiable, but they did not manage to quell the pressure of the capitalist lobby on land and many other rights. The ordinance on land acquisition is a violation of the most basic guarantee of swaraj, the right to claim sovereignty over land, thereby allowing citizens to help define their relationship with the state.

The Constitution and the legal framework are in fact going to be a primary battleground of the immediate future. In all likelihood, it is ordinary people who are going to repeatedly swear allegiance to the Constitution. Whereas, ironically enough, it is the rulers who will want to set it aside, change it and, if these attempts fail, undermine it and make it irrelevant.

In large part, the phase beginning with market globalisation in the early 1990s has been the most threatening for constitutional principles. The contradiction between the market and its principles of competition and profit on the one hand, and the Constitution and its principles of equality and justice on the other, was bound to come to a head. Given the importance of the Constitution to India's polity and democratic future, the dilution of its principles could only begin in a piecemeal manner. This has now steadily grown to a point where the rulers have dispensed with even the attempt to show that policies are in keeping with the Constitution.

People, however, have felt the effects and strengths of these policies, and have now become the most vocal proponents of basic constitutional principles. These differences have led to a new area of contention – the need to protect the freedom of expression, which also is enshrined in the Constitution.

Contemporary attacks on the Constitution are no longer piecemeal. Basic concepts are being questioned. The preamble to the Constitution is for many an invocation to democracy – one of the few secular chants we have. A prominent government advertisement deliberately omitted the words 'socialist and secular', and an explanation was offered that the words were not present in the original version of the Constitution. That the words which caused conceptual discomfort to the ruling regime were also the ones to have been omitted was (we were informed) apparently just a coincidence. Announcements were subsequently made that only the current 'official' version will be used. Nevertheless, the so-called fringe elements grabbed the opportunity to say that the time had come to debate the utility of the concepts themselves – and one realises that there is method in this madness.

Nothing could be a bigger mistake. More direct attacks on the fundamental right to equality, liberty and fraternity are carried out through legislative measures, in the name of 'opening up' the economy to investment. No amount of state violence can really quell people's power or protest. The consequent attempts to suppress questioning and critique, through the denial of fundamental rights, have exposed the real plan.

In this context, it is even more important to reinforce the centrality of the Constitution. The fact that Dr B. R. Ambedkar chaired the Drafting Committee of the Constitution not only resulted in a legal framework that expressly emancipated the most oppressed, but also protected the democratic rights of all people to express themselves freely – especially to articulate distress. Three challenges were understood and sought to be secured for all citizens: freedom from want and access to the basic necessities; dignity and the equality of all; and the freedom to speak out, convey disagreement and express dissent. All three are crucial, and they together define Indian democracy and its relevance to its citizens.

Capitalism, in theory and in practice, finds it difficult to operate in the realm of justice and equality. It is competitive, single-minded and ruthless in its drive for profits. It uses the power of money to drive itself, buying allies, the media, and even elections along the way. Within a democratic framework, it is deeply insecure and threatened by voices that might burst its bubble, or expose the inequality and injustice that might be an outcome of capitalist policies.

That is why there are repeated attempts to suppress difference of opinion, from the incarceration of Binayak Sen for sedition some years ago,[4] to the targeting of NGOs critical of nuclear energy or GM foods. The change in regime at the centre has only amplified a discourse made public by the Intelligence Bureau that these voices are anti-development, and therefore anti-national. The sometimes uneasy alliance between communal and market forces is sustained by the state looking the other way, when 'unconstitutional' attacks are made on prominent public intellectuals. The threats to U. R. Ananthamurthy, a great Kannada writer, or the killings of Narendra Dabholkar and Govind Pansare for expressing views which the majoritarian fundamentalists could not tolerate, are all part of the package to intimidate people who may set an example, and foster a popular discourse that might be difficult to withstand.

The atmosphere of intolerance has got steadily worse over the last 15 years. The shameful hounding of M. F. Husain, and the recent Shiv Sena editorial in its mouthpiece *Saamana* demanding that Muslims be denied the vote, show how much state tolerance there is for those who launch blatantly unconstitutional attacks on the idea of an inclusive India. The apparent and real disregard for a plural India places many uncomfortable questions at the door of the literate, often confused with the 'educated', electorate. Not the least of them is the straightforward question: how much freedom are we willing to barter for comfort and 'the good life'?

Constant vigilance is necessary. Even seemingly weak or quiet suggestions to dilute those principles in the law or Constitution which protect democratic expression and minority rights cannot therefore be taken lightly. Any attempt to whittle down protection for equality and justice in existing structures of the Constitution and the law must be viewed with concern. In essence, the Constitution laid down principles to protect the freedom of people and for the exercise of equality in a country with a web of discriminatory interests and a feudal hierarchy entrenched in tradition. A constitutional democracy was sought to be built which would give economic, social and political opportunity to all citizens – an almost impossible challenge.

An Assertion of Constitutional Rights

In this new and more hostile atmosphere after economic liberalisation – that theoretically and politically prioritised selective 'freedom' in and for 'the market' over other forms of freedom or political rights – marginalised communities had to reorganise their struggles. On the political side, deepening democracy and democratic rights became a natural corollary. On the economic side, a demand for universal basic development rights was the new paradigm of a rights-based approach to development. During the transition to a market economy, the state began talking of inclusive development and 'growth with a human face'. The people's movements were making demands to move beyond safety nets to a rights-based approach. The result of those struggles was the slew of rights-based entitlements such as the Right to Information (RTI), MGNREGA, the Forest Rights Act (FRA), the Right to Education Act, the National Food Security Act (NFSA), etc. These legislations were the result of people asserting democratic equality to claim economic and social rights. The marginalised poor were collectively claiming a minimal level of entitlements in a 'free and democratic' society. On the other hand, legislations such as the Special Economic Zones (SEZ) Act were a simultaneous concession to marauding capitalist interests. Uneasy as the tension between the two contradictory forces was, there was an attempt by the first United Progressive Alliance government to recognise and legislate the right of all India's citizens to some basic protection or services.

This new assertion of legal entitlements to access basic rights arose from the continued appalling condition of the people, although many governments came and went at the centre and in the states. The people had waited on the sidelines, hungry and beset by innumerable problems for half a century after independence. The slow and sometimes absent delivery system also brought a focus on issues of democratic governance. There was a widely acknowledged recognition of the failure of delivery by a bureaucratic and political system that had inherited a colonial apparatus of elite control. It was no longer a secret that all the political parties that had ruled India had failed to really reflect the aspirations of the people in planning or implementation, because the citizens had not been empowered, or even allowed to seek their own remedies.

Within this narrative is the marginalised Indian citizenry – weaker and more populous – which has used egalitarian yearnings to come together occasionally and attempt to build a shared vision, bridge the multiple gaps and reduce discriminations. The vast majority of India's population has understood the connection between the vote and governance. But the links between the vote and economic and social rights, which seemed to be getting clearer, have been muddied. Greater economic and social equality as promised in the Directive Principles of State Policy seem to have been pushed aside. With the new economic order, those at the margins are suddenly even more marginalised, and have nowhere to turn to. From being ignored by the race to achieve high growth rates, they have now become its victims. In a theoretical sense, they have every reason to demand the deepening of the manifestations of the fundamental principle of political equality underlying one person, one vote.

The Challenge: To Bring Together Social Justice, Economic Equality and Political Expression

Let us recall what Dr Ambedkar said in his address to the Constituent Assembly on 25 November 1949 at the dawn of the Indian republic, as the Constitution was placed before the people of India:

> On the 26th of January 1950, we are going to enter into a life of contradictions. In politics we will have equality and in social and economic life we will have inequality. In politics we will be recognising the principle of one man one vote and one vote one value. In our social and economic life, we shall by reason of our social and economic structure, continue to deny the principle of one man one value. How long shall we continue to live this life of contradictions? How long shall we continue to deny equality in our social and economic life? If we continue to deny it for

long, we will do so only by putting our political democracy in peril. We must remove this contradiction at the earliest possible moment else those who suffer from inequality will blow up the structure of democracy which this Constituent Assembly has so laboriously built up.[5]

Even as India rejoiced at its freedom, the country saw the violence accompanying Partition and some of the obvious challenges posed by its celebrated plurality. Before India even gave itself a Constitution, Gandhiji was assassinated. The independence movement had created a powerful legacy of civil disobedience, struggle and political protest under very adverse circumstances. After independence, the different shades of the political spectrum were left to battle it out within the framework of a democratic polity. While the electoral and parliamentary structures have received great attention as the 'mainstream' political process, it is actually within the texture of the constitutional framework of rights and decision making that the more fundamental issues are being contested and addressed.

The situation has changed once again after the 2014 elections. The people who are sought to be dismissed as 'fringe elements' in fact reflect some of the priorities of the ruling regime. Today, this fringe can create a larger-than-life message through the virtual domain. Even the democratic legitimacy of numbers can be purchased through the click of a mouse. The propaganda machine is overactive on social media, even proposing the obliteration of Newton and Akbar from textbooks. There is a veiled attack on the scientific temper, while technology for profit is enthusiastically promoted. Books are pulped, people killed, and those presenting dissenting views are blatantly attacked. The right to freedom of expression is threatened, and when fatal attacks are made on people who dissent, like Dabholkar and Pansare, the state is silent. Till a year ago, those who toasted Gandhi's assassin were truly 'fringe elements' restricted to a small section which was largely unseen and unheard. There is an almost absurdly loud proposal that Nathuram Godse's statues should be put up as the 'true nationalist' as against the 'usurper' to such a claim – Gandhiji. Gandhiji's worst critics would have been appalled at even the mention of elevating Godse to a national hero. Both the state and civil society did not allow such statements to occupy public space in the past. While the official representatives of the state are so busy on the 2nd of October (his birth anniversary) reducing the message of Gandhi to a broom, they are just as deafeningly silent on the attack on his life and his essential message. What has enabled this shift and made it so easy?

Unbridled Capitalism
Growth for Some versus Empowerment for All

Ambedkar recognised that the power of money is often, if not always, too strong and overpowers ethical and democratic scruples: 'History shows that where ethics and economics come in conflict, victory is always with economics. Vested interests have never been known to have willingly divested themselves unless there was sufficient force to compel them' (Ambedkar 1945: 197). The theoretical frameworks and principles of both Ambedkar and Gandhi are under attack, as the ground shifts from empowerment to growth at any cost. Constitutional rights are being implicitly and explicitly undermined. The right to decentralised decision making, the protection of natural resources and self-reliance are threatened as never before.

The objective of addressing and removing poverty and economic inequality was written into the constitutional framework, although the obligations of the state were diluted by placing them in the 'advisory' section of the Directive Principles of State Policy. Gandhi's India was an India where hands would not be idle and the capacity for production in already existing skills would be recognised and promoted. There was an emphasis on the economics of self-reliance. While their concerns were never addressed before or after independence, those being uprooted periodically and displaced by 'development' projects have been enabled by the spaces opened up by democratic rights enshrined in the Constitution to at least articulate their deep distress. Coming together in organised campaigns and in people's movements has given them a theoretical framework for their struggles, while using enabling constitutional provisions. Marginalised and oppressed communities found support not only in the Constitution but also in a decision-making framework that at least paid lip service to socialism, secularism, affirmative action, and the goals of a welfare state.

The current attack on Nehruvian India, cloaked in the phraseology of the political discrediting of dynastic rule, blames the structures he introduced. The claim is that his socialist outlook set India back economically and, on the basis of this, the public sector in India is being dismantled, including the winding up of the Planning Commission. But there is an underlying intent that is not articulated. Nehru promoted a secular and scientific India within rational paradigms. He also chose to introduce a socialist model to promote the growth of infrastructure and create a base for industrialisation in India. The current dispensation promotes an ideological position that favours inequality in social structure and in economic access, and is bound to have problems with the words 'socialist' and 'secular'. When scientific principles are replaced by myths, mysteries and prejudices, the rational paradigm is broken. The business management structure comes from a universe that would be happy to see the end of the use of words like 'socialist', but would be embarrassed by the throwback to ignorance, prejudice, unscientific attitudes, and the rubbishing of scientific temper. The discourse promoted in the public domain is therefore shallow and incomplete. The mode for selling toothpaste and 'fair and lovely' creams does not allow space for anything more than a jingle.

Asking questions is fundamental to the scientific temper and to democracy. India understood that development and growth were not possible without reducing inequality and addressing injustice. Even as the big dams and the steel plants were commissioned, the attitude to welfare was still a priority for a new India, and the independent Indian government tried to bridge the two divergent interests through protecting constitutional guarantees. But, whatever the differences, no one could argue against the necessity for the state to assume responsibility for the welfare of its most vulnerable. There were nuanced differences between and among the ruling elite. However, independence was largely seen as not merely freedom from the colonial government but as freedom from want. Development for this country could not be achieved without addressing development on terms of equality and justice.

The Era of Market Globalisation

The direction of aspirations changed in the early 1990s. Neoliberal globalisation of the 'free' global market accompanied by economic liberalisation in India fundamentally altered the discourse of the so-called 'mainstream'. The basic constitutional structure remained, but the lip service paid by decision makers to egalitarian principles of socialism and the welfare state was slowly and deliberately replaced by an enthusiastic endorsement of the driving force of profit and consumerism. Newfound 'freedom' was said to have come in a package – the political freedom of democracy, and the economic freedom of profit and growth. The capitalist victory over the 'socialist world' allowed political freedom to be interwoven with a model of profit-driven economic growth. The inherent contradictions of capitalism and democracy were not only ignored but a model of capitalist democracy was also propagated across the world as inherently complementary rather than contradictory.

The popular apprehensions about the form of governance in socialist countries were related to its totalitarian structure and repression of freedoms. The delivery of promised equality was also compromised because of corruption within an unquestioned structure that was intolerant of dissent, criticism and critique. The capitalist alternative, touted as the opposite of a totalitarian regime, may in fact be just as totalitarian in a very manipulative and insidious way. It uses the invisible power of money to manipulate and impose monopolies, to restrict freedom of speech by buying up and creating media monoliths, and ultimately by financing elections to manipulate policy, legislation and governance. In India, where the chasm between intent and action is colossal, the doublespeak and manipulations are more explicit and apparent.

Constitutional guarantees have become subservient to profit and money. The red herring and the holy cow – a weird hybrid if ever there was one – is the word, 'growth'. This very ambiguous and strange species has become the facade, the cover and the excuse for the undemocratic perversion of policy, legislation and performance.

Growth and Economic Inequality

In fact, the warped priorities reflected in the unequal distribution of the fruits of growth are only too obvious when we look at the analysis of different indices that Amartya Sen and Jean Drèze made in an article published in 2011:

> Indeed, even today, after 20 years of rapid growth, India is still one of the poorest countries in the world. This fact is something that is often lost sight of, especially by those who enjoy world-class living standards thanks to the inequalities in the income distribution. According to World Development Indicators 2011, only 16 countries outside Africa had a lower 'gross national income per capita' than India in 2010: Afghanistan, Bangladesh, Cambodia, Haiti, Iraq, Kyrgyzstan, Laos, Moldova, Nepal, Nicaragua, Pakistan, Papua New Guinea, Tajikistan, Uzbekistan, Vietnam and Yemen.
>
> The progress of living standards for common people, as opposed to a favoured minority, has been dreadfully slow – so slow that India's social indicators are still abysmal. For instance, according to World Bank data, only five countries outside Africa (Afghanistan, Bhutan, Pakistan, Papua New Guinea and Yemen) have a lower 'youth female literacy rate' than India (World Development Indicators 2011). To take some other examples, only five countries (Afghanistan, Cambodia, Haiti, Myanmar and Pakistan) do worse than India in child mortality rate; only three have lower levels of 'access to improved sanitation' (Bolivia, Cambodia and Haiti); and none (nowhere – not even in Africa) have a higher proportion of underweight children. Almost any composite index of these and related indicators of health, education and nutrition would place India very close to the bottom in a ranking of all countries outside Africa.

. . . There is probably no other example in the history of world development of an economy growing so fast for so long with such limited results in terms of broad-based social progress. (Sen and Drèze 2011)

Ideology or Jargon?

Capitalism, like Democracy, is a trendy word, and the idea of it has been linked essentially with a free market and the notion of profit and material well-being. The 'free market' remains a mythical notion as control of the market and its workings are pre-decided and manipulated by the elite working within a hierarchy of affluence and power, which is jealously guarded and preserved at all costs. The starting line allows for no handicaps. In other words, we expect the most endowed and privileged as well as those from the lowest rung of the class and caste hierarchy to have a 'fair competition' so that the best man win! An anti–affirmative action group of elite students at Delhi University calls itself 'Youth for Equality'! As much as we might call this equality and justice, it is obvious to the poor that the system remains loaded against them. Stiglitz, echoing Ambedkar, says of the market:

> [E]conomic inequality puts our democracy in peril by undermining our basic principles of one person, one vote; and . . . our notion of America as a land of opportunity has been undermined and our principle of justice for all has been perverted into justice for those who can afford it. If you go through almost every social and important political economic debate, it's being shaped by the massive inequality we're facing today. . . .
>
> High levels of economic inequality lead to imbalances in political power as those at the top use their economic weight to shape our politics in ways that give them more economic power. If you look at so many of the outcomes in our political process, no one can say that they reflect the interests of most Americans.
>
> . . . What they're doing is moving money from the bottom to the top. But they're not creating wealth; they're just shifting wealth around. And the people who have been exploited are not better off; in fact, they're worse off. (Stiglitz 2012)

Democracy with Equality and Justice
Exploring the Democratic Framework

India established a legal framework of constitutional democracy first, before the new economic paradigm made inroads. Those who are distressed and displaced because of 'development' have asked for, and continue to assert, their democratic rights. These are expressed in multiple ways – through democratic institutions and democratic practice, including expression of dissent and disagreement, and through satyagraha and public protest. The numbers are too large to quell. The state tries to ignore uncomfortable questions, but is occasionally forced to respond and accept. It is unable to act completely contrary to the laws it has framed, and sometimes finds itself bound by legalities and due process. While giving the new economic paradigm full control, people's access to legal recourse became an impediment. As it is not possible to completely deny them legal recourse, the laws were changed so that they would further empower the capitalist class! Ironically, laws had to be made so that the highest priority could be given to foreign direct investment, foreign companies and corporates. Never mind if the 'rule of law' itself would be unconstitutional, affecting the right to equality, access and justice. Unrest and protest had to be stopped and stopped legally – law and justice did not have to be complementary. The attack on rights-based legislations by the present dispensation proves the point. That's not all. Stumped by democratic processes and the persistent assertion by poor communities in India, irate investors see the laws to ensure equality, justice and constitutional guarantees as impediments in themselves. Prabhat Patnaik (2012) comments:

> The starting point of the answer to such questions is the basic social philosophical position which underlies the argument both for the welfare State and for socialism, namely that material deprivation is the result not of some individual failing on the part of the deprived but of the social arrangement within which they live. If there are people in society who are hungry and malnourished, then it is not their fault but that of the social arrangement under which they live; if there are people who are involuntarily unemployed then the reason for that lies in the social arrangement under which they live; if there is concentration of wealth at one pole and of poverty and destitution at another, then this is reflective not of some 'natural order of things' but of the specific social arrangement under which people live. And this social philosophical position is not a matter of faith, but is analytically sustainable.

Propaganda or Informed Choices?

The use of propaganda, including simplistic accusations and carefully created myths, has been part of the modus operandi of today's politico-corporate complex. One such myth currently generated and placed in the public domain is that the country's growth rate has been badly affected by rights-based legislations. There is an opinion that the social policy of the last decade has set India back. The spurious argument is that democratic dissent related to economic reform is disastrous for growth, and therefore anti-national, and that what India needs is a capitalist dictatorship!

In a survey done by Children's Movement for Civic Awareness, an NGO based in Bengaluru – covering 'about 10,000 high-school and college students from 11 cities across the country' – 50 per cent of the respondents reportedly 'preferred military rule to democracy' (Arora 2015). Though the survey, as highlighted by NDTV, was very slim in its coverage, the notion of a 'strong' leadership, and of anointing one person to sort everything out, undermines democracy itself. Talking of dictatorship portends ill for this country's youth and for the millions who do not live in consuming-and-purchasing affluent India. Most of the poor and marginalised in India also fall out of the net and ambit of cameras, surveys and opinion polls. For most of them, democracy is a means to express their distress. Sometimes it is a means to support someone who promises to secure for them a small share of independent India's affluence and comfort.

The politicians pretend to listen to them when cornered; the civil servants look at them as trouble – as 'mobs'. A current new coinage is 'professional protesters' who come to unsettle them and their 'weightier' issues. When they assemble in strength and protest, the state comes down heavily on them. The conflict that has arisen is at a much more fundamental level – between a burgeoning understanding of democracy and its use by poor people, and the onslaught on them by the moving forces of capitalism, namely investment, money, profit, and consumerism.

Democratic Rights and People's Movements

India has a rich and creative tradition of people's movements. This is a legacy from the independence movement. Leaders across the spectrum – Gandhi, Ambedkar, Bhagat Singh, the communists – knew that mass mobilisation and people's participation in political processes were the strongest vehicles of real change. Mahatma Gandhi refused to take office and continued to fight against injustice even after independence. Even single-issue struggles against injustice in any sphere in India have broader implications and impact the larger political edifice. There are millions of protests, and when they develop into movements and campaigns, they create a new kind of engagement and space, forcing the system to work democratically. Sometimes even the seemingly impossible has been achieved through determined pursuit, by using non-violent means to put pressure on the system. Whether it is the unequal battle against a nuclear power plant in Kudankulam,[6] or the sustained struggle against a big dam by the Narmada Bachao Andolan (NBA), or the struggle against POSCO in Odisha, people have had to take on the might of the state and corporate power through creative modes of resistance and democratic protest. Many of these are inspired by the Indian independence movement, particularly by Gandhi and his mode of satyagraha and civil disobedience.

As we all take the essence of the mode from Gandhi, we also lay claim to his legacy. People's movements have also had to aspire to build the combination of moral strength, humility, honesty, and political shrewdness that made the Indian independence movement a unique struggle against colonial power. The tradition of revolutionary non-violent protest continued with Jayaprakash Narayan and his call for total revolution. What we need to remember is that this breadth and depth of vision and action will only be born out of the struggles of the people on the margins – the disenfranchised and the oppressed, who have been fighting collective battles with a strong commitment to principles and values. Real change takes place when democratic space is given to those struggles to assert the voice of the marginalised, till a point of true inclusiveness is reached.

Ambedkar had personal experience of discrimination, and in his search for justice had gained first-hand experience of the importance of collective action and struggle. He knew that for the socially and economically marginalised communities in India, the fight for justice was much more imbalanced. He therefore sought to provide a strong legal framework for equality so that the law would support those fighting for equality and justice. Having made space for the aspirations of the marginalised within the Constitution, he was determined to ensure that the legal system not only created rights, but also supported the oppressed as they fought to realise their rights. He was keen that their struggles take place within the constitutional framework.

This legal and constitutional assertion of democratic equality, coming as it does from the poorest and the lowest in the social and caste hierarchies, has been unacceptable to the power elite. The truth is that the poor are not only the greatest defenders of democracy – since it gives them space, voice and equality – they are also its most creative theoreticians and practitioners. This combined legacy of Gandhi and Ambedkar, of satyagraha and constitutionally protected struggle, has resulted in a tradition of creative and successful people's movements in India. It is the questions of the poor that initiated and strengthened the journey for the people's right to information, and subsequently led to a vigorous demand for transparency and accountability. The issues raised by poor and marginalised communities – either proactively, as in the case of the right to information, or in defence, as in the case of displacement – have found their way into the theoretical and legal framework. Those fighting with their backs to the wall are persistent and tenacious in their struggles. They were, in many cases, initially ignored by the state, the media and policy makers. They have, however, used the lexicon of democracy and democratic rights to build a number of other important basic rights. Despite the many crises, the volume of protest has increased, and so has the capacity to shape the discourse in the modern democratic idiom.

People have developed the capacity to ask for political accountability, exposing hollow arguments as well as election rhetoric and promises. Unable to answer them logically and equally unwilling to enter into a real dialogue, the state is resorting to violence and has begun its attempts to change the legal framework. It also views dissent as anti-development and equates it with anti-nationalism. Unfortunately for the modern corporate state, people have learned to keep a watch on the legal framework, defend the Constitution, and fight exploitative law making.

Capitalism and the Rights-Based Framework

An electoral mainstream dominated by the need and desire for money is predictably open to and supportive of the capital- and profit-driven model of growth. Control over natural resources, as well as the right to commercialise and appropriate knowledge systems for profit, become the potential flashpoints in obvious ways. People's movements, using the Directive Principles and the guarantee of fundamental rights as sacrosanct, have fought to protect the Constitution and democracy. In areas such as the Narmada valley or Niyamgiri hills,[7] the issue of control over land, water and natural resources made the battle stark and adversarial. The NBA's slogan 'Vikaas chaahiye, vinaash nahin' (Development wanted, not destruction) conveys the clash of worldviews as the development of one community comes at the cost of another. With forced displacement, the 'project-affected people' (mostly tribal communities) have the struggle for survival thrust upon them. As they fought for the right to protest and express dissent, they had to turn to the Constitution that guaranteed them political equality. This was part of the battle for control over state power and decision making.

Ultimately, independent decision making and the use and accountability of democratic institutions are important factors in guaranteeing equality. The ruling elites claim that this struggle for equality has destabilised the growth agenda. Hasty investment and growth come into direct conflict with the demand for political equality promised to all citizens, poor or rich. Amending the land acquisition and rehabilitation laws through ordinance is an example of how the ruling class reacts to people's democratic pressure. In one stroke, it denies rights to the common people while exploiting the available legislative space by bringing in an ordinance. The vote will have to remain as it is; no category can be denied equal franchise. The easiest to attack are the enabling legislations, which for the first time in independent India have made an attempt to create a level playing field. The rights-based legislations have been the target.

Political Engagement and Deliberative Democracy
Political Formations for Realising People's Rights

A new assertion of entitlement to basic rights arose from amongst the people who had lived on the sidelines under appalling conditions, beset by innumerable problems for over half a century after independence. The slow and sometimes absent delivery system pointed to a poor system of democratic accountability and governance. As top-down development and governance structures failed, it became clear that citizens had not been empowered to seek their own remedies either.

People's movements had begun to respond to these challenges and forge their own paradigms of equality to gain some control over their collective future. However, the overwhelming concentration on growth rates meant that those who demanded capital investment and growth would be favoured regardless of its costs to other segments of society. Such was the greed of this segment of society that all rights-based entitlements such as RTI, MGNREGA, FRA, etc. were opposed and sought to be diluted. Even during the period when these basic legislations were passed, concessions were made to the corporate sector through legislations like the SEZ Act.

The RTI Act, MGNREGA, FRA, and NFSA went through long debates and consultative processes inside and outside Parliament. The movements for these laws exemplified the assertion of democratic rights by disadvantaged citizens, who claimed the economic and social rights that are theirs in a 'free and equal' society. The SEZ Act, on the other hand, was passed without deliberation and discussion. Today, attempts are being made to amend the Land Acquisition Act, but citizens' groups have been watching these processes and happenings like a hawk.

Grassroots Realities and Terra Firma

It would perhaps be relevant to explore the contours of the journey of the MKSS over the last 25 years. When the MKSS was formed in 1990, everything about it was seemingly out of fashion; its name denoted an organisation of labour and peasants, and its motto was *Nyaaya samaanta ho aadhaar, aisaa rachenge hum sansaar* (We will make a world with justice and equality as its foundations). An organisation like the MKSS could not and cannot afford to be merely rhetorical. It has to connect with the practical everyday needs of its primary constituents. The beginnings of an alternative future arise out of the hundreds of practical questions and solutions, as well as the struggles for equality and justice. The wisdom of the Constitution and its vision of equality, the legacy of satyagraha and civil disobedience left by Gandhi, and the Marxian lens of class struggle— all enabled the poor to begin using their strengths. While the conditions of the poor make most of them natural Marxists, they are Ambedkarites and satyagrahis in their mode of protest. These factors have shaped the history and contributed to the strength of people's movements. It has been a search for democratic space and broad alliances.

Popular Resistance

The model of neoliberal growth (officially defined as 'development') is now being relentlessly pursued by the Indian government, and resolutely resisted by many local communities. These dogged protesters and their supporters are labelled as troublemakers, professional protesters, anti-growth and anti-development blackmailers, and are finally declared anti-national. Any attempt to show resistance to a project is painted as contrary to the nation's interest. Some of these flashpoints convey the nature of the ongoing battle in India. They are illustrations of people using democratic spaces to resist a model of economic growth that benefits the capitalist class at great cost to the rest of the population, and at a near fatal cost to local communities.

As practitioners, people are often advised to remain within the confines of public action, and leave the analysis of the situation to the 'thinkers and researchers'. Divorcing action from reflection would be a grave error. We will not go into the endless debate about whether thought precedes action or whether action prepares the ground for thought. I would go along with Yeats (1935), who said:

> God guard me from those thoughts men think
> In the mind alone;
> He that sings a lasting song
> Thinks in a marrow-bone; . . .

Who Gains and How Much

The neoliberal bait of a better life first bought over the rising middle class with its desire for new brands of luxury goods and the consumerist lifestyle of the Western world. Rapture over rare 'foreign goods' was replaced by conspicuous consumption of goods and services. Management positions, salaries at international rates, and the economic advantages of outsourcing for the private sector ushered in a new, richer and assertive middle class. This is the group that felt and said that India was 'shining'. The general election in 2005 made it clear that the majority of people had not benefited from this boom, and they were now using democracy (the vote) to demand basic development rights.

One section of society continues to describe the slew of rights-based legislations as no more than social safety nets. What is more important is the political implication of asserting basic development and economic rights for all citizens. As questions of accountability and implementation are raised alongside the battle for a share of national resources, the ideological framework of democratic equality is seen on a bigger canvas.

But, even the middle class has faced several rounds of market-induced vulnerability. It is beginning to see how the windfall gains are being cornered by big corporations – whether in the awarding of captive coal blocks or in the selling of airwaves. Like in the West, failed corporations are bailed out and their top executives' salaries are protected. The middle-class farmer in India has already understood the stranglehold of a credit-oriented capitalist agriculture, and has found no escape except in suicide. As waves of recession hit economies in different parts of the world and result in layoffs in faraway places, there is a fear that educated youth with huge debts and no jobs may go the way of the farmers. The state steps in to extend a \$1 billion loan for the Adani group's coal project in Australia through the nationalised State Bank of India, but subsidies are cut even when they are meant for the rural economy and the poor.

The gap between the rich and the poor is increasing. Unemployment, minimum wages and labour rights are seen as disruptive non-issues. Since the 'Occupy Movement' and other protests,[8] there has been a growing understanding that the political dispensation all over the world is controlled by corporations, billionaires and international banking institutions. There is resistance even in the US and Europe. The aspiring class in other market-oriented economies has had to take notice. In these difficult times of resistance, protest and revolt, the state expectedly increases its expenditure on security and surveillance, while development measures and basic needs get smaller allocations and less attention.

The Movements: People as Makers of Policy and Law
The RTI as a Transformative Right

The RTI Act was to bring transparency and help make the state accountable to the Indian citizen. In addition, the RTI further strengthened constitutional equality, according citizens equal access to matters and processes of governance.

When the RTI is seen through this wider prism, it becomes an effective tool to fight corruption and the arbitrary exercise of power. Corruption is not just an illegal transaction of money, but also a manifestation of injustice in different forms. That is why it is not enough to have a broad coalition against corruption without linking it with injustice. Similarly, it is not enough to have a movement against corruption without a commitment to democratic principles.

The bureaucratic tradition and structure in India make the bureaucrat vulnerable to arrogance and self-interest. It draws grandeur from the 'glory' of a colonial legacy that created a force of civil servants that would wield power over the people while strictly following orders from the top. The bureaucracy is getting confused, squirming under the questionable leadership and arbitrariness of an increasingly delegitimised political class. Moreover, the evolving democratic demands for scrutiny are making the bureaucracy accountable to people they do not necessarily see as their equals. Their exclusivity – a distancing from the very people they take an oath to serve – needs no elaboration. Their confusion often leads to greater arbitrariness and aggression with those they perceive as 'weak', and to abject subservience to their political bosses. The mere 'adjustments' with a new democratic order have not really worked, and we continue to pay the price for not creating a bureaucratic architecture that would be committed to the principles of democracy and participation.

The political class must be held responsible for this failure. Leaders who had spent decades or a lifetime by the side of the people, away from the trappings of power and position, quickly and easily slid into the comfort zone of established power. The steady dilution of ethical principles was inevitable as they lost personal touch with the needs of ordinary people. The Constitution, made during the transition into an independent nation, therefore remains our strongest legacy of the hopes of building a democratic country, which will recognise the aspirations of equality, justice and freedom of expression for those at the margins.

The political class of independent India has never been more lacking in principles and ethics. It searches for immediate justifications and exemplifies a politics of convenience. Ideological alternatives are to be expected and can be debated. But the dismissal of all ideological moorings is, in effect, trivialising the citizen and the voter by denying prior information to make informed choices. A disclosure of the basic promises of governance should be the basis for seeking votes in any rational democracy. The 'post-ideology' rhetoric is an excellent cover for political opportunism. While some politicians are indeed opportunists, it is also an excellent red herring to divert attention from more sinister designs.

In the deliberately created mess of incompatible ideologies, political opportunism has won with the support of capitalist investment. The capitalist, in the neoliberal age of market fundamentalism, has managed to take full advantage of these weaknesses and has bought almost everyone in power, including those who shape the discourse. For the investors, every action is measured and evaluated by profit, and not by the parameters of the Constitution. The leaders are projected on a giant screen and endowed with all the attributes of indomitability. Dressed regally with the aura of celluloid heroes, they have captured the imagination of befuddled voters. Tired of the chaos the leaders themselves add to by deepening class, caste, gender, and religious fault lines, citizens are surrendering to the magic of authority and the promise of better days. Fatigue with incessant bickering and mismanagement has brought in the cult of a 'strong' leader, along with cold, rational strategies of capital and profit. The mainstream did not use their reason to ask what the 'good days' would get translated into. Only this time, the emperor's new clothes had a bill that could have fed many thousand hungry citizens. And this time, at least after the elections, the questions are getting asked!

Two Indias

Social activists and people's protests are considered irritants, serving as reminders of how the 'anarchy and disorder' of a democracy are used to 'unreasonably' claim social and economic rights. The administration's horror at being questioned is the final straw. Those who protest against the 'assault' by capital (resources) as part of the new economic order are deemed anti-development activists.

People are no longer satisfied with what the vote gives them. They are using powerful democratic means such as the RTI and public hearings to discuss governance. By asserting development rights through new laws – that were fought for and drafted bottom-up – people are demanding their share of democratic decision making and governance.

Those of us who work with the poor in rural India are worried by the lack of real understanding of these powerful democratic processes, and the deliberate myopia of the ruling elite. The consequent anti-democratic, elitist legitimisation of sanctioned plunder of natural resources, as well as the profit-driven business encouraged by leaders across parties, has reduced the space for dissent. The loss of lives, livelihood and natural resources is casually written off as 'collateral damage'. While we talk of sustainable growth, over-exploitation of natural and human resources by capitalists cannot get us anywhere close to our goal. It also fuels aspirations to maintain this level of consumption and exploitation. The disastrous effect on the environment, so obvious to everyone, is not even being addressed any more. A new justification by our rulers is 'that the poor of India and China have the right to "develop"'! Never mind that the ones protesting against this model of 'development' are the tribals and impoverished citizens of India. Quite apart from robbing these huge communities of their habitats, we are following a trajectory that will lead the earth to self-destruct.

Parameters for Policy

In India, competing interests and ideologies and contradictory visions of future are getting played out in the political domain. Any attempt to bring to the forefront the constitutional provisions addressing the concerns of those at the economic and social margins is now countered by marginalising the Constitution itself. The Constitution was shaped to steadily and incrementally balance the inequality embedded in social and economic structures. The Directive Principles of State Policy read like a manifesto for a better India; they address the inequalities in the poorer India consisting of more than half of the population. Articles 36–51 of the Constitution read in essence like an agenda for action. They call for the state to secure a social order for promoting people's welfare, elucidating principles of policy to be followed by the state: Article 38 (State to secure a social order for the promotion of welfare of the people) says:

(1) The State shall strive to promote the welfare of the people by securing and protecting as effectively as it may a social order in which justice, social, economic and political, shall inform all the institutions of the national life.

(2) The State shall, in particular, strive to minimise the inequalities in income, and endeavour to eliminate inequalities in status, facilities and opportunities, not only amongst individuals but also amongst groups of people residing in different areas or engaged in different vocations.

All this is, however, resisted strongly by the rulers of the day. The manner in which basic principles of the Constitution are being set aside shows how unconstitutional the current 'growth-based' development model actually is. In the year of Ambedkar's 125th birth anniversary, market forces will ensure that his birthday will be celebrated and his image sold, diluting his ideas with vacuous words and tinsel decorations.

The Expectations of Independent India

Independent India defined for itself a democratic structure ensuring economic and social freedoms. It provided reservations for people oppressed by a discriminatory caste system worse than apartheid, with social handicaps for centuries. The middle class and elite castes have resented reservation for Dalits. Today, every middle- and upper-caste group clamours for reservation of its own social constituency! Unable to upset the status quo, this new demand for reservation is aggressive, backed by privilege, and is apparently a claim for justice. It is a political tool that tries to use the symbol of 'equality' to further entrench and protect inequity. Sadly, it only manages to parody the seriousness of the original, mocking the genuine need for reservation. It turns upside down the need to protect traditionally deprived communities.

Ambedkar's predicted contradiction now re-emerges from an economic 'model' superimposed and forced on a people who have begun to ask intelligent democratic questions relating to governance, fiscal viability, regulatory mandates, fulfilling the democratic dream of a people aware of their rights. They are the real keepers of Indian democracy and yet are targets of the system, which declares that they are indulging in acts of sedition.

In other cases, they become the targets of a system that professes to address their concerns. They have fought the myths that seek to keep them where they are and the traditions that pin them down. The great political analyst Eduardo Galeano (1989) writes:

> Fleas dream of buying themselves a dog, and nobodies dream of escaping poverty: that one magical day good luck will suddenly rain down on them – will rain down in buckets. But good luck doesn't rain down yesterday, today, tomorrow, or ever. Good luck doesn't even fall in a fine drizzle, no matter how hard the nobodies summon it, even if their left hand is tickling, or if they begin the new day with their right foot, or start the new year with a change of brooms.
>
> The nobodies: nobody's children, owners of nothing. The nobodies: the no ones, the nobodied, running like rabbits, dying through life, screwed every which way.
>
> Who are not, but could be.
> Who don't speak languages, but dialects.
> Who don't have religions, but superstitions.
> Who don't create art, but handicrafts.
> Who don't have culture, but folklore.
> Who are not human beings, but human resources.
> Who do not have faces, but arms.
> Who do not have names, but numbers.
> Who do not appear in the history of the world, but in the police blotter of the local paper.
> The nobodies, who are not worth the bullet that kills them.

When they emerge from this 'destiny' of subjugation, they face a new set of superstitions. The future is glossy with an array of consumer goods that will turn their attention away from injustice and hunger! What continues is the modern mirage of *achhe din* (good days).

Who Decides: People as Policy Makers

In India, the people who have gained equality through the vote but largely remain disenfranchised economically and socially, constitute a numerical majority. The current economic model that is being imposed essentially dispossesses people of land and livelihood or, as in Kudankulam, threatens to bring in technology the after-effects of which are irreversible. This debate goes into very many issues, fundamental to which is the basic question of democratic governance: Who decides? Can we decide on behalf of the people whose safety may be threatened, and pronounce their fears invalid and, more heinously, illegitimate, without even attempting to enter into a dialogue? Who decides costs, and on what parameters? Is 'cost' calculated only financially or is it measured by factoring in the possible irreversible genetic damage and dysfunction of a million people? Can future costs of decommissioning a plant be transferred to a later generation? Why are local populations so concerned about the future (when they will not be around) and why are policy makers so quick to underestimate future costs? Is the common sense of people senseless rabble rousing when countered by experts with many years of academic and technical study behind them?

Sceptical citizens in India have begun to believe that many claims made by the so-called experts and policy makers are just dangerous doublespeak. There is an ostensible argument about economic growth, trickle-down theories and shared revenues, but there is a growing understanding that the push and the shove come from profit and greed. This suspicion has now been confirmed by the various scams that have unfolded in India. The stated objectives of development and growth are often a smokescreen for siphoning off huge amounts of money.

One of the central principles of a democracy is sharing 'governance' (the exercise of power) with the people. A population that elects a government has a right to be consulted and involved in every stage of planning, implementation and monitoring. Although this was not denied, it was never really a part of the grand design either before or even immediately after independence. This bankruptcy of understanding has just become much starker, etching a scenario bleaker than ever before. The dissonance between the sovereign people and the ruling elite is now substantially worse because of a serious threat from the capital which has entered through the front door of a free market economy, and is welcomed as a powerful, influential player.

Information, Knowledge, Dialogue

What we then bring to you is the logic, the understanding and the theory that come out of being in, and being a part of, public action. It is a process that forces people to examine the status quo, to go beyond what is apparent to be able to see the links among what appear to be unconnected issues, to evolve a discourse to help the struggle for better life with equality and justice.

The broader contribution of the RTI campaign to the common person's understanding of democracy was its unpacking of the basic constitutional right of sovereignty. This movement demonstrates that we can claim a share in governance and decision making in a more comprehensive way and not only in issues of immediate concern. Spontaneous uprisings and protests make a mark, but reasoned understanding comes with the ownership of an idea that can come only through sustained struggle, rooted in shared principles and ideology. Campaigns shaped on those premises and following participatory processes survive to change systems. This is a collective exploration of an understanding that has emerged from various struggles.

Perhaps we should see this as the beginning of a conversation. Despite the nature of the mode of discourse – a speaker facing an audience – we will not assume a continuing divide between the speaker and the listeners. It is in the nature of such issues and concerns that conversations must (and do) continue in different ways over a period of time. Let us therefore see this as the beginning of a longer set of dialogues and discussions. There will be no definite charting of a 'road map', a topical term indicative of a definitive end of a journey, this evening. We should rather think that *manzil door hai* (the destination is far), and prepare for a long journey to fashion a world of equality and reason, where the assertion of the larger good defined by people will shape political structures and economic policies. We also have to understand the nature of the parallel and contradictory forces at work. I belong to a community of actors whose articulation is almost as marginalised as its existence. Yet, this marginalisation should not be allowed to obliterate the power of concepts and ideas born through its democratic struggles. The stories of courage and persistence tell us a great deal more about the potential of essential democratic processes which have established even the preliminary right to protest. Some of the poorest people, deprived of all material advantages, unarmed and largely unsupported, have managed to stave off the ire of the state with peaceful resistance.

The fact is that the ideas they have inherently understood, shaped and sustained have to be acknowledged and sometimes followed by a completely antithetical ruling elite. These concepts undermine illegitimate concentrations of power. The fact that in these neoliberal times we have laws that enshrine the right to information and the economic rights of poor and marginalised people is a tribute to their struggles, to democracy, and to the power of their ideas. This evening can at best end with a set of agreements on convictions, borne out by the logic of common-sense arguments and the veracity of facts tabled. We may perhaps begin shifting both perception and action.

Despite the indifference of the electronic media controlled by corporate interests, a corrupt administrative system, and the systematic betrayal by the elected political class, people have managed to keep the battle alive. In some cases, they have even prevailed enough to claim partial victory. Maybe capital shifts only to find another spot, but what we see repeatedly every day is the sharp political wisdom of the poor. Though some of them are illiterate, they understand the authority that the democratic system and the vote have given them. Political educational levels of the people in rural India should be seen through their sustained engagement with power. It makes them the real protectors of democracy. The deviants are those who talk of democracy but plan methods of siphoning off profits at the cost of people's lives and livelihood.

People have to use their knowledge and their voice. Jeremy Cronin, writer and political activist in South Africa, said of citizenship in a democracy that it is 'not so much to speak truth to power as to make truth powerful and, the hardest of all, power truthful' (Cronin 2008: 526).

Shaping Democracy

The RTI movement in India has been powerful because it has asserted and begun to define democratic participation and accountability to the citizen. The movement that was initially shaped and sustained by poor people gave birth to simple questions that inextricably linked corruption with injustice. As mentioned earlier, the MKSS was born in 1990 with the motto of remaking the world with justice and equality as its foundations. It was natural, therefore, that in the struggle for the right to information, the questions that were framed and the issues that were taken up related to the same dream of justice and equality that the MKSS began with.

It is also this democratic understanding and assertion that allowed the RTI to move into more incisive areas of accountability and participation such as the right to public audit. The RTI movement has deepened and widened like a river that sustains a civilisation. The various campaigners and associated campaigns have begun to assert the right to frame legislation through a transparent pre-legislative process. The right to demand democratic accountability becomes far more comprehensible after the engagement begins through the right to information. Processes of public audit begin from stages of planning, implementation and participation in the framing of legislation. Underlying all these simultaneous and growing demands are two simple but powerful democratic rights and one duty – the right to know and the right to decide; and democratic accountability to the people on the part of all those in positions of power.

At the heart of the democratic exercise are the principles of justice and equality, walking side by side, like the justice and freedom Eduardo Galeano (2001) speaks of so eloquently:

> The capitalist system, the so-called 'market economy', has sacrificed justice in the name of freedom, and the so-called 'real socialism' has sacrificed freedom in the name of justice. Beginning the new millennium, this is the challenge: we want justice and freedom, Siamese twins, living and walking together.

On the 125th birth anniversary of Ambedkar, we need to draw inspiration from his faith in principles in these difficult times. He has been, is and will continue to be a touchstone for those of us who cherish equality and justice as twin values in all matters of socio-economic and political life. In 1942, he gave the following advice to his followers:

> My final words of advice to you are educate, agitate and organise; have faith in yourself. With justice on our side I do not see how we can lose our battle. The battle to me is a matter of joy. The battle is in the fullest sense spiritual. There is nothing material or social in it. For ours is a battle not for wealth or for power. It is battle for freedom. It is the battle of reclamation of human personality. (Quoted in Keer 1971: 351)

Seventh Ambedkar Memorial Lecture, 14 April 2014, Ambedkar University Delhi.

Notes

[1] The Gini index measures the extent to which the distribution of income or consumption expenditure among individuals or households within an economy deviates from a perfectly equal distribution. A Lorenz curve plots the cumulative percentages of total income received against the cumulative number of recipients, starting with the poorest individual or household. The Gini index measures the area between the Lorenz curve and a hypothetical line of absolute equality, expressed as a percentage of the maximum area under the line. Thus a Gini index of 0 represents perfect equality, while an index of 100 implies perfect inequality.

[2] The incident refers to the alleged decision of the State Bank of India to extend a $1 billion loan to the Gautam Adani group in 2015 for funding the group's $7

billion coal project in Australia. The issue became hugely controversial in India. The bank reportedly did not extend the loan, eventually.

[3] Priya Pillai, an environmental activist with Greenpeace India, was offloaded from a Delhi–London flight in January 2015 to prevent her from testifying before a British parliamentary committee on the activity of a firm registered in the UK but having business interests in Madhya Pradesh. While the central government justified the decision on grounds of national interest, the Delhi High Court eventually expunged the ban on Pillai's travel.

[4] Binayak Sen is an Indian paediatrician and public health specialist who extended healthcare to poor people in the rural-tribal areas of Chhattisgarh state. He was also a human rights activist. He was arrested in 2007 and was tried in the Raipur Sessions Court under the Chhattisgarh Special Security Act, 2005, and the Unlawful Activities (Prevention) Act, 1967. In 2010, the sessions court sentenced him to life imprisonment under charges of sedition. He appealed for bail before the Chhattisgarh High Court. Since the bail was denied to him, he appealed to the Supreme Court, which granted him bail on 15 April 2011. The whole issue precipitated a stormy debate on issues of citizenship, dissent and sedition in India.

[5] See Constituent Assembly Debates (Proceedings), vol. XI, 25 November 1949, http://164.100.47.132/LssNew/constituent/vol11p11.html (accessed on 26 May 2018).

[6] Kudankulam is the nuclear power station in the Tirunelveli district of Tamil Nadu. The power plant, which was started in 2002, met with strong opposition from the local population. The state employed strong-arm tactics to subdue this movement continuously and a large number of activists came to be arrested and were put behind bars. The plant started producing power from 2013 onwards.

[7] In the Niyamgiri hills in Odisha, the permission given to the mining firm Vedanta Resources was scrapped in 2013 due to widespread local protests and the unanimous decision made by local tribal communities in their respective village council meetings. The decision of the tribal village council was sought on the direction of the Supreme Court.

[8] The Occupy Movement was a widespread mass movement against social and economic inequality and lack of democracy. Beginning in 2010, it spread to several cities across the world, particularly in the US. One of its most important slogans was: 'We are the 99%.' Social media and web technologies were widely employed in this movement. By 2012, the movement had begun to dissipate.

References

Ambedkar, B. R. 1945. *What Congress and Gandhi Have Done to the Untouchables.* Bombay: Thacker & Co.

Arora, Nikita Niraj. 2015. 'Young India Says "Yes" to Military Rule, "No" to Inter-religious Mingling: Survey', NDTV, 23 January, https://www.ndtv.com/india-news/young-india-says-yes-to-military-rule-no-to-inter-religious-mingling-survey-731336 (accessed on 1 June 2018).

Cronin, Jeremy. 2008. 'An Interview with Jeremy Cronin' by Andrew van der Vlies, *Contemporary Literature*, 49(4): 514–40.

Galeano, Eduardo. 1989. 'The Nobodies', in *The Book of Embraces*, trans. Cedric Belfrage, https://holywaters.wordpress.com/2011/12/08/los-nadiesthe-nobodies-by-eduardo-galeano/ (accessed on 2 June 2018).

————. 2001. 'Eduardo Galeano', interview by Jaime Manrique, *Bomb*, 75, https://bombmagazine.org/articles/eduardo-galeano/ (accessed on 2 June 2018).

Keer, Dhananjay. 1971. *Dr Ambedkar: Life and Mission*. Mumbai: Popular Prakashan.

Patnaik, Prabhat. 2012. 'For a Universal Old-Age Pension Scheme', *People's Democracy*, 36(19), http://archives.peoplesdemocracy.in/2012/0513_pd/05132012_8.html (accessed on 1 June 2018).

Sen, Amartya, and Jean Drèze. 2011. 'Putting Growth in Its Place', *Outlook*, 14 November, https://www.outlookindia.com/magazine/story/putting-growth-in-its-place/278843 (accessed on 31 May 2018).

Stiglitz, Joseph E. 2012. 'The Price of Inequality: Interview with Joseph E. Stiglitz' by Jared Bernstein, *Rolling Stone*, 25 June, https://www.rollingstone.com/politics/news/the-price-of-inequality-interview-with-joseph-e-stiglitz-20120625 (accessed on 31 May 2018).

Yeats, W. B. 1935. 'A Prayer for Old Age', https://rpo.library.utoronto.ca/poems/prayer-old-age (accessed on 2 June 2018).

8

Rethinking the Concept of Civilisation as History

Romila Thapar

The concept of civilisation has underlined our understanding of world history over the last couple of centuries but is now becoming rather paradoxical. The idea of a civilisation is a construction that emerges at a particular point in history. It is one way of comprehending the past. The question is whether it can continue to be used despite the substantial changes in how we perceive the histories of what have been called 'civilisations'.

The term implies a kind of package with specific characteristics. Initially, religion and language were the most visible of these, but more recently the concept has been expanded to include others. The territory of a civilisation has to be demarcated; it is identified with a period of high intellectual and aesthetic achievement – what, in short, is sometimes called 'high culture'. It is articulated in a single representative language; it is symbolised in a single religion; it assumes a complex society and elaborate governance; its elite is distinctive and dominates its surroundings; and, above all, a civilisation records its knowledge of the world and attempts to advance it.

Civilisations identify places and cultures. But identities change in the course of history, especially of those creating the concept of civilisation, as indeed of those who are the subject of this construction. Concepts help us understand social reality, but they in turn have to be investigated, particularly where they claim to be foundational to understanding history. These are some of my concerns in this lecture.

The somewhat spare definition that I have just given needs enlargement. The territory is expansive, resulting from the ultimate success of one state from among a number of competing others. The dominant culture forms the focus around which the erstwhile lesser units now coalesce. It monopolises that which is defined by civilisation, to the near exclusion in historical terms of the lesser cultures. The lesser cultures in such descriptions tend to get hidden or fade out.

Change is endemic in all societies. This happens either from within the society or from contact with other societies in various ways. This disturbs the social equilibrium and can result in either increasing or decreasing the degree of integration of the earlier smaller units. Can a civilisation therefore be static or is it required to change?

Let me turn to how and when the concept of civilisation first came to be constructed. It was used in France and England in the 18th century. Derived from the verb 'to civilise', it postulated a prior condition of not being civilised. The Enlightenment understanding of history, together with social Darwinism in the subsequent century, gave human society the status of an advanced evolutionary stage, and incorporated the definition. The Enlightenment underlined humanistic values embedded in the literature of a civilisation, and also the belief that rational beings could control the world around them. The pattern of control was of interest.

Another view has argued that apart from 'high culture', civilisation placed a premium on sophisticated behaviour associated with the elite. In medieval feudal times people had to be socialised into behaving in a civilised manner. Much emphasis was placed on social manners derived from the mores of the elite. The civilising process could come from the state claiming a monopoly of power, or from norms created by influential members of society. It assumes the idea of mutation in human behaviour.

German writers differentiated between civilisation and Kultur/culture. Culture referred to what was thought of as intellectual and artistic in terms of values and ideals, as well as to morality. These were specific to nations. But cultures were not compact, enclosed and static. Civilisation, however, had a broader spread and, as the definition suggests, included more than what constituted culture. Was this a middle-class culture searching for self-expression?

Civilisation assumed that the historically preceding societies were uncivilised, and they were labelled as barbarians. It became a recognised dichotomy. The question was how ancient societies constructed the two. The answer was simple. Those that were 'the Others' were assumed to be not civilised. For the Greeks it was the non-Greeks, for the Chinese the non-Han, and for the Aryas of India it was the Mleccha. If the Greeks called them barbarians, Sanskrit speakers referred to them as *barbara-karoti* (speaking in a confused way). The barbarians were those who spoke a language different from that of the civilised. Some lived among the civilised; others lived in isolation.

The concept of civilisation assumed the existence of the barbarian as a counterpoint to the civilised. In the 19th century, the dichotomy between the two was further elaborated. It was said that human society went through three stages of change. Starting with savagery, it improved somewhat when it reached barbarism, and this was prior to civilisation. The change to the third stage could come through either a kind of osmosis or even evolution. This was the imprint of social Darwinism. But it was used less frequently to suggest social evolution and more often to point out the distinction between the stages.

The other more effective route was seen in the imposition of the civilised on the barbarian through conquest, an obvious attempt to justify colonialism. A classic example was the argument that the Aztecs as the less civilised performed human sacrifice that the civilised Spanish conquest and the Catholic Church had to bring to an end.

Civilisation was the marker that separated the isolated societies from those that claimed to have achieved a high state of progress of every kind – social, cultural, political, economic, and technological – combined with laws that ensured morality and human values. Taken a step further was its association with a sophisticated urban culture and the existence of the state as a source of governance.

The concept was now used in two ways. One was its role in colonial thinking and the other was the detailed social evolution that entered studies in anthropology, archaeology and history.

Colonialism was clear about the distinction between the civilised and the alternate – the primitive. The coloniser was the representative of civilisation and brought it to the colonised, the uncivilised primitive. In India there were, however, two views on this as expounded by British colonial writers – the utilitarian and the orientalist. One was the view of James Mill and other utilitarian thinkers writing on the Indian past. They saw the territory of India as hosting two nations – the Hindu and the Muslim – both heavily hostile to each other. The system of governance was what was called 'oriental despotism', and this was not characteristic of civilisation. The colonised were viewed as requiring substantial correction in order to be fully civilised.

The other view came to be known as orientalist. Sir William Jones on arriving in India in the late 18th century enquired of the learned brahmanas as to the texts he should study to understand ancient India. He was directed to the *Vedas* and to classical Sanskrit literature. His take on this was to undertake comparative studies of language and religion in an effort to suggest parallels with ancient European civilisation. He set out his views on the closeness of Sanskrit, Greek and Persian.

The orientalists disagreed with the utilitarians and argued that

India did have a civilisation and that this had to be researched. Sanskritists in Europe continued these studies. Influential among them was Max Mueller who focused on the Vedic texts that he regarded as the foundation of Indian/Hindu civilisation. Seeing the area as a single unitary civilisation, specifically defined, made it easier for the colonisers to understand the colony, irrespective of how problematic these definitions were. We have inherited these problematic views about religion and language with which we still struggle.

The world as divided up into civilisations provided portals to the study of global history. The definition of a civilisation drew on the earlier discussions of cultures, grouped together as a civilisation. The essential components, after defining its territory, were the high intellectual achievements as reflected in its texts that gave the civilisation its identity. This was either through the initial texts or those of a period that accompanied associated achievements in aesthetics and values. Such a period of history was viewed as the mainspring that kept the history of the civilisation going for centuries. This required a single representative language and preferably a single religion that encapsulated the civilisation. The exemplar was Greco-Roman Europe.

Asia could boast of three civilisations named after language or religion: the Islamic civilisation of Arabia and Persia with Arabic as the language; the Sanskritic Hindu civilisation of India; and the Chinese civilisation of East Asia associated with Confucianism. I have often asked myself as to why Buddhism was lost sight of in all of this. It was once the interconnecting thread through most of Asia. It was made to disappear in India; it faded in Central Asia and was persecuted in China. But even today it remains a crucial link in what are admired as ways of thinking and ethical values. A deeper investigation of Buddhist culture in terms of the critique that it posed to many existing Asian cultures might help us redefine some civilisations.

Civilisation associated with archaeology took a different turn. Patterns of the development of human societies in archaeological research drew from the theory of evolution postulating a trajectory from the simple to the complex and arguing for the survival of the fittest.

Human society, it was said, began with the stage of savagery in the bands of hunter-gatherers. These societies used minimal stone tools as aids. Some of these societies evolved into agro-pastoralists through efforts to grow food and breed animals. The institution of family and notions of property, that radically changed society, emerged slowly. This took them to the stage of barbarism, extensive and diverse. Some remained at that stage; others moved to the third and highest stage (or urbanism). As in the case of animal life, evolution did not move in a straight vertical line for all societies. For some, a horizontal movement became permanent. Many agro-pastoralists asserted themselves by developing a rich tradition of herding domesticated animals, especially cattle and horses, and by working out efficient systems of cultivating crops.

Such societies had the leisure to hone the systems they used to the point where they could be identified by the quality of the material goods they produced, ranging from pottery to metal ornaments and objects. But they were not recognised as civilisations and instead were described as cultures. A culture was defined as a pattern of life and could be applied to any system, whereas a civilisation had specific features defined differently. The primary features of a civilisation were urban centres and literacy, although many other features of our present-day definition of civilisation were also listed.

This seemed a fairly direct trajectory. But it was problematic in some instances where earlier definitions of civilisation were already in use, as for example in India. According to the archaeological definition of civilisation and the evidence available, the Harappan cities are the foundation of India's civilisation. They predate the generally accepted date of Vedic culture by quite a few centuries. There is so far no proof of their conforming to Aryan culture. The orientalists had argued that Vedic culture was the foundation of civilisation, but by the new definition, this culture lacked urbanisation and literacy. So, there was a contradiction.

Harappan cities are not only sophisticated urban centres but give every indication of having been carefully planned by people who understood the requirements of urban settlements. Such settlements had a complexity of functioning, such as demarcating the area where public functioning was concentrated as distinct from an expansive residential area. Other features are familiar to us from our schoolbooks – a sensible layout with planned roads, a remarkable drainage system, and the complex defences at the gates to the cities. Among the many other aspects of trade and an advanced material culture was the central role of a system of writing. So, we now have a situation where archaeology informs us that the foundations of Indian civilisation lie in the cities of the Indus civilisation, dated to well before the *Veda*s, but the orientalists of half a century earlier had projected the *Veda*s as its foundation. In the latter definition of civilisation, neither urban centres nor literacy were required. Therefore, the Vedic period could be called a civilisation. Inevitably, there are controversies about the origins of Indian civilisation.

But the concept of civilisation popular among 19th-century

historians was of course not the archaeological one. I would like to return to the definition of Indian civilisation that has prevailed in many works on the subject since the 19th century, and look more carefully at its features.

The territory chosen was that of British India. The confidence of colonialism made it seem that it would be permanent and stable. This was unlike the geographically changeable boundaries of names used for parts of the subcontinent such as Jambudvipa, Aryavarta, Bharatavarsha, or even al-Hind. However, British India did break up into three nations in the 20th century. This was not unusual, as every century has seen changing alignments in the borders of the many states and kingdoms comprising the subcontinent. There were no fixed boundaries.

In pre-cartographic times, when there were no maps, it was problematic to define boundaries with any precision. The more common usage lay in frontier zones being marked by natural and geographical features. If we make a study of such frontier zones, we may find that often they were where the much more interesting historical formations sometimes took shape. Frontier zones have the advantage of looking both inwards and outwards, and they even had the choice of deciding which was which.

The geographical focus of regions also shifted for a variety of reasons. The Harappans occupied the Indus plain, and their contacts seem to have lain westwards towards Mesopotamia. The authors of the Vedic texts who were settled in the Panjab moved in the opposite direction, going eastwards to the Ganga plain. The second urbanisation had its epicentre in the middle Ganga plain. The peninsula and the south are generally off the radar at this point, probably because, as their archaeology shows, their impressive Megalithic cultures differed substantially from the cultures of northern India.

Interestingly, the Mauryan and the Mughal states had somewhat similar boundaries – incorporating the northwest borderlands but not controlling the far south. Territorially, neither made it to being a fully subcontinental empire. The Kushanas were half in and half out. Their fulcrum was the Oxus valley, whereas we treat them as integrated into northern India. We could ask whether they looked upon northwestern India as a frontier zone of their empire. And if so, how did they see it? Did the Kushana polity focus more on Central Asia and China? Indian texts have little to say about the Kushanas but they are a presence in the Chinese annals of the time, the *Hou Hanshu*.

In terms of the wish to control territory within India, the Guptas and the Cholas were virtually mirror images, one having a northern base and the other a southern one, separated by a few centuries. The Cholas, however, had maritime connections that the Guptas lacked. The Turks, Afghans and Mughals, irrespective of their roots, were firmly ensconced in northern India and the Deccan.

So, in terms of the territorial base of the civilisation, we are not speaking of a compact area but of parts of a large area that hosted a variety of cultures. The variations are pertinent to the notion of constructing a single civilisation. But these are frequently ignored when we think of civilisation as a package. The same would be true of West Asia and China. What this suggests is that we should be sensitive to changes in the frontier areas, both overland and maritime, and be open to how they may have contributed to the creation of what we call 'civilisation'. The view from the other side cannot be overlooked. At the same time we have to concede that cultures within themselves also evolve over time. This makes it necessary to see civilisation not as a fixed package but as a continuous process registering change.

Language is often a good barometer of historical change. This becomes significant now that we know that all languages, even those in relative isolation, undergo change. Given the array of languages spoken and written in India, the change was impressive – both from evolution resulting from using a language, and that which comes from contact between languages. The earliest carefully preserved language that we know about was Vedic Sanskrit, used by a select few who maintained that its ritual efficacy, which was its primary use, would be annulled if it was contaminated by other languages, and it therefore had to be protected from them. This was the language that was said to be at the foundation of Indian civilisation. This poses a couple of questions for the historian.

One is that we don't as yet know what language the Harappans spoke. Attempts to read the Harappan symbols through the Indo-Aryan language have so far failed. An alternative is to assume that the Harappans spoke a Dravidian language and that the symbols were later translated into Indo-Aryan. This has yet to be proved. This is partly based on the theory of the presence of some Dravidian linguistic forms in Vedic Sanskrit. Would this suggest bilingualism among speakers of the two languages?

Mention is made of the *dasas* who are different from the Aryas. They cannot speak Aryan correctly, they worship different gods and they observe different customs. There is also the puzzling group referred to as the *dasi-putra brahmanas*, something of an oxymoron. How can the sons of *dasis* be brahmanas? But there they are and are a respected category. Let's leave aside the yet inexplicable and turn to certainties. For almost a millennium, the language most widely used by royalty and commoners was not Sanskrit but Prakrit. The Jaina texts were initially composed in

Prakrit, the Buddhist in Pali. Discussions on causality in thought, dharma and ahimsa, degrees of rationality, the questioning of the existence of deity, and many such ideas were first discussed in these languages. Learned brahmanas often preferred to set these aside as the thinking of *nastika*s – non-believers. Prakrit was the language that travelled to Kushana centres in Central Asia, to parts of Southeast Asia and, together with Tamil, to West Asia.

The adoption of Sanskrit, or the emergence of what has recently been called 'the Sanskrit cosmopolis', dates to the much later period from the Guptas onwards. This was when it had a monopoly as the language of learning, of creative literature, of administration, and was used by all those aspiring to high status. Existing institutions using Sanskrit received substantial patronage. It expanded further with courtly culture in newly established kingdoms requiring its use by local court poets, but also in official documents, where occasionally it was used incorrectly. The competition with the new official language, mainly Persian, was more in kingdoms with long histories. Newer kingdoms, when hard pressed, would use the emerging regional languages, especially when new castes of local origin became upwardly mobile. Sanskrit was pre-eminent for a millennium in virtually every branch of learning and more so in courtly literature and in religious scholarship, composed more frequently by upper-caste authors.

The history of this prior patronage explains in part the high status of Sanskrit at the Mughal court, where brahmana and Jaina authors interacted with scholars of Persian, also patronised by the Mughals. Patronage to Sanskrit in medieval times as one of the languages of learning and formal religion is borne out by the number of texts, commentaries and digests that were composed in the last thousand years under multiple patrons.

This was continued with the patronage from the colonial state, conscious of its upper-caste connections. Other languages and their literatures received less attention as carriers of civilisation. It might be worth doing a survey of what was composed in languages other than Sanskrit throughout history, to gauge the lineages of thought and articulation. This in itself would be insightful in evaluating the role of a single language in the concept of civilisation.

Any text of any kind and in whatever language assumes an audience. All composition is in essence a dialogue. If a text is composed by the elite and uses the language of the elite, it can only indirectly reflect the culture of others. To that extent it curtails our understanding of the civilisation.

Much the same can be said about choosing a particular religion as the prominent one in a civilisation. Religions in India were described as monolithic in colonial readings of Indian cultures. But, were they so? Most colonial scholars saw Indian religions through their experience from the medieval European past, with its single religion of Catholicism that had virtually denuded Europe of its multiple existing religions. In India, religion was articulated and propagated through a range of sects, each having the choice of being autonomous or associated with another. These religious sects have a long history. Their survival is also in part conditioned by their closeness to particular castes or caste clusters. This may coincide, but need not, with the patronage of royalty or the wealthy. This highlights the interface between religion and society, an aspect of culture that was not given prominence in the concept of civilisation. By bunching together every religious articulation under the label of Hinduism, the essential nature of religion in India, with its unique multiplicity, was denied.

Dharma, which we today take to mean religion, was viewed as consisting of two streams. One was Vedic Brahmanism that required a belief in Vedic and other deities, maintained the sanctity of the *Veda*s as composed by the gods, and held that each mortal had an immortal soul. Strongly opposed to these beliefs were various groups jointly referred to as Shramanas, who doubted or rejected deities, treated the *Veda*s as human utterances, and rejected the idea of an immortal soul. Across the centuries, dharma was referred to as the two streams of the Brahmana and the Shramana, or the *astika*/believers and the *nastika*/non-believers, which we today would regard as the orthodox and the heterodox. The nastika consisted of Buddhists, Jainas, Ajivikas, and those of such persuasion, including the Charvaka, the school of materialism. Far from maintaining that Charvaka thinking had declined, it is given importance in a 14th-century compendium of Indian philosophy, although the author states clearly that he disagrees with it.

The dual division was recognised in the edicts of Ashoka Maurya, in the account of Megasthenes as well as that of Xuanzang, and up to the time of Alberuni – a period of 1,500 years. A specific reference is made in the grammar of Patanjali of the early centuries AD, who adds that the relationship between the two can be compared to that of the snake and the mongoose. The Shramanas in some *Purana*s are referred to as the great deceivers – *mahamoha* – who teach people the wrong doctrines. They are therefore *pashanda*s – frauds. The Buddhists sometimes use the same epithet for the Brahmanas. Occasions are recorded when the relationship between the two became violent. That Indian civilisation had a singular and monolithic religion can be seriously questioned.

Yet, at another quite different level, there was dialogue and much discussion between the Brahmanas and Shramanas on philosophical questions, a major subject being the definition and use of logic. Many philosophical schools were involved in these discussions. Reference is made these days to important monasteries that were the location of philosophical discussion. Interestingly, most of these are Buddhist or Jaina. These were places where teaching was open to all and the monks came from high and low castes. Brahmanical learning was located in *matha*s and *ashrama*s. These were more closed in terms of kinship and caste, and were largely the preserve of the brahmanas.

The last thousand years have been quite striking in terms of the changes that were introduced at various levels in what we would regard as aspects of civilisation. The landscape changed. Buddhist monasteries and stupas receded, and the new features were temples and mosques. Some of the most magnificent Hindu and Jaina temples were constructed in this period. These were heavily endowed with land, and their committees of control were into substantial commerce in all the powerful kingdoms, as had been some of the Buddhist monasteries in earlier times. Obviously, there was much wealth available. The focus was on sectarian worship. Those temples that were involved in the politics of the time, such as the temple of the Bundellas in Mathura, suffered from the crossfire of Mughal–Bundella politics. Others received impressive grants from the Mughals and from the Hindu elite, converting them into rich institutions.

At another level, there were preachers and teachers who, since an earlier period in south India, were now, at a later time, becoming prominent in the north as well. These were the Bhakti *sant*s, who encouraged worship in devotional forms, taught in local languages, and gave a new shape to the religion that we now call Hinduism. For the majority of its followers, Vedic belief and ritual were marginal. Much of the Bhakti teaching was oral and therefore attracted vast followings from the majority of the people, who were in any case not literate. The result was a multiplicity of sects of every kind, either drawing from or opposing the more formal religions. Discussion of who the followers of the various religious sects were unfortunately often gets left out of the classic descriptions of civilisation.

These descriptions draw essentially on elite cultures and give little or no space to the contributions of the rest. The concept of Indian civilisation says little or nothing on the relationship between people at different levels in society. It is salutary to remember that the 'golden age' of Indian civilisation, earlier taken to be the Gupta period, justifiably regarded as a high point from the perspective of art and literature in particular, was nevertheless a period when social ethics reached an abysmally low level. At the same time that Kalidasa was composing his brilliantly sophisticated poems and plays, the *Dharmashastra*s were propagating the theory of the social exclusion of some sections of society, thought to be impure to such a degree that they should not even be touched. This discrimination applied even to their descendants. They are described as people who were ghettoised, living outside the village or town, and they had to strike a clapper every time they entered the settlement, so that the other non-polluted people could move away from them. Their numbers are sizeable and they are referred to as the *avarna*s, outside the *varna*s, and therefore outcastes, and as *asprishya*, untouchable. This was a period of high aesthetic values but divorced from social ethics.

What I am suggesting is that the conventional description of what constitutes Indian civilisation is partial, in the sense that it does not include contributions beyond those of the elite and the upper castes, and that it ignores the social ethic. The ethic of such extreme discrimination is difficult to reconcile with the norms of social values, even in ancient times when social ethics did not have a central place among such values. There were many inequities that characterised what we call civilisations, such as the long history of varieties of slavery, and sometimes quite vicious, in many parts of the world. But to reduce a section of society to being genetically polluted as it were, and therefore untouchable, seems to be, ethically, the worst. If the concept of civilisation continues to be used, we need to revisit it so as to include a far wider spectrum of social behaviour than we have allowed for until now. This critique would apply to all civilisations and one may argue that the meaning we have given to the concept is in itself far too limited. Its relevance may have to be reconsidered.

The evaluation and the prioritising of the cultural forms that go into the making of a civilisation need to be examined afresh if the concept is to be retained. Let me try and explain this. The compactness of civilisation is viewed in part by the demarcated territory where it prevails. But many of the historical achievements resulted from the commingling of groups, elite and non-elite, both within this territory and those on its frontiers. The commissioning of a monument or a cultural object may lie in the hands of a wealthy patron, but its creator is often a lower-caste professional. Styles can therefore be a reflection of localities and popular trends. The early images of the Buddha illustrate this. The Gandhara image from the northwest is Indo-Greco-Bactrian in style; the one from Mathura is strikingly different as is also the one from Amaravati in the south. It then changes in Borobudur and Angkor in Southeast Asia, as also in Dunhuang and Longmen in Central Asia and China. The images do not conform to a single aesthetic, but do suggest the richness of the dialogues that must have taken place, unfortunately unrecorded, among the sculptors that created them. Did some *shilpin*s and *sthapati*s – artisans, masons, craftsmen, and their supervisors – also travel with the traders, brahmanas and Buddhist monks to Southeast Asia in the early periods, to assist with questions of architectural forms, or the aesthetics of iconography? The diversity of the image is only one example that points to the inspiration not being limited to single elite sources.

Texts requiring scholarship travelled with brahmanas, Buddhist monks and traders with access to upper-caste activities. Many ventured beyond the frontiers, creating new mixed cultures that challenged the existing civilisational models, possibly even assisting in the forming of new states. In the intense competition for patronage, Indian texts were rewritten in local languages and adjusted to local perspectives. The variations are culturally fascinating. In the controversial additions to the story of Rama, the Hikayat Seri Rama of Malaysia, the patriarch Adam is brought into the story as is communication between Ravana and Allah. Other variations strike a familiar note as variations were common in India. Adaptations provide another perspective. It has been interestingly argued that the early story of Rama in Old Javanese was not based on the Valmiki text but on the later *Bhattikavya*. The reasons for the diversity of sources remain unexplained. Nor do we concede that some sources of significance in the creation of texts need not be from the elite. Such explanations are what we need to hear, especially from those that insist on cultural singularity.

A parallel example comes from Central Asia. The carriers of the cultures were the same but the Buddhists drew the greater attention. Buddhist monasteries marked the staging points of the trade routes that went from China through Central Asia to the eastern Mediterranean with offshoots into India. The location of the monasteries virtually marks the routes that were taken. A healthy patronage encouraged each to host murals of the highest quality illustrating narratives from the Buddhist texts, sometimes with a background of local history. Their version of the narratives becomes a commentary on the Indian texts, an attempt to see a part of India from the other side; or do they represent only the perspective from China? Did their perceptions confirm some of our current views of Indian civilisation?

The involvement of Indians in this trade continued until the last century, interspersed with varieties of exchange. Named as the Old Silk Road in recent times, the route linked places over land from China to the eastern Mediterranean. For over a millennium it cut across the civilisations of Asia, civilisations whose distinctiveness we have thought of as being crucial to the history of the region. But the achievements in philosophy, religion and the arts came out of the interaction of these cultures and not from the isolation of each.

Indians and Chinese in the past arrived in Southeast Asia through a maritime exploration. This linked ports and hinterlands servicing routes across the Arabian Sea, the Bay of Bengal and the South China Sea – a kind of Indian Ocean route linking segments to form a continuous chain from North Africa to the eastern Mediterranean, and via South and Southeast Asia to south China. This of course is not a compact land mass, but it informs us of the kind of contacts that fuelled civilisations. It boasted multiple high cultures, literatures in a variety of languages, architecture and art that competed with the quality of that which we regard as coming from established civilisations. Above all, it demonstrated that ultimately knowledge advances when there is an exchange between those in the know.

The study of astronomy, mathematics and medicine in Asia was dependent on this exchange and continued to be so for many centuries. This was not just a casual mixing of ideas. It involved the careful sifting of what goes into a knowledge system so as to understand it better. This surely is an essential requirement of being a civilisation.

When we start to think of the concept of civilisation as not something territorially compact and pertaining to a limited period of history, we perhaps need to pause. What is now emerging from the swathes of the cultures that we study, is the porosity of their frontiers. Territories, languages, religions, however stable we would like them to be, are in fact constantly taking new forms. The change comes from many sources: internal pressures that alter social hierarchies; alien cultures that accrete to them and take on new identities; mutations that transform the cultures of the frontiers; and the ensuing perceptions that those beyond the frontiers have of us.

Civilisation is not a sudden occurrence. I like to think of it as a process that evolves over a long period, mutating as it goes along, and we have to recognise the mutations. The concept of a civilisation is a construct, as is what we call a civilisation. Early histories as studied in our time, recognising the nature of interactions at various levels, tend to question the idea of each civilisation being singular and compact. The sheer span of a civilisation would make it susceptible to diversities and they reformulate the features. If the concept is not to be discarded and a redefinition is sought, existing ideas about it will, nevertheless, need to be unpacked. Some will be rejected and some replaced by current explanations. Such explanations of the past are likely to change the contours of the concept. I would like to suggest an emphasis on two: its porosity in reacting to cultural contacts requires civilisation to be seen as a process arising out of both evolving and intrusive cultural interventions; such articulations have to go beyond elite upper-caste activities and incorporate the dialogue between varying social groups in the societies that constitute the players.

If we think at all of a civilisation, it would have to be thought of not as a self-contained homogeneous entity for all time, but rather as a pulsating universe using the present to link the past in creating a future.

Eighth Ambedkar Memorial Lecture, 14 April 2016, Ambedkar University Delhi.

9
Is There a Conception of the Exemplar in Babasaheb Ambedkar?

Gopal Guru

Individual exemplary action may be worth respecting, but most of the time it is not worth repeating or imitating. Collective action is exemplary and hence millions of time superior to individual action. – B. R. Ambedkar (2005: 35)

[E]very act of independent thinking puts some portion of [the] apparently stable world in peril. – B. R. Ambedkar (1979a: 95)

It indeed is a great pleasure to speak at the annual Ambedkar Memorial Lecture that Ambedkar University Delhi has been organising for the last eight years. I am equally pleased to know that the scholars who spoke before me in this series seem to have focused their attention in and around Ambedkar's thoughts. In some cases, the themes taken up by these scholars had a direct bearing on Ambedkar's thought, while others chose to speak on themes that had an indirect bearing on the philosophical/theoretical core of Ambedkar's metaphysics of emancipation. On this occasion, 14 April 2017, Babasaheb Ambedkar's 126th birthday, I acknowledge the scholarship of these renowned scholars. However, to be honest, I am self-conscious about the scholarly limitations with which I will speak on this particular occasion. While I thank the university for providing me this opportunity, it has also placed enormous moral as well as intellectual pressure on somebody like me, who does not possess the intellectual calibre of the speakers who preceded me. Therefore, I consider myself quite adventurous, if not arrogant, to speak in the same series. However, as Ambedkar has taught us, taking the plunge into independent thinking is likely to put anyone's reputation in peril. To put this differently, I might disappoint, if not annoy, several among you for not being able to come close to the height and depth that the previous scholars attained in their talks. It is this element of anxiety about my own calibre that has compelled me to drop the idea of having a discussant for my talk.

Having said this, let me now try and put before you *my* ideas about the theme, ideas that have hardly received any attention from Ambedkar scholars. I am going to make an argument, which in my opinion is quite difficult to defend, particularly on intellectual grounds. The argument is as follows: the attribution of the position of an exemplar does not sit well with Ambedkar as he is himself an autonomous, enlightened being. Adopting the conception of the exemplar, however, becomes a historical necessity when contemporary figures do not measure up to the intellectual and political imagination of Dalits, who then seek to work out the metaphysics of emancipation by critically appropriating exemplars from the past.

I have tried to develop this talk in three sections. In the first two sections, I focus my attention on two points: the Dalit cultural imagination that involves the construction of Babasaheb Ambedkar as an exemplar; and its subsequent rejection by different traditional adversaries of Ambedkar. I will argue that there are three types of adversaries who seek to deny Ambedkar the status of an exemplar. These include members of the Hindu right who reject outright the Dalits' assertion of Ambedkar as an exemplar, and poststructuralists who deny Ambedkar the undisputed/undiluted status of an exemplar. Finally, a third type includes liberal conservatives who seek to grant Ambedkar the status of an exemplar; however, for them Ambedkar is a role model only for the Dalits. This particularised characterisation by the liberal conservatives can be seen as a parochial apportioning of Ambedkar. In the second section, I thus seek to question both the poststructuralist and the liberal conservative reading of Ambedkar. In the third section, I will discuss Ambedkar's own conception of the exemplar, and will end by arguing that in Ambedkar's own writings, there is a categorical refutation of such a conception.

Ambedkar as an Impeccable Exemplar for Dalits

In the Dalit cultural imagination, the positioning of Ambedkar as an exemplar emerges more from convention than from reason. Dalits do not need to find reasons to establish their association with Ambedkar. The reason is implicit in their estimation of Ambedkar as an impeccable exemplar. Hence, for Dalits it is convention, in fact, radical conviction, which makes them place their faith in Ambedkar. This faith, which is not without the force of cultivated reason, can be summarised in the Dalit common sense in Maharashtra. This common sense is constitutive of the following estimation of Ambedkar: 'Babasaheb Ambedkar, the tallest, the bravest, most honest and universal thinker, and world philosopher, direct us! Ambedkar is the clearest conception of virtue and hence has to be held imaginatively, at some distance from the immediate importunities of our own lives.'

Dalits, thus, place their full trust in Ambedkar. In fact, their trust in Ambedkar is based on a subtle and unrelenting suspicion of their own motives, as well as a steady contemplation of ethical models which are wholly independent of their immediate desires. It is in this sense that their estimation of Ambedkar does not reek of instrumentality. The withholding of reason by Dalits has a transcendental charge to it. The ordinary Dalit evokes the idea of Ambedkar not for some personal gain but to sustain their aspirations for a better future.

In the cultural imagination of Dalits in India, Ambedkar appears as a perfect exemplar not just for India, but for the entire world. Hence, for Dalits he is not only a Bharat *ratna* (jewel of India) but also a *vishwa ratna* (jewel of the world). The affirmation of Ambedkar as an exemplar has a resounding significance for the ordinary Dalit. The cultural space within which one can visualise the emergence of Ambedkar as an exemplar – inhabiting the socio-cultural imagery of ordinary Dalits – has to be understood in a counter-cultural or counter-intellectual context, which, to a large extent, has been rendered insignificant by the self-serving politics of 'official' Dalit intellectuals. These intellectuals seek to 'governmentalise' Ambedkar to the extent that his essence appears relevant for the policy purposes of the state, or he is turned into an instrument for silencing political opponents. But, for ordinary Dalits, Ambedkar serves as an inspiring figure whose teachings empower them to maintain their self-respect. He provides the intellectual and moral energy that is so critical to the Dalit struggle for *manuski* (dignity), as expressed by Ambedkar in Marathi. In fact, Dalits assign an exemplary moral value to Babasaheb, whose moral, ethical and intellectual qualities elevate him above the world of *laukika* (ordinary/ worldly) human relationships. It is quite common for Dalits, particularly the subaltern sections, to organise their lifeworld(s) in accordance with moral values that they shuffle and reshuffle with complete freedom to put Ambedkar, their exemplar, at the centre of their moral universe. In their hierarchical ordering of values, they have placed Babasaheb right at the top. To put it differently, Dalits have, without hesitation, subordinated their mundane and material values to the power of moral reason. This is manifested in their extraordinary defence of Ambedkar as an exemplar.

Here, let me cite an example from the lived reality of Dalits to show us the impact of Ambedkar's normative philosophy on their moral judgement. Some years ago, a woman, an Ambedkarite from Mumbai, offered to sell her *mangal sutra* (a symbol of her sacred tie to her husband) to a bookseller in exchange for a book that contained a pictorial biography of Ambedkar.[1] This, in a moral sense, is quite an exemplary act by a Dalit woman, who sought to subordinate the traditional value of the mangal sutra to the emancipatory value embedded in Ambedkar's text. The example shows the defence of Ambedkar's ideals by assigning them a superior moral value. This moral hierarchy is evident in the exemplary acts with which Dalits defend Ambedkar's emancipatory legacy. These acts show their readiness to make huge sacrifices for a superior cause. Needless to say, committed Dalits expose themselves to grave risk while defending Ambedkar's ideals. Dalits take this risk in the face of anti-Ambedkar social forces seeking to erase his ideals from their cultural memory. Let us not forget the 1997 Ramabai Nagar killings in which 10 Dalits lost their lives when the police fired upon a crowd protesting against the desecration of an Ambedkar statue.[2] The vandalising of Ambedkar's statues and resultant Dalit protests against such a hostile anti-Dalit mood have become a regular cultural phenomenon that we continue to witness across the country today.

Ambedkar as an exemplar has acquired moral significance in terms of helping individual Dalits develop a transcendental world view. Put differently, it has taken the Dalits immense moral stamina to overcome a paralysing sense of fate as they plan the future keeping in sight the illuminating power of Ambedkar as an ideal. Let me offer the example of my father for whom Babasaheb Ambedkar, a morally universalisable father figure, was an impeccable exemplar. My father, following Ambedkar's example, took the decision to send me 250 kilometres away to Nagsen Van in Aurangabad, Maharashtra, to study in the college that Ambedkar had established in 1950. In my father's estimation, Ambedkar's efforts to establish educational institutions were exemplary as they provided Dalits the opportunity to become guiding forces in the enlightenment tradition inaugurated by Ambedkar himself. Using an inspiring analogy, my father would often say, 'Vani cha pohnar ani Aurangabad cha lihinar kuthehi tarun jato.' In other words, anyone capable of swimming in the strong currents of the Van river can swim anywhere in the world, just like those who study in Ambedkar's Nagsen Van, in Aurangabad, can survive in the competitive world.

My father, however, did not adopt a utilitarian attitude. He did not view Ambedkar as an exemplar who would lead me on the path of self-centred, possessive individualism. He did not expect me to take up a more materially lucrative profession. To him, Ambedkar was a guide who would inspire me to become a *vidwan* (a learned person). Thus, my father found in Ambedkar's ideal not just redemptive content but, much more importantly, a transformative energy to leap out of existential despair into a promising future. He saw in Ambedkar's ideal a mediating force – to move out of the 'sensational' body into the mode of an intellectually vibrant mind. Thus, it can be safely argued that the Dalit cultural imagination acquires moral significance as it reveals to us the Dalit's efforts to put a premium on transcendental aspirations.

Dalits today seek to transform their social lives by keeping Ambedkar at the centre of their imagination. Ambedkar, the ideal exemplar, is the form of their social life. Dalit cultural politics which is built around such an exemplar does not reduce Ambedkar to an empty dream; in fact, for them, he is part of their everyday forms of inspiration and resistance. This, in effect, has created recalcitrant adversaries of Ambedkar, particularly among right-wing Hindus. Ambedkar, though an inspiring exemplar for Dalits, has his adversaries.

Ambedkar and His Adversaries

The struggle of Dalits to uphold their cultural claim on Ambedkar as an exemplar does not find easy recognition in the caste-ridden Indian society. In fact, the elite members of society actively oppose their claim. Ambedkar's adversaries tend to articulate their opposition to the claims of Ambedkar as an ideal using three different expressions. The first expression, by some members, involves a contemptuous rejection of Ambedkar. This expression, as we shall see in the following sections, is the result of a dishonest intellectual disagreement with Ambedkar, but it has its origin in the self-limits of those who use such offensive language. The second expression is different from the first inasmuch as it uses an element of cultural relativism to undermine Dalit claims which see universal qualities in Ambedkar's ideal. In the second category of opponents, we can arguably put scholars particularly with a poststructuralist orientation. Finally, we come across some scholars who neither reject nor seek to relativise Ambedkar's universalisable stature; instead, they seek to reduce it from its universal essence to the particularities of Dalit existence. Let us briefly discuss each of these adversaries.

Right-Wing Adversaries of Ambedkar

Ambedkar, the exemplar, has faced direct, and that too quite contemptuous, rejection by members of society who lack both the social and the cognitive generosity to accept him as a universal ideal. This lack of generosity stems from a loss of the intellectual calibre that these members were invested with, in the pre-modern days, by virtue of their caste position. The ideology of caste unilaterally conferred on these members the status of *bhudeo* (lord of the earth).[3] The desire to retain the bhudeo self-image through a rejection of any parallel exemplar from the lower castes has its basis in the *Manusmriti* (Laws of Manu), treated as the law book for Hindu life. It is interesting to note that for Manu, lower-caste Shudras could never be exemplars for the higher castes. As has been noted by Professor Rajendra Prasad, even the preaching of moral precepts by a Shudra is considered a crime, and a serious crime at that, not an ordinary lapse. It is worthy of severe punishment (Prasad 2008: 308). In Maharashtra, another possible explanation for the discounting of Ambedkar's status as an exemplar for Dalits is that his upper-caste adversaries follow the Marathi Ramdasi tradition of the 18th century, which does not consider any lower-caste person worthy of such a status.

In fact, such opponents, filled with hate and contempt, brazenly reject Ambedkar as an exemplary model. Let me give just three examples to show the feeling of contempt they nurse towards Ambedkar. In the first category are people who seem to textually reject Ambedkar as an exemplar. Even amidst this textual denial, these scholars do not show any restraint while expressing contempt for Ambedkar. This morally crippling overflow of contempt can be evidenced in sarcastic titles such as *Worshipping False Gods* (see Shourie 1997). Others, who follow the same logic as the first group, try to ridicule Dalit efforts at institutionalising Ambedkar as a modern exemplar.[4] One has to ask: why this anger? The social idealism that is inherent in Ambedkar's example seeks to challenge upper-caste domination. Being a challenge from below, this becomes a necessary, 'logical' provocation for the moral as well as physical violence perpetrated against Dalits by upper-caste adversaries. The growing atrocities against Dalits are, sadly, a validation of Ambedkar's ideas.

The 'touchables' constantly attack Dalits on the grounds that they *live out* Ambedkar's words. The Dalits' struggle for equality and dignity continues to bring Ambedkar's thoughts alive. He is a 'live' example for Dalits. He lives among millions of them through his ideas. He lives in their cultural and political assertions, modernist aspirations and emancipatory projects. He thus refuses to become a mere reified idea in History. His ideas with their emancipatory intention have sought to mobilise the political actions of Dalits, and in turn their political action has sought to make his ideas relevant to their political project. We may support this reading of Ambedkar by Dalits by taking our cue from Quentin Skinner, who would argue that the history of ideas does not discuss texts or timeless concepts, but the social context within which the text seeks to mobilise people (Skinner 1969: 48). As Ambedkar is a living text, at least when it comes to Dalits, he cannot be studied from the perspective of a history of ideas removed from a living social context. Ambedkar's ideas, unlike the ideas of other thinkers, have not become a part of History. It is this aspect of the exemplar that annoys his adversaries, who attempt to attack him by attacking Dalits. Finally, the denial of exemplary status to Ambedkar has to be understood as upper-caste efforts to compensate for what has been 'lost' in the present moment by turning to tradition. To put it differently, the opposition to Ambedkar's ideas has to be seen in terms of the upper-caste rivals' descension into irrational individuals who are unable to accept the exemplary qualities of a person irrespective of his/her social/gender/territorial background.

The Poststructuralist Dilution of Ambedkar as an Exemplar

Scholars of a poststructuralist persuasion undermine the logical claims for Ambedkar as an exemplar by using the non-linear method of placing him alongside other Dalit exemplars.[5] Poststructuralist scholars argue that Ambedkar is not the only ideal available within the Dalit social landscape.[6] In fact, they argue, there are other hidden ideals in different Dalit contexts across the country.

One need not find this move particularly objectionable on two grounds. First, this move to relativise Ambedkar's importance as an exemplar may seem morally sound inasmuch as it seeks to put the focus on all those Dalit exemplars who, according to a non-linear logic, would otherwise be overshadowed by Ambedkar's towering presence. Second, there isn't much need to oppose such efforts as long as they seek to 'democratise' the cultural imagination of Dalits by making other Dalit leaders stand in Ambedkar's company. This move would also be acceptable to those who would see in such efforts the potential to undermine the Hegelian element of insinuation – which would accommodate the other who has been elevated from the state of a slave to one that is closer, but not identical, to that of the master.

One fails to understand why these people, who support the non-linear 'understating' of the exemplar, choose to dispute the Dalit community's claim to Ambedkar as their sole exemplar. One needs to point out to them the grave error of assuming that either Ambedkar or his supporters nurtured the idea of his becoming an exemplar. This is shown to be inaccurate by the evidence Ambedkar provides in his own writing. He does not have the desire to become a messiah or a Moses. Nor does he want everybody in the community to become a self-referential 'bhudeo'. Furthermore, this non-linear mode, which seeks to flatten Ambedkar's moral essence, does not tell us why those who claim to stand with the 'overshadowed' Dalit exemplars dispute the Dalits' upholding of Ambedkar as an exemplar.

The question that needs to be raised is why the poststructuralists choose not to historicise the conception of exemplar. This would ensure parity in terms of disputing the claims that make other thinkers exemplars. Why is it that the other exemplars serve as a paradigm but not Ambedkar? Why do they repeatedly choose Ambedkar as the privileged target while seeking to democratise the Dalit conception of exemplar? Would it not be fair to adopt a more egalitarian conception of exemplar by implicating a non-Dalit exemplar? To put this more provocatively, these scholars do not seem to be interested in historicising the conception of exemplar in relation to thinkers such as Rabindranath Tagore and M. K. Gandhi. Arguably, Tagore does not share his essence with any thinker other than Gandhi, whom he gave the name 'Mahatma'. For Tagore, the name/title 'Mahatma' is the ultimate description and is therefore exemplary. For Gandhi, Tagore becomes 'Gurudev'. Tagore may continue to remain *the* poet for many people, including the poststructuralists. Similarly, these scholars do not position any other exemplar alongside Gandhi and therefore he remains *the* Mahatma for them. We will come back to this point in greater detail in the next section where we will discuss Akeel Bilgrami's portrayal of Gandhi as an exemplar (Bilgrami 2003: 4161). While the poststructuralists attempt to dilute Ambedkar's status by denying him the advantage of becoming a singular exemplar, the liberal conservatives in India seek to deny Ambedkar's universal status as an exemplar by adopting the approach of 'proportionate exemplar', in the sense that Ambedkar's status as an exemplar is directly proportionate to the cultural aspirations of Dalits.

Liberal Conservatives: Their Conception of 'Proportionate Exemplar'

Let me begin this section by posing two interrelated questions: what does one mean by the idea of a proportionate exemplar, and why is the Indian liberal conservative interested in defining the proportionate exemplar with particular reference to Ambedkar? Let us first attempt to address the question of the proportionate exemplar. One can define the idea of the proportionate exemplar in terms of the parity between an exemplar and his/her moral essence. There is a fairness principle involved in the word 'parity'. But this fairness suffers great damage when one attempts to replace this kind of parity with the one between an exemplar and his/her social identity. In other words, the principle of fairness suffers further damage when the moral essence of an exemplar is ontologically reduced to the sociological proportion of his or her social constituency. According to such a reading, Ambedkar is an exemplar only to Dalits. He may embody universal principles but he is not universalisable in the sense of his principles being followed by people across the board.[7] In this regard, we often encounter a rather naïve suggestion from the upper castes who say that Dalits (alone) should follow examples from within the Dalit community.

Attempts by the liberal conservatives to define Ambedkar's exemplary character in proportion to the cultural aspirations of Dalits – or their hesitation to grant him the advantage of being universalisable – shows them to be conservative in their evaluative judgements. This conservative element forces them to apportion the universal meanings of certain concepts to narrow spheres in the present contexts of Dalit life. Among political thinkers in modern India, such a conservative reading of the exemplar tends to make social justice coterminous with Ambedkar's exemplary figure. As a corollary to this phenomenological move, liberal conservatives seek to bracket Dalit aspiration for social justice with Ambedkar. This conservative reading of the exemplar has other consequences for an accurate characterisation of Ambedkar. For example, characterising him as a political philosopher would be inaccurate on certain grounds.

The ideal of social justice defines political philosophers. Hence, for liberal conservatives, the proportionate exemplar gets defined only in relation to a single principle which stands narrowly defined, in this case, for example, the principle of social justice. If these scholars had been liberals, in their spirit and practice, they would without hesitation grant Ambedkar the comprehensive status of being the embodiment of several emancipatory ideas, with social justice being one among these. Correspondingly, such a clearly defined principle provides narrow ground for the acknowledgement of Ambedkar as an exemplar. Through the conception of a proportionate exemplar, liberal conservatives make a phenomenological attempt to try and filter out the crucial component of social justice from the set of principles which are constitutive of the metaphysics of emancipation as suggested by Ambedkar. One finds a symbolic acknowledgement of such an exemplar in the government's rhetorical act of putting Ambedkar's portraits in the offices of the Department of Social Justice. This tendency is also evident in the government's policies and efforts to publish Babasaheb Ambedkar's unpublished writings and speeches. It should be noted that this literature is being brought out by the Ministry of Social Justice and Empowerment and not by the Ministry of Culture. The ontological link between the narrow principle and the social origin of the exemplar, thus, decides the proportionality frame within which a particular thinker is condemned to remain confined. This kind of reading also suggests that the Dalit conception of the exemplar is in proportion to their life plans, which, according to these adversaries, do not extend beyond social justice. By implication, such a reading leads to a compressed conception of social justice, which in a Rawlsian sense (Rawls 1971) has universal validity.

One may in a liberal spirit argue that liberal conservatives are cognitively more generous than poststructuralists in as much as they do not seek to even out or balance the essence of Ambedkar with other Dalit exemplars. In their evaluative judgement, they do grant Ambedkar the status of an exemplar to Dalits, and it is in this sense that they are liberal, unlike Ambedkar's diehard and intolerant opponents of whom I have spoken above. But they are conservative in that they grant Ambedkar only a partial status; to them, he can be an exemplar for just the downtrodden. In fact, they seem quite reluctant to grant Ambedkar the full status of a universal exemplar. Thus, as part of this conservative logic, Ambedkar is seen only as a Dalit thinker, or as a messiah of the Dalits, or as a social reformer. Interestingly, such reductive expressions keep appearing regularly in the academic writings of other Ambedkar scholars. However, one needs to appreciate the discursive skill demonstrated in the way they size Ambedkar into narrow compartments or shade in the normative dimensions of his universalisable personality. They reduce him in proportion to the cultural aspiration of Dalits. Put differently, they project Ambedkar as a particularised exemplar.

It is also interesting, if not intriguing, to note that liberal conservatives seek to particularise the exemplar in terms of both space and time. They seek to reduce the operational conceptual space of universal ideas such as social justice that form the intellectual basis of Ambedkar's metaphysics of emancipation. Their moves are discursive inasmuch as such moves seek a balance between the conceptual space of justice and the sociological place into which Ambedkar is thrown. In a way, such efforts try to achieve a kind of reconciliation between ontology and epistemology. Moreover, such efforts tend to narrow the universal range of ideas by filtering them out or isolating them from their ontological location. The entire normative thrust of Ambedkar as a complete exemplar gets reduced to the single objective of the annihilation of caste, which then overdetermines the social agenda of Dalit emancipation. Thus, Ambedkar is seen and studied, if at all he finds a place in the curriculum, only as a social thinker or political philosopher. Liberal conservatives, therefore, seek to particularise both his universal principles and also the universalisability of these principles. Ambedkar's influence, therefore, as a complete exemplar gets compressed in terms of time as well.

Liberal conservatives expect Dalits in particular to follow Ambedkar's principles in their social and political practice. Although liberal conservatives have some definite intention behind such a particularised reading of the exemplar in Ambedkar, such a reading may not weaken the moral commitment that Dalits have to Ambedkar – both as the embodiment of a universal ideal, and as the possessor of a social identity, which they share not just as sociological entities but as human beings. Liberal conservatives need to be sensitive to the heavy social cost of the Dalits' efforts to publicly affirm their association with Ambedkar as an exemplar. Such efforts are often met with violent opposition from the upper castes. As we have seen in the section above, Dalits have made supreme sacrifices to defend the universal human values that Ambedkar embodies.

It is paradoxical to note that the non-Dalit castes – such as the Brahmans, the Gujjars from Rajasthan, Jats from western Uttar Pradesh and Haryana, and Marathas from Maharashtra – often attempt to identify with the idea of social justice as operationalised through the policy of reservation. These castes now demand reservations. Like Dalits, they may want to be the beneficiaries of the social justice principle, but they do not follow Dalits in terms of identifying with Ambedkar as a pioneering thinker on social justice. Without taking Ambedkar's name, they may be the silent beneficiaries of social justice. But they and their mentors, the liberal conservatives, need to keep in mind that Ambedkar's universalisability is not the same as silently following the principle of an exemplar. On the contrary, it involves an open identification both with the idea of Ambedkar as well as with Ambedkar as a universal embodied identity.

It is important to not only question but also actively defy the phenomenological design that liberal conservatives have used to apportion Ambedkar's universal ideas to a narrow social base. The moral question that one needs to raise here is this: will the upper castes rise above their caste considerations and, in turn, allow Ambedkar to rise above his? This paradox of the 'touchable' castes is co-extensive with the paradox of the liberal conservatives. The liberal conservative understanding demands from Ambedkar that he remain a 'perfect Untouchable' or an 'ideal Untouchable' only for the 'Untouchables'. One can express the upper-caste attitude towards Ambedkar in the following manner: for these reluctant liberals, Ambedkar as an exemplar is less than the universal exemplar, but he is more than the lesser exemplar that exists within and for the Dalit community.

Undoubtedly, this kind of reading of exemplars seeks to counter the poststructuralist conception of epistemic justice, which its proponents would like to achieve through the cultural relativisation of Ambedkar's significance as the paradigmatic figure for the Dalit community. The social orientation of the 'touchable' castes, and that of the subcastes of Dalits or Maha Dalits, a majority of whom have complaints against Ambedkar, tends to endorse the viewpoint of the liberal conservatives, who believe in the inevitability of granting Ambedkar the status of a proportionate exemplar. This implies that his relevance would not encompass the upper castes, but that he would establish an ontological identification with the Dalits.

One has to ask why Indian liberals are liberal in some instances and conservative in others. Why do these scholars adopt a conservative attitude towards Ambedkar? We could offer a 'non-ascriptive' answer to this question and suggest that the Indian conservatives are reluctant to give Ambedkar his due, or are reluctant to consider him a universalisable exemplar, because they are selfish. A second, more generous explanation might be found in the individualising (or ascribing) of blame. This would entail holding the selfish individual responsible for his reluctance to give Ambedkar his due. A third reason could be the caste consciousness that prevents Indians from becoming fully liberal and assigning the full status of exemplar to Ambedkar. A genuine liberal would acknowledge Ambedkar's articulation of universal principles. A thinker's universalisability depends on the moral actions he or she performs. However, in India, the success of universalisability depends not on moral actions but on the caste background of the person concerned. Ambedkar, in fact, considers moral action an important criterion for articulating the idea of the exemplar.

This brings us to a critical question: is there a conception of the exemplar in Ambedkar? My answer will include a qualification. The conception of the exemplar exists in Ambedkar, yet it is present only as an initial condition. In the final analysis, Ambedkar discounts the need for an exemplar. But, before we defend the claim that there is no conception of the exemplar in Ambedkar's work, let us discuss in some detail the concept as it exists there.

The Exemplar as a Historical Inevitability for Dalits

Ambedkar's conception of the exemplar follows a particular historical trajectory. It is ethically constituted and emerges at a certain time in history, and then disappears after having played its hermeneutic role. To Ambedkar, the exemplar is a concrete human being who originates from, and is shaped by, an ethical relationship between two human beings. Thus, within Ambedkar's framework, the exemplar is conceptualised outside the sphere of both theology and mythology. It is in this sense that the possibility of God being an exemplar for the human being is ruled out. Some critical thinkers would not consider even a mythical exemplar as impeccable or worth imitating (Prasad 2008: 297). While Ambedkar does not draw upon mythology for his conception of the exemplar, Jotirao Phule's exemplar, King Baliraja, a benevolent peasant king, emerges from a heterodox reading of mythology. Phule's exemplar becomes an ideal to be followed when considered alongside the presiding deities of the 'twice-born' castes.[8] We would, however, need to elaborate on this in a separate space.

To return to Ambedkar, his exemplar is not only historical but also moral. This is evident in his adoption of the Buddha, Kabir and Jotirao Phule as the three exemplars he would follow initially as a moral necessity. As against a theological model, Ambedkar's exemplar is defined in terms of the concrete ethical relationship between two human beings. It is the ethical that creates the ground for defining the exemplar. It is in this inverse sense that Ambedkar lays the groundwork on which other thinkers are forced to find limits to their claims of being an exemplar. Ambedkar's own socially corrosive personal experience undercuts the moral grounds on which others' claims to the status of exemplar could be established. Thus, thinkers on Ambedkar, particularly from the mainstream, who are implicated in the 'Ambedkar question', have no independent ground other than the one set by Ambedkar. Since Gandhi associates himself with the Ambedkar question, he is an exemplar not only for the Dalits, but, more importantly, for upper-caste Hindus. Gandhi exhorts the upper castes to join the struggle against untouchability. Thus, Gandhi and others like him are not exemplars with an independent standing. In this way, Ambedkar is able to establish the limits to the claims of being an exemplar. This is particularly relevant to those who are part of what can be termed as the social mainstream. Since Ambedkar was pushed out of this mainstream, there was no ground upon which he could limit his own claims. The exemplar does not become an ideal in an a priori or predetermined fashion. In fact, their claims to the status of an exemplar are based on the validity of their claims to interrogate the conception of their opponent's ideal. For example, Ambedkar is an exemplar by virtue of his interrogation of Gandhi's conception of an ideal such as Ramarajya (rule of Rama). One need not therefore conclude that Ambedkar's ideal is derivative as it emerges from a critique of the Gandhian ideal. In fact, it emerges from a dialectical process.

Ambedkar's conception of the exemplar underscores the word 'instructive' rather than the word 'imitative'. The choice of this word acquires cognitive importance in a context where one has to select from different kinds of exemplars that become historically available to a person like Ambedkar. Ambedkar, like persons from the 'other' castes or communities, was not privileged enough to inherit, from within his own historical trajectory, an exemplar with imitable qualities. Furthermore, he argues that following the ideas of a particular thinker is not a linear hermeneutic process. In fact, such an interrogation involves radical choices through the process of 'relativising' thought. This happens as part of a historical process (Kamble 1992: 167). Ambedkar's historical and social contexts explain the care with which he appropriated critical impulses drawn from heterodox traditions of thought in India. Hence, Ambedkar prefers the instructive over the imitative. In his conception, the word 'instructive' is more reflective than the word 'imitative' (Ambedkar 1979b: 225). To Ambedkar, such comparisons were instructive in so far as they helped historicise the options for the choice of exemplars. These choices were critical in a situation where intellectual resources were being mobilised for emancipatory purposes. In the absence of a relevant historical lineage, Ambedkar had to be selective in his choice of exemplar, favouring the instructive over the imitative.

Ambedkar's Conception of Exemplar

Needless to say, there is a conception of the exemplar in Ambedkar. This is part of his common sense, evident in the acceptance of the Buddha, Kabir, Phule, and Justice Ranade as the thinkers who would be his exemplars. Ambedkar lays down certain moral criteria for the exemplar. In his opinion, the exemplar could be located in the congruence between self-expression and its public reception. In other words, the opinions expressed by an exemplar would have to confirm their truth claims on the level of experience (Ambedkar 1979b: 223–24). In Ambedkar's view, figures like Jotirao Phule and Justice M. G. Ranade could claim public support and recognition for their truth claims. To become an exemplar, a person also needs the moral capacity to confront the system of social relationships of which he/she is an organic part. He/she should also have a robust internal critique of the caste system, of which he/she is a part. Those who consistently take up the fight against local configurations of power (i.e., Brahmanism and casteism) are genuine exemplars. By his own admission, Ambedkar defines the exemplar as an instructor and not as someone whose principles or actions are worth imitating. In Ambedkar's opinion, making an exemplar worthy of imitation involves a serious moral problem. The 'follower' of a particular exemplar, instead of taking moral responsibility for his/her actions, tends to invoke the principles defined either by the exemplar or by a sanctified text such as the *Manusmriti*, the most important *Dharmashastra*. The followers who are in an imitative mode seek to justify their actions through the exemplar or the authority of a text. In a caste-ridden society like India, such a shifting of responsibility has been quite prevalent.

The exemplar taken as a moral instructor invests the individual with an element of autonomy. The individual can use the exemplar's instructions to both guide and morally fine-tune his/her actions. Such instructions from the exemplar become necessary, particularly in a context where one does not have a clear road map or the authority, for instance, of texts such as the *Dharmashastra*s. Thus, in the final count, one has to take responsibility for one's actions because the exemplar is looked up to as only a temporary source of instruction. Ambedkar, however, rules out even the need for a temporary exemplar as an instructor. For historical reasons, he considers the exemplar as only the initial, and not the essential, condition. He restores complete autonomy to the individual who can then, along with others, participate in concretising a vision of society based on universally attractive principles such as friendship. Ambedkar finds such promises of intellectual independence or self-determination in the Buddhist principle of *atta dippo bhava*, which gives rise to the metaphysics that is a source of instruction for him as well.

Replacing the Exemplar with the Buddhist 'Atta Dippo Bhava' of Ambedkar

'Atta dippo bhava' in Ambedkar's conception of Buddhism means a being that is self-illuminating. Before we move further into defending our main argument, it is necessary to offer some clarification about the overlapping meanings that the word 'dippo' has acquired in Buddhist political and pedagogical practices. 'Dippo' in the Buddhist Pali language means 'island'. The same word acquires an entirely different meaning when it is rendered in Sanskrit. In Sanskrit it is translated into 'lamp'. Ambedkar in his own writings has used the Sanskrit version of 'dippo'. His followers continue to use and understand 'dippo' as 'lamp'. There is an overlap in the use of this word. Interestingly, Ambedkar does not pick up this meaning of the word from the Western tradition, though he is well versed in the Kantian and Emersonian traditions of Enlightenment. We know the idea of self-illumination belongs to an Enlightenment tradition thickly associated with Kant and Emerson.

Ambedkar is self-conscious about the affirmative energies that are an integral part of the enlightened self. 'Atta dippo bhava' implies the unfolding of the awareness of confinement into the selves of broken men. He argues that one begins to unfold oneself in the light that is self-generated through one's own experience, as well as through universal principles that people internalise during the course of their mutual interactions. In Ambedkar's understanding of neo-Buddhism, action trumps principles. One acquires self-awareness or inner light only through reacting to or acting on the forces that seek to torment us, for example, an experience such as that of untouchability. The moral as well as intellectual actions which interrogate the social production of broken men (Ambedkar's expression) will continue to remain broken if they are not attended to with coherent principles. Ambedkar suggests that one has to bring purpose to action by measuring its impact on the capacity of that action to resolve the problem. Truth for Ambedkar is not a given; on the contrary, it has to be attested through the concrete practice of principles, in his case, Buddhist principles. Measuring purpose presupposes the idea that while action may access the truth, it may deviate from it. 'Atta dippo bhava' essentially means moving from truth to truth, through the radical overcoming of self-limits. Overcoming self-limits means being expansive in terms of extending the self into the other through the conception of *maitry*, or unconditional friendship.

On the other hand, the non-Brahman thought which has been influenced by Gandhi defines the exemplar not in terms of its ethical extension into the other, but in terms of the capacity to realise that one's limits are coterminous with the limits of the 'other'. The exemplar in non-Brahman thought, for example of Vithal Ramji Shinde, is self-conscious, not only about its expansive thrust or qualities, but also its self-limiting ethical capacity. Ambedkar, unlike Shinde, does not have the choice to become small. He has been already relegated to the margins, thanks to the caste system, which plays a determinate role in Ambedkar's banishment. Since Ambedkar and the entire Dalit community were banished to their ghettos, they needed to acquire an expansive character, and it is only after this expansion that they can think of limiting their 'self'. These limits would then become coterminous with the other's ethical limits. Modernity becomes one important mediating ethical force which would not allow the other to become too big or seek to become small. So, Ambedkar's withdrawal is contingent upon his becoming big in the first instance.

In the last section of this talk, let me attempt to defend the core argument. I am taking my reference from the Kantian maxim. In the Kantian conception there is no exemplar. A person has to give moral law to himself. This is a scenario of self-legislation, which was an integral part of the Enlightenment project. Ambedkar's approach to the exemplar is dialectical inasmuch as it accommodates the exemplar as the initial condition but not the essential condition. In Babasaheb's emancipatory project, the need for the exemplar appears only as an initial condition. He is convinced that for historical as well as structural reasons, Dalits have to depend on historical figures who stood on the side of normative values which form a constitutive part of the Dalit self. Ambedkar, imbued with the normative desire to protect his dignity, 'manuski', seeks to move away from the dependence on an exemplar in order to become intellectually autonomous through self-determination. Ambedkar does not consider the exemplar as an essential precondition for mobilisation. He, thus, eliminates the possibility of the exemplar by taking recourse to the famous Buddhist principle, 'atta dippo bhava' (be your own guide).

'Atta dippo bhava' can be defined as the autonomous consciousness charged with the self-generated moral and intellectual power to illuminate those who were pushed into, to use Plato's allegory, the 'dark caves'. It is the moral power to gain insight into one's self-discovery.

'Atta dippo bhava', in the Buddhist sense, is a kind of epistemic capacity to intellectually present oneself to oneself. To put this differently, to accept the other's description of the self is to accept the defeat of the self. It is for this reason that Dalits from Maharashtra do not accept the descriptions of the community by either Sir R. D. Bhandarkar or Mahatma Gandhi. Bhandarkar described Mahars as *mruthari* (those who eat the flesh of dead animals). Gandhi, in turn, described the 'Untouchables' as Harijans. 'Atta dippo bhava', on the other hand, can be understood as the capacity for self-determination whose cognitive function is to negate the degraded consciousness of repulsion (Sartre 1988: 23). It also refuses representation by another consciousness, such as S. M. Mate's Brahmanical representation of the 'Untouchables' as *aaspustha*, a Sanskritised version of the word 'untouchable'. More importantly, 'atta dippo bhava' marks the absence of anything concretely given, such as the 'name' Untouchable or the denial of re-description as Dalits or neo-Buddhists. The autonomy to adopt a new description of the self or a reflective re-description is an integral part of this process of self-determination (Khairmode 1985: 194). In this regard, it is worth stating that Dalits consider Gandhi's re-description of their selves as humiliating (*ibid*.: 215).

Ambedkar's adoption of the philosophy of 'atta dippo bhava' is an uncompromising statement about Dalits' right to self-determination, challenging the given descriptions of the 'Untouchables' as broken men. This philosophy as self-determination empowers the broken men to challenge the practice of untouchability that seeks to overdetermine their existence, destroying their human essence.

Accepting 'atta dippo bhava' as a credo of self-illumination would summon, on priority, the most critical questions that Ambedkar raised: Why were the 'Untouchables' reduced to the pathological status of broken men? How long will they remain severed from the human bonds fostered through maitry (friendship)? What is the normative basis which would make the 'Untouchables' an integral part of the larger human connection? 'Atta dippo bhava' enlightens and encourages every single Dalit to take the initiative without waiting for someone else to act. It directly interrogates the intentions of customary caste tormentors with Ambedkar's question, '[I]t may be your interest to be our masters, but how can it be ours to be your slaves?' (Ambedkar 1945: iii). Ambedkar borrowed this formulation from the Greek philosopher Thucydides. Ambedkar's question is a generic question, a question that applies to everybody, and a question that everybody should ask. 'Atta dippo bhava', perceived as the intrinsic capacity of self-determination, comes very close to the Cartesian dictum, 'I think therefore I am,' inasmuch as it rejects the counter-dictum, 'I think therefore you are.' 'Atta dippo bhava' shows a thick familiarity with the Bahujan intellectual traditions represented by Jotirao Phule, and later by V. R. Shinde. Shinde's Marathi dictum suggests the following, 'Aplachy khanduwar aplech doke' (One's head is placed on one's shoulders) (Shinde 1989: 181). In such a tradition of thinking, there is no exemplar, one stands on one's own feet. I am, therefore, at the centre of the canvas, my limits are coterminous with the limits of others. Brahmans, on the other hand, seem to desire a 'bhudeo' exemplar, a self-contained totality.

With 'atta dippo bhava', you do not require floodlights to guide you towards your emancipatory destination. You become the self-illuminating source by internalising the universal principle of emancipation. As Ambedkar says, '[w]e have internalised the principle, hence we do not require an exemplar. We do not submit to anyone's patronage' (Ambedkar 1989: 317).

Let me close this talk, however, with a caveat. One can perceive a problem even in Ambedkar's Buddhist conception of 'atta dippo bhava'. The concept has the potential to render an individual egotistical, a person who can think only of herself and who imagines that she has her destiny in her own hands. There is a possibility that such a person would find herself alone and finally shut herself in to the lonely solitude of her self-illuminating image. Ambedkar provides a normative alternative that is available in another Buddhist conception, that of 'maitry'. For Ambedkar, maitry is an all-encompassing moral value which is encapsulated in the radical ethics of friendship.

Ninth Ambedkar Memorial Lecture, 14 April 2017, Ambedkar University Delhi.

Notes

[1] Subodh More, a prominent Mumbai-based social activist, shared this narrative with me.

[2] The residents of the Ramabai Ambedkar Nagar colony, Mumbai, were fired at by a team of the State Reserve Police Force on 11 July 1997 while they were protesting against the desecration of a statue of Ambedkar. Ten Dalits were killed and 26 got injured. For a better understanding of the tragic narrative, see the powerful documentary *Jai Bhim Comrade* (2011) by Anand Patwardhan.

[3] As is clear from the socio-intellectual history of India, Brahmans regarded themselves the only knowing subjects. Others also treated them as the fountainhead of all knowledge. This construction of the community as a self-referential authority was considered the intellectual virtue of the Brahmans in India. Claims to complete knowledge, without conversation/dialogue with others, implied that others needed to derive their knowledge from Brahmans, a self-contained totality. The bhudeo lacks the quality of self-consciousness as his sense of superiority is rooted in self-referentiality.

[4] An important leader from Maharashtra reportedly asked why the poor and hungry Dalits were demanding that a university be renamed after Ambedkar when they didn't have the resources to feed themselves ('*Ghari nahi pith ani magtat vidypith*'). The jibe was made when Dalits across the country were agitating to rename Marathwada University after Ambedkar. The elevation of Ambedkar by Dalits becomes a necessary provocation for their humiliation. An NRI (non-resident Indian) scholar in Brussels is reported to have contemptuously denied Ambedkar exemplary status.

[5] See the Introduction to Satyanarayana and Tharu (2013).

[6] *Ibid.*

[7] In the essay 'Gandhi's Integrity: The Philosophy behind the Politics', Akeel Bilgrami emphasises the distinction between universality and universalisability. According to him, the idea of universality suggests that 'a moral value, whether or not someone in particular holds it, applies to all persons', whereas universalisability points to how 'if someone in particular holds a moral value, then *he* must think that it applies to all others' (2006: 255).

[8] In the varna system, a child has to go through the sacred thread ceremony (*upanayana sanskaara*) before he can receive education. After the ceremony, the individual is born again in a metaphorical sense. Shudras are not allowed to undergo this ceremony. They are thus denied the distinction of being 'twice-born' (Prasad 2008: 182).

References

Ambedkar, B. R. 1945. *What Congress and Gandhi Have Done to the Untouchables*. New Delhi: Gautam Book Centre.

———. 1979a. *Annihilation of Caste*, in *Dr Babasaheb Ambedkar: Writings and Speeches*, vol. 1, pp. 23–96. Bombay: Education Department, Government of Maharashtra.

———. 1979b. 'Ranade, Gandhi and Jinnah', in *Dr Babasaheb Ambedkar: Writings and Speeches*, vol. 1, pp. 211–40. Bombay: Education Department, Government of Maharashtra.

———. 1989. *Dr Babasaheb Ambedkar: Writings and Speeches*, vol. 5. Bombay: Education Department, Government of Maharashtra.

———. 2005. *Dr. B. R. Ambedkar and His Egalitarian Revolution (Dr Babasaheb Ambedkar: Writings and Speeches*, vol. 17, part I). Bombay: Education Department, Government of Maharashtra.

Bilgrami, Akeel. 2003. 'Gandhi, the Philosopher', *Economic and Political Weekly*, 38(39): 4159–65.

————. 2006. 'Gandhi's Integrity: The Philosophy behind the Politics', in A. Raghurama-raju (ed.), *Debating Gandhi: A Reader*, pp. 248–68. New Delhi: Oxford University Press.

Kamble, Arun (ed.). 1992. *Babasaheb Ambedkaranche Janatatil Agralekh* (Marathi). Mumbai: Popular Prakashan and Mumbai University.

Khairmode, Changdeo. 1985. *Babasaheb Ambedkaranche Charitra*, vol. 6. Pune: Sugava Publication.

Prasad, Rajendra. 2008. *A Conceptual-Analytic Study of Classical Indian Philosophy of Morals* (*History of Science, Philosophy and Culture in Indian Civilization*, gen. ed. D. P. Chattopadhyaya, vol. XII, part 1). New Delhi: Concept Publishing.

Rawls, John. 1971. *A Theory of Justice*. Cambridge, MA: Harvard University Press.

Sartre, Jean-Paul. 1988. *The Transcendence of the Ego*. New York: Routledge.

Satyanarayana, K., and Susie Tharu (eds). 2013. *Steel Nibs Are Sprouting: New Dalit Writing from South India*. New Delhi: HarperCollins.

Shinde, V. R. 1989. *Jivan ani tatyadnyan*. Bombay: Cultural Department, Government of Maharashtra.

Shourie, Arun. 1997. *Worshipping False Gods: Ambedkar, and the Facts Which Have Been Erased*. Delhi: ASA Publications.

Skinner, Quentin. 1969. 'Meaning and Understanding of History of Ideas', *History and Theory*, 8(1): 3–53.

10

The Burdened Life

Ambedkar, Arendt and the Perplexity of Rights

Homi K. Bhabha[1]

For this is your home, my friend, do not be driven from
it; great men have done great things here, and will
again, and we can make America what America
must become. It will be hard, James, but you come
from sturdy, peasant stock, men who picked cotton
and dammed rivers and built railroads, and, in the
teeth of the most terrifying odds, achieved an unassailable
and monumental dignity.
– James Baldwin, *The Fire Next Time* (1993: 10)

'Whose House Is This?'
Whose house is this?
Whose night keeps out the light
In here?
Say, who owns this house?
It's not mine.
I had another sweeter, brighter,
With a view of lakes crossed in painted boats;
Of fields wide as arms open for me.
This house is strange.
Its shadows lie.
Say, tell me,
why does its lock fit my key?
– Toni Morrison, *Home* (2013)

Citizenship and Alterity

Toni Morrison's atonal lyric, with its chromatic wandering between notes, represents the music's reluctance to resolve or to be reconciled to a 'home-note'. The music stalks the lyric with cadences of custom and familiarity, and then its anxious tones and soaring scales fail to provide any sign of return or repose. *This dark house of the nation's history is not mine,* the lyric declares. *It has dispossessed me and discriminated against me; it has unhomed my history and darkened my presence. I am untouchable, I am enslaved, I am trafficked, I am lynched. This house is strange. . . . And yet, Say, tell me, why does its lock fit my key?*

In 2006, Toni Morrison developed this double-toned theme of the nation's home strangely turning into an unrecognisable 'homeland'. At the Louvre, Morrison staged a multi-media project titled *The Foreigner's Home*. On that occasion, she extended the vision of her lyric to address the international condition of migration and displacement.

> *Who is the foreigner?* is a question that leads us to the perception of an implicit and heightened threat within 'difference'. We see it in the defense of the local against the outsider: personal discomfort with one's own sense of belonging. *Am I the foreigner in my own home?*[2]

I have chosen to begin my lecture today with Morrison's question *'Am I the foreigner in my own home?'* – a sentiment that could easily be misunderstood and wilfully misused by those who espouse the persecutory politics of ethno-nationalism. Morrison wilfully places herself alongside the 'foreigner' or the migrant in order to contest the violence mobilised by populists against the 'other' on the grounds of ethnicity and race (African-Americans, Kurds, Rohingyas, etc.), caste (Dalits), belief (Muslims, Jews, etc.), political status (minorities, undocumented, *sans papiers*, migrants, refugees). There is a kind of poetic justice in Morrison's role reversal as she interrogates her own American citizenship from the perspective of the alienage of the African-American subject. *'Am I the foreigner in my own home?'* sunders the concept of the nation's people, pitting the cause of the subaltern subject against the claims of the sovereign citizen. The link between territory and belonging is now effectively broken, and it is from this breach that the poet speaks. Morrison recognises the country as the memory of her homeland – *'With a view of lakes crossed in painted boats'* – as if to say, this land is my land and the natural landscape belongs to me, as I to it. In the same breath, she feels alienated from the nation's *Heim*, which is a strange house that is *not* mine, and I am *not* an integral part of its imagined community.

Such a double consciousness is an instance of citizenship's alterity, not merely a default or deficit of sovereignty in the citizen's formal standing. *Alteritas* or Otherness, Hannah Arendt writes, is the fundamental gesture of human consciousness caught in the midst of the world's plurality. Alterity is an ontological awareness of 'a difference [that] is inserted in my Oneness' (Arendt 1978: 183); and the difference inserted in the oneness of citizenship creates a cleft subject caught in-between agonistic self-identification and ambivalent civic recognition. When confronted by institutional forces of inequity – legal or governmental – and the systemic pressures of prejudice – policy and police – ontological alterity has to be translated into the alterity of political and ethical agency. The cutting edge of agency develops its power and profile through its engagement with the steel of unrelenting hegemonic power. *This house is strange:* my memory of belonging is agonistically pitted against the anxiety of displacement; my *amor patria* is at war with the hate that disempowers me. *Am I the foreigner in my own home:* as a discriminated minority, am I not ambivalently placed in the national community? Am I not, at once, positioned *within* its legal jurisdiction and *without* its civic dignity?

Morrison's lyric has its counterpart in an imaginary dialogue staged by W. E. B. Du Bois to dramatise the dark dilemma of 'partial citizens'. Discriminated minorities are entitled to formal rights which are undermined by everyday customs of exclusion and humiliation. Although the social geography of discrimination tends to be spatial – margins, peripheries, borders, ghettoes, police cordons – migrants and minorities are also trapped in temporal envelopes of vigilant uncertainty and anguished vulnerability. Time inflicts injuries of exclusion that are no less severe than the prejudices of place. When a pale friend ironically inquires of Du Bois whether he can seriously claim to be discriminated against *every day*, this is what he has to say:

> Not all each day, – surely not. But now and then – now seldom, now, sudden; now after a week, now in a chain of awful minutes; not everywhere, but anywhere – in Boston, in Atlanta. That's the hell of it. . . . blows that are not always but ever; not each day, but each week, each month, each year. (Du Bois 1999: 131)

Morrison and Du Bois, in their different ways, ask the same question: *Am I the foreigner in my own home?* The domestic colour line that marks the boundaries of American discrimination and segregation echoes the politics and polities of exclusion elsewhere in the world. The title of one of Dr Ambedkar's seminal works, *Untouchables, or the Children of India's Ghetto* (1989), says as much. Ambedkar's severe indictment of the caste-rule of the Hindu state passionately convenes persecuted Indian

Dalits in community with African-Americans and Jews – all of them peoples consigned to ghettos. In its critique of the concept of citizenship, alterity reveals the contradictions and disavowals inherent in the concept of 'dignity' as the moral ground of the citizen's 'standing'.

Dignity and respect endow the subject with standing; and it is standing that empowers the citizen's role as agent. In his important essay 'Citizenship and Dignity', Jeremy Waldron drives the point home:

> By and large, those subject to state power are not to be treated as mere subjects, but as active and empowered members of the political community for which the state is responsible. . . . This equality of concern and respect goes far beyond the dignity of citizenship in the narrow sense. (Waldron 2014: 334–35)

In a broader sense, the aura of dignity reaches beyond constitutional rights to transform the ordinary subject from a state of 'abject vulnerability' to the elevated status of dignity with standing. 'To dignify the status of citizen we tell ourselves stories about the social contract,' Waldron continues. 'We are dealing with a fiction, but the fiction may be the best way of tracing the contours of respect that we think are required. The strategy here is a version of the Kantian hypothetical contractarianism' (*ibid.*: 341).

Alterity shifts our understanding of the mythic grounds of the citizen's standing. Dignity's auratic quality, Waldron proposes, transforms the ordinary subject from abject vulnerability to empowered citizen by 'according her [the citizen] the respect that would be due to one of the framers of the country's legal and constitutional arrangements' (Waldron 2014: 341). How, then, does this fiction work its mythic magic? How does the aura of dignity create a character worthy of playing the role of the citizen? These questions are as important for law and politics as they are pertinent to the study of narrative. The empowering fiction of entitlement is achieved by establishing the ubiquitous visibility of the citizen's *presentness* in historical time and public discourse. As a narrative form, then, dignity is not only a moral quality attributed to the citizen's person ensuring her rights and respect; dignity is, equally, a fabrication of historical time as it attaches to the citizen's *persona* rather than to her particular person. And an elevated *persona of dignity* is a symbolic representation of public personhood – a surrogate for the subject – even as it dignifies the citizen's individual presence. Indeed, the persona of dignity – the aura of dignity in Waldron's phrase – masks the abject vulnerability of the empirical, singular citizen in an atemporal norm of universal human value enshrined prominently in discourses of human rights.

The contours of civic dignity (Waldron's phrase) are inscribed in serial, homogenous temporalities that trace the unbroken identity of the citizen from the founding framers to the contemporary citizen. The 'timeless' link that proposes a linear progression between the nation's origin and the citizen's identity shields the subject from her 'abject vulnerability', compensates for her 'modicum of protection', and obscures her 'microscopic quantum of political power' (Waldron 2014: 341). Alterity disturbs the citizen's aura and reveals the abject vulnerabilities hidden beneath the contours of dignity. Sovereignty's 'other' members – minorities, migrants, the rightless or stateless – can no longer be relegated to the shadowy half-life of citizenship. Deprived of rights and respect, they are no 'ordinary citizens'; subjected to fragmented times and prejudicial places ('not always but ever'), they can claim no mythic lineage to the framers of the constitution. So much is true. However, alterity makes possible other ways of thinking about the rights of belonging and the wrongs of sovereign citizenship. The interrupted injuries of time and place – *not everywhere, but anywhere* – gives presence to a subaltern subject whose agency is belated and iterative. You can hear the belated agency of record and retrieval in Morrison's lyric protagonist. She is the foreigner in her own home who *returns* to take possession as best she can – of herself, her home, her lifeworld – in temporal conditions of affective ambivalence and ethical risk. The risk lies in taking political action – and, indeed, making the poem – in the teeth of abject vulnerability, by putting the key in the door and entering the strange house of history's horror and poetry's hope:

> This house is strange.
> Its shadows lie.
> Say, tell me,
> why does its lock fit my key?

The paradoxes of public standing, at the heart of the perspective of alterity, tarnish dignity's aura and disrupt the fiction of the living link between the founding fathers and contemporary citizens. Such a sundering of the temporal narrative of seamless succession creates a significant shift in the grounds of dignity and the time of agency. If the Kantian mould of dignity shapes a morality of inherence and natality (exemplified, for instance, by the Universal Declaration of Human Rights [UDHR]), then the dignity of risk emerges in the very midst of the perils of mortality and fatality with which minorities and migrants struggle to make their presence felt and their voices heard in the civic *habitus* (beyond the voting booth). The dignity of risk is often seen to lack respect, and indeed to be disrespectful of the civic order of things and disruptive of the powers that be.

This is a narrow, negative view of the dignity of risk that does not take into account the distinctive ambivalent agency that informs the alterity of citizenship. What is routinely disavowed or suppressed, in the name of the respectful aura of dignity, is the compelling case to be made for a dignity of risk that afflicts citizens who are abjectly vulnerable, or political subjects *in extremis*: the stateless and rightless, those who are victims of distress migration, or hostages to discrimination and harassment at the hands of the surveillant state. Citizens in states of alterity, I have argued, are purposeful, performative subjects whose speech and action are as affective as they are deliberative although their life-threatening (or life-enhancing) decisions and judgements have to be made in split seconds or in jagged temporalities that mark time in history's calendar of oppressions: 'now seldom, now, sudden; now after a week, now in a chain of awful minutes; not everywhere, but anywhere.'

In the 'teeth of the most terrifying odds', James Baldwin writes, is 'achieved an unassailable and monumental dignity' (1993: 10). Freeing oneself, or giving others their freedom, I believe, is only possible by putting oneself at risk – taking an ethical risk – in the cause of the emancipation of the other – the neighbour – who is also at risk. It is in this spirit that Baldwin continues: 'One can give nothing whatever without giving oneself – that is to say, risking oneself. If one cannot risk oneself, then one is simply incapable of giving. And, after all, one can give freedom only by setting someone free' (*ibid.*: 86).

If the aura of citizenship is a kind of fiction, a smoke-and-mirrors mode of 'dignification' (if I might be allowed to graft dignity with legitimation), then how do we recognise the place of the living dead amongst us when the smoke-machine splutters and the mythic mirrors crack?

The Rubbish Dumps of Zarzis

Zarzis, a town on the south-eastern coast of Tunisia, is known for its thriving fishing industry and its prodigious olive production. Zarzis has, in the last decade, become a beachhead for beleaguered refugees from Africa, Asia and the Middle East. Syrians, Eritreans, Libyans, Ethiopians, Bangladeshis, and Afghanis head for Zarzis in their attempts to reach Tunisia's long Mediterranean coast. Refugees (like migrants more generally) soon lose their singular identities to the sovereign denomination of legal status and political designation. Migrants and refugees are ironically named after the very nations that have driven them into the wilderness and rendered them rightless: Syrian refugees, Eritrean refugees, Bangladeshi refugees. Names lost in life are anonymous in death. To identify corpses retrieved from the sea or the shore on the evidence of DNA is an expense the Tunisian state does everything to avoid. Death's dominion, however, waits for no one. The stench of decaying 'foreign' bodies hangs heavy in the air, and the citizens of Zarzis create a *cordon sanitaire* around the polluting presence of refugees, dead or alive, to protect the protesting citizens of Zarzis.

Fisherfolk refuse to cast their nets in waters they believe to be polluted. The people of Zarzis refuse to admit foreign corpses into local morgues because their very existence defiles the sacred deaths of local families. Underfunded municipal authorities, unqualified for the task, dump the bodies on waste ground outside the town limits. 'A sense of fear and revulsion surrounds the whole process,' a local journalist observes. 'If they are brought to the hospital, the smell and fear of disease angers local citizens. They do not want the bodies buried in the town's cemeteries' (Reidy 2015a). The cemeteries for refugees in Zarzis are open mounds of earth piled high with garbage; they are, indeed, the town's garbage dumps. 'Without access to an ambulance, or storage, or a recognized place to bury them', a local activist explains, 'the corpses are dumped into a municipal garbage truck and taken directly to a plot of unused land about five miles outside of Zarzis, designated as a burial ground by the local authorities' (*ibid.*). Steve Saint Amour, a deep-water search and recovery expert in Zarzis, draws the unforgiving conclusion: 'You only have stateless people. . . . Which country has a national interest to find out what happened?' (Reidy 2015b).

Hauling migrant bodies out of the water like shoals of dead and decaying fish – 70 corpses in Zarzis between June and July 2014 – makes Saint Amour despair. Attending to the stateless, day after day – the naked and the dead – echoes Hannah Arendt's unforgettable description of the stateless in inter-war Europe: 'the abstract nakedness of being nothing but human was their greatest danger' (Arendt 1973: 297). For Arendt, rightless people are, as she says, those who are 'expelled from the "human condition" and thrown back into the peculiar state of nature' (*ibid.*: 300); and for the migrants and refugees in Zarzis, we might say, they are thrown back into the Mediterranean or cast out on the rubbish dumps. At a rough count, there have been over 22,500 migrant drownings since 2014.

Mohamed Trabelsi of the Tunisian Red Crescent will not give in to Saint Amour's sense of agitated resignation. The harsh sentence on statelessness, delivered by national neglect, cannot be allowed to have the last word. Outraged by the *rigor mortis* relegated to the dumps of Zarzis – death as a kind of detritus – Trabelsi is provoked to speak of the dead as though they are still alive, deserving not only of proper burial rites, but the dignity of human rights: 'For me, these corpses are people who have human rights. They should be treated with respect. After all, we never know how our lives can change at some point and we can become those people' (Reidy 2015a).

At first sight, Trabelsi's statement seems to refer to respect for the dead: every corpse should be respectfully laid to rest, and every individual identified before being interred. However, the counterfactual claim made in the present imperative – 'For me, these corpses are people who have human rights' – shifts the conversation from burial rites to human rights. In what sense are corpses people who have the rights to have rights? It is clear that Trabelsi is not speaking as a political theorist or a legal philosopher, but the ethical passion that spurs his figurative language should be carefully heard.

Our respect for 'these dead people' acknowledges the sympathy we feel for the tragedy of wasteful and wanton deaths – casualties of civil wars and terrorist states, victims of Euro-American imperial interventions, targets of tribal-nationalist xenophobia, bought and sold by smugglers, incarcerated in detention camps, embroiled in an overwhelmed and incapacitated international refugee system. Trabelsi's figures of speech – *corpses are people who have human rights* – turn the life and loss of the stateless into real presences, or better still, surreal presences: 'surreal' in the sense invoked by Walter Benjamin as the aesthetic sign that marks the historian's rude awakening to the *'now* of recognisability in which things put on their true – surrealist – face' (Benjamin 1999: 464). 'In maritime legal black holes', the legal scholar Itamar Mann has written, 'killing typically occurs while all involved actors express their dismay, their shame, and indeed their horror – but can avoid extending their help' (Mann 2017: 29). Statistical data, like the 1,200 adults and children who drowned in the Mediterranean in a 'black week' in April 2015, turn corpses into cyphers that numb the nerves.

Refugee corpses, raised from their *rigor mortis* by Trabelsi's moral imagination, become spectres of an ethical agency that foreshadows the precarious history of the present. These corpses do not only signify the haunting past of refugee drownings. Moving beyond horror and empathy, Trabelsi proposes a more agonistic, if ambiguous, ethical form of identification based not only on the exigencies of the present but on the contingencies of a future conditional: 'After all, we never know how our lives can change at some point and we can become those people.' The 'we' that signifies the shared community of rights and the political solidarity of the human condition is itself in a state of alterity. At one moment, 'we' represents the universal subject of natural rights that establishes an inclusive, timeless identity between 'we', the living, and 'those people', the refugee corpses. This moral equivalence, inherent in the discourse of human rights, is underscored by another 'we' that is less ontological (and universal) and more agential (historically contingent). This is the 'we' that represents the ethical agency of citizenship *in extremis*, and demands a form of 'distress' identification (in keeping with 'distress migration') with those who are stateless or rightless.

Such a mode of identification is founded on a subject caught in a proleptic temporality – a future conditional – in which the citizen-subject is moved by an affective empathy with the 'other' premised on a radical internal 'unknowability' – 'we *never know* how our lives can change at some point. . . .' A proleptic temporality prefigures or foreshadows the narration of an event at a point earlier than its chronological place in a story.[3] Figuratively, it ushers the future into our presence in order to bear witness to the moral choices we make in the present. Ironically, proleptic thinking intensifies the importance of the necessity of political punctuality: '*For me, these corpses are people who have human rights.*' It is the very opposite of deferral or irresponsibility; it emphasises the dire necessity of taking imminent action *in the present* (in the interest of an-other) through an ethical enlargement brought about by the alterity of being and time – an expansion of the rights and representation of Others by inserting a difference into the Oneness of citizenship, to echo Arendt's deft formulation of alterity which serves as the groundnote of her critical concept of 'the right to have rights'.

The 'future conditional' is, I grant, an unfamiliar way of thinking of how we conceive of the *timeliness* of our ethical commitments and our political actions. It is also an unusual way of talking about the temporality of rights which are traditionally considered to be either embodied in the inherent status of the human being (the moral value of dignity), or projected into an aspirational 'future perfect' which is most commonly heard in the phrase 'Never Again'. The future conditional is in tension with each one although it is in conversation with both. The alterity of the citizen-subject unsettles the inherence of rights while recognising the need for the 'we' of recognition and identification; and the proleptic agent, displaced into the ethical domain of the future conditional, acknowledges the importance of aspiration even as she returns anachronistically into the present – from the time lag of the future conditional – in order to act *just* in time. Indeed, to do justice to the cause of the Other in a time that is not yours, and a place that is the foreigner's home, is the ethic of hospitality to which the future conditional aspires.

Trabelsi's claim for the rights of and respect for dead refugees exceeds the 'moral intuitionism' that underscores the concept of universal human values enacted in the UDHR. Moral intuitionism – the grounds of dignity in the discourse of human rights – proposes that 'people everywhere have a moral sense or faculty … that gives them unaided access to basic truths of morality' (Morsink 1999: 37). Moral intuitionism was introduced to condemn the barbarism of the Third Reich and to rebut claims to historical or moral relativism in the drafting and intent of the UDHR. Moral intuitionism often results in a benevolent moral equivalence – 'they are human beings just like ourselves, *and there, but for the grace of god, go I*' – and it is this ahistorical and 'unaided access' to human identity and empathy on the grounds of similitude that Trabelsi avoids. I construe his claim as saying: 'We' – the international community, the individual bystander, the attendant media, the political activist – have to first confront the violence implicit in this differential co-existence that defines the dissensus of our contradictory and yet proximate political proximity: 'a paradoxical world that puts together two separate worlds', 'mak[ing] visible that which had no reason to be seen' (Rancière 2010: 39, 38).

Trabelsi's demand is, indeed, a paradoxical thing. On the surface he seems to echo the norms of moral intuitionism – the unaided moral sense that ensures universal rights for all human persons. At another level, there is an elliptical argument stirring from the sidelines of his statement which resonates with Rancière's concept of political dissensus. A paradoxical world that puts together separate worlds – the surviving citizen, the drowned refugee, the migrant on the move – discloses something that can only be seen, and known, through an ironic and displaced double vision. In Trabelsi's case, figurative language is best able to convey an elusive ethical and political message 'that had no reason to be seen'. What gains visibility *now*, in the imminence of the present moment, is the future conditional that mediates the *political rights* of citizen and migrant, and the *human fate* of the drowned and the saved.

All Europe contributed to the making of Kurtz, Joseph Conrad once said of African genocide in the *Heart of Darkness*; much the same, on a global scale, may be said of the migration crisis in these dark times of neoliberal hegemony and majoritarian xenophobia. More than the universality of moral intuitionism, Trabelsi seems to be saying, we need to cultivate a sense of historical alterity. Trabelsi's claim for the rights and respect for migrants *in extremis* is a speech-act in the future conditional to intensify the moral agency and urgency *within* our own times: 'After all, we never know how our lives can change at some point and we can become those people.' 'Say, who owns this house? / Its shadows lie.'

At some point, in the unknowable future, our rights to citizenship may (or may not) become so worthless and compromised as to render us unprotected, vulnerable and homeless: minorities in our own homeland or refugees adrift in someone else's. *There is no knowing.* And since we cannot know at what point we may be in the place of the 'other', it is this very indeterminacy of time and intention (not its universality) that makes our ethical commitments historically 'principled', precisely because they are non-contractual, non-instrumental, non-dogmatic.

Ethical principles that pivot on the 'future conditional' do not neglect long-standing structural social injustices and power asymmetries that belong to the long past: they only intensify their necessity and visibility. If there are echoes of the ontological ethics of Emmanuel Levinas in my more politically driven thoughts, it is due to his insistence that the 'rights of man' must question their Eurocentric privilege and their Enlightenment prejudice in order to elaborate what he describes as a 'new development of the rights of man' (Levinas 1993: 121) with respect to the global South, 'threatened by disease, hunger . . . the development of destructive armaments, and the abusive manipulation of societies and souls' (*ibid.*). In a stirring sentence that could have been spoken amidst the dead strangers in Zarzis, Levinas writes, 'men may [ethically] seek one another in [the] [in]condition [unconditionality] of strangers' (2006: 66). The lives of strangers, whether they are national minorities or international migrants, are claimants to 'the defense of the rights of man [which] correspond to a vocation outside the state' (Levinas 1993: 123): a kind of extraterritoriality within a political society 'that upholds justice in its limitations' (*ibid.*) or law at its limits.

If my argument sounds somewhat theoretically abstruse, it is because I believe that legality and ethicality are joined in their purpose, and their articulation cannot simply be left to specialists and professionals. By turning a blind eye to Levinas's 'extraterritorial' ethical spaces that uphold justice at its limits, we create legal black holes, and as the migration lawyer Itamar Mann argues, 'whether pushed to sea by the increasingly violent condition in [Syria, Libya, Burma, Eritrea, or Iraq], or "pulled" by the hope of being saved, the operation [sees] a continued swell in migrant departures – and continued deaths at sea' (Mann 2017: 9–10). 'States [then] seek to leave migrants beyond the scope of their legal duties under constitutional and/or international law' (*ibid.*: 7). The corpses of Zarzis represent one person in every 113 living in the world today; 65.3 million people constituting the largest mobile territory in the world today (UNHCR 2016). This is a population on the move, in detention, or waiting for asylum or visas on a scale that makes them inhabitants of the 21st largest country in the world, even if they have failed to become citizens of any nation. 'The pertinent underlying problem is displacement,' write Alexander Betts and Paul Collier of the Oxford Refugee Project. 'Global refugee numbers are

at their highest since the early 1990s . . . the highest figure ever recorded'
(Collier and Betts 2017: 15).

Abu Jana, a Syrian refugee on his way to Sweden, speaks:
'Right now Syrians consider themselves dead. Maybe not physically but
psychologically and socially' (Kingsley and Diab 2015). 'If the chance of
making it to Europe [across the Mediterranean] is even one percent, then
that means there is a one-percent chance of your leading an actual life'
(Schmidle 2015). Nizam, from Iraq:

> In a paradoxical mixture of fearlessness and paranoia, anxiety about
> what's to come, but the simultaneous confidence that it's hardly worse
> than what's come before . . . Nizam is running through possible
> scenarios in his head; making a run for it; getting caught; having to
> try again. But he also remembers what he is running from in the first
> place. Compulsory conscription. The advance of Isis. . . . The experience
> of wandering, with no let-out clause, through a wild and unknown
> continent . . . increasingly defined by radicalism at both ends of the
> spectrum, the dwindling of solidarity between European states, and the
> scapegoating of refugees and persecuted minorities – starts to mirror
> that of the 1930s. (Kingsley 2017: 221–23)

To hold on to the human right of 'dignity' *in extremis* – to struggle
for the right to movement, the right to life and the right to security, because
we never know how our lives can change – is to enter that precarious
territoriality where the jurisdiction of international justice is pushed to its
limits. A limit first noticed in the drafting of Article 13 of the UDHR on
the right to movement, during which delegates were consistently worried
about the right to move between countries. Trabelsi, Abu Jana and Nizam
bear witness to a perilous condition described in the early 1930s as the
crime of transnational barbarity by the Polish jurist Raphael Lemkin,
who would go on to draft the Genocide Convention in 1948. Acts of
barbarity attack dignity and cause humiliation which, when taken together,
Lemkin writes, 'bring harm not only to human rights, but also and most
especially [undermine] the fundamental basis of the social order' (Lemkin
1933). With a prescience relevant to ethnic cleansing, racial violence,
cultural destruction, and the migration crises of our own times, Lemkin
defines barbarity as a process of transnational contagion directed against
collectivities: 'similar to epidemics, they can pass from one country to
another . . .. Indeed, acts of barbarity . . . often cause the emigration or
the disorganized flight of the population of one State to another' (*ibid.*).

Disrupted time and disorganised flight are matters of life and
death for both Abu Jana and Nizam. Trabelsi, citizen of Tunisia, has

stared into the 'black hole' of the burial dump of the stateless in Zarzis and seen for himself what lawyers know only too well: 'without jurisdiction there are no human rights applicable and hence no duties' (Besson 2012: 867). 'These migrants are losing their lives due to jurisdictional rules, and therefore can reasonably be described as rightless' (Mann 2017: 14). In demanding the rights of the dead as if they are people amongst us now, Trabelsi only emphasises this larger legal-ethical issue that pertains to the living, to survivors. Like Giacometti's haunted walking figures, these corpses are still in themselves, but they move us forward in thought, as we rise to meet their truths in a frozen right to movement. Trabelsi is now burdened by what I have proposed as the ethics of alterity. The 'future conditional' – 'we can never know at what point we will become these people' – has crept up on him *now and here*. In what circumstances can the 'citizen' also be a 'refugee'?

Outside the Fold

Santu, who lives in a village in Maharashtra, has a problem with his worn, wet chappals. His feet keep slipping out of the slimy leather thongs and threaten to give way. The road is treacherous, and it's hard to get a firm foothold. As Santu makes his way, losing his balance repeatedly – tripping, falling – he finds it difficult to pursue a forward path or to get a toehold in the slippery soil. It feels as if the very ground on which he stands is trying to trip him up; the earth itself wants to throw him off its back. Santu's sense of himself is dark and dead. Like for Abu Jana, the Syrian refugee, free thought and free movement are extinguished:

> Was it not a feat of trying to keep his balance, standing in the mire of slimy customs . . . the tenuous fold of casteism would hem in his mind, but it would still struggle to break out. He slipped on a rock in the path and his wet chappal snapped. . . . Cursing he walked on, barefoot. . . . My name itself is a curse. (Dolas 2009: 217)

'The Refugee', a short story by the celebrated Marathi Dalit writer Avinash Dolas, is set in a Mahar village, similar to what Ambedkar calls 'the Indian ghetto', the black hole of the Republic. Ambedkar writes:

> The republic is an Empire of the Hindus over the Untouchables. It is a kind of colonialism of the Hindus designed to exploit the Untouchables. The Untouchables have no rights. They are there only to wait, serve and submit. They are there to do or to die. They have no rights because they are outside the village republic and because they are outside the so-called village republic, they are outside the Hindu fold. This is a

vicious circle. But this is a fact which cannot be gainsaid. (Ambedkar 1989: 26)

The Untouchable is the 'colonised citizen', or what Ambedkar elsewhere names the 'half-fledged citizen' (*ibid.*: 76) living 'outside the fold' (*ibid.*: 19); Ambedkar's African-American correspondent W. E. B. Du Bois considers segregated minorities to be partial citizens who dwell in the great veil of the colour line that cuts across what he calls the quasi-colonial world (Du Bois 1985: 195–97); and, finally, this iterative, itinerant figure – half-fledged-partial-quasi-citizen – reappears as 'the internal emigrant' in Adrienne Rich's remarkable anti-war, anti-nationalist lyric, 'An Atlas of the Difficult World':

> . . . a citizen trying to wake
> from the burnt-out dream of innocence . . .
> to remember . . .
> that blessing and cursing are born as twins and separated at birth
> to meet again in mourning
> that the internal emigrant is the most homesick of all
> women and of all men
> that every flag that flies today is a cry of pain.
> Where are we moored?
> Where are the bindings?
> What behooves us? (Rich 1991: 23)

Santu is untouchability's 'colonised citizen'; he is also the Mahar village's 'internal emigrant'; and he is unmoored and has lost his bindings: 'Go away from here, my son' (Dolas 2009: 216) is the first searing line of the story, as Santu's mother banishes him from the family fold for having struggled against the stranglehold of caste injury and its prejudicial laws. The worst of it, Ambedkar writes, is 'isolation and exclusiveness . . . not out of routine but out of faith' (Ambedkar 2009: 185). Abu Jana's words reverberate in Santu's sense of his own corpse-like, immobile condition, constrained in thought and action. 'Right now Syrians consider themselves dead. Maybe not physically but psychologically and socially.' A *rigor mortis* also settles upon Santu's *imago* of his own persona, assembled from prosthetic parts, dead limbs, his dog-like life.

> Like a piece of iron sought by someone for no particular purpose, heated, hammered, pounded flat at will – *that's what he was* – iron at first inflamed, then enduring blow after blow of the hammer, till finally one day it snapped. (Dolas 2009: 216)

As Dolas cleverly uses 'body parts' to signify the bio-politics of untouchability, Santu's sense of himself as an agent of liberty and liberation is pitted against what Antonio Gramsci once described as the 'tidal wave' of hegemonic power that renders subaltern agency 'chaotic, formless, extempore' (Gramsci 1971: 111). Santu's precarious water-logged chappals, losing their balance in the slimy grounds of the segregated village, create a destiny that is, in part, chaotic, formless and extempore. Dolas externalises the somatic dialectics of the caste system as it passes through the body in violent amputations and prosthetic displacements: the Untouchable as a dog, or a piece of molten iron, or a body branded with the merciless insignias of caste gradations. Ambedkar is only too aware of the role played by the political unconscious in the un-making of citizenship.

> To tell an Untouchable 'you are free, you are a citizen, you have all the rights of a citizen', and to tighten the rope in such a way as to leave him no opportunity to realise the ideal is a cruel deception. It is enslavement without making the Untouchables conscious of their enslavement. It is slavery though it is untouchability. It is real though it is indirect. It is enduring because it is unconscious. (Ambedkar 1989: 15)

Dolas's depiction of the Untouchable body as a prosthetic of the victim of caste power – 'a broken man' in Ambedkar's phrase – exposes the empty ideal of citizenship held out to the half-fledged citizen who is impeded at every step – in every mode of speech and action – from achieving the agency or dignity of citizenly 'standing'. Dolas passionately paints the picture: 'Was it not a feat of trying to keep his balance, standing in the mire of slimy customs. . . . Cursing, he walked on, barefoot.' Directionless in his dilemma, North, South, East, West all seem equally discriminatory and disorienting. Santu decides to flee, like a refugee, to Bombay. And it is on the train to Bombay, when Santu meets Surji, a refugee from Bangladesh, that he enters the temporal realm of ethical alterity, as I have defined it: *After all, we never know how our lives can change at some point and we can become those people.*

The unbearable contradictions of the citizen-cum-Untouchable are revealed through a glass darkly, and Dolas reveals Santu's paradoxical status as citizen-refugee:

> Bangla Desh – massacre – refugees. A whole series of scenes passed before his eyes. A man leaves Bangla Desh to see his relations in Bombay. . . . And here I am, a citizen of this country! . . . I argued, I protested, for my rights. But my own mother finally told me, My son go away from here! . . . The whole scene came alive again before his eyes. On one side

there was Bangla Desh in turmoil, and on the other, the community of Mahars in Agony. One homeless Bangladeshi refugee was going back to his relatives after twenty years. And one Mahar, even after twenty years was homeless in his own country. (Dolas 2009: 220)

As this comity of the homeless develops between lost refugee and fleeing citizen, on the train to Bombay – associated no doubt with the *Train to Pakistan* and other migrant and refugee transports – a theoretical scene passes before my eyes. A scene conjured up by Partha Chatterjee in his exposition of 'political society' in *The Politics of the Governed*. The direction of my argument today finds common ground with the comity of 'political society'. 'Refugees, landless people, day labourers, homestead, below the poverty line – are all demographic categories of the governmentality [of political society],' Chatterjee writes (2006: 59). And then his informant from Rail Colony Gate Number One takes on the story. 'We have somehow built a shelter of our own. If . . . we are evicted from the shanties, we have nowhere to go' (*ibid.*). And that is what is reflected in Dolas's double mirror: Refugee and Untouchable, by no means political or moral equivalents, are related through alterity; and alterity, as Hannah Arendt once cleverly said, is the political recognition of the 'difference [that] is inserted in my Oneness'. Citizen/Refugee.

The dilemma of the 'moving home' has haunted the lives and laws of refugees, minorities and migrants, national and international. Think, for a moment, of the poignancy of the artist Zarina Hashmi's multiples of homes-on-wheels (spectres of the escape from Aligarh), or the pained poetry of her void floor plans marking her own itineraries of exile and isolation. The primary purpose of Article 13 of the UDHR which deals with 'the right to movement' – national and international – was minoritarian in intent: 'the prevention of discrimination on grounds of race, color, where people might live and how they might move from place to place' (quoted in Morsink 1999: 14). However, there remained a serious worry about the status of the international right to move between countries.

Despite opposition in the third session of the drafting process, Rama Mehta, the Indian delegate, resisted writing any limits into the article on the grounds that the right to movement, she submitted, 'aimed at establishing the principle of freedom of movement, which like freedom of speech, freedom of meeting etc. was a fundamental human right'.[4] Mehta's insight lies in the vital link she makes between the right to the freedom of movement and its intimate and integral connection to the very idea of freedoms or the thought of liberty itself. Freedoms of movement, expression and association are all embodied affective practices, embedded in enunciation-as-action, and aimed at contextual and relational (rather than individual) freedoms. And the right to movement as the matrix of the agency of freedom is, I believe, the foundation of Hannah Arendt's advocacy for minorities and the stateless, forcefully argued in her celebrated Lessing Lecture:

> Of all the specific liberties which may come into our minds when we hear the word 'freedom', freedom of movement is historically the oldest and also the most elementary. Being able to depart for where we will is the prototypical gesture of being free, as limitation of freedom of movement has from time immemorial been the precondition for enslavement. Freedom of movement is also the indispensable condition for action, and it is in action that men primarily experience freedom in the world. . . . both action and thought occur in the form of movement and . . . therefore, freedom underlies both: freedom of movement. (Arendt 1993)

Think back to Nizam's testimony: the freedom of movement is his vehicle for formulating the very thought of the freedom of action as he runs through various paradoxical and anxious scenarios of liberty and security in his head: 'making a run for it; getting caught; having to try again . . . remembering what he is running from in the first place. Compulsory conscription'. Remember the leitmotif in Dolas's 'Refugee'. It is Santu's shackled and slippery chappals that serve as a symbol of the insecurity and oppression of the Untouchables in the Hindu village. Standing in the mire of slimy 'caste' customs, he loses his balance as he attempts to exercise a right of movement and expression that is met with upper-caste violence and arson. It is when the chappals break that he throws them off and begins to stand on his feet, so to speak. And in realising his right to movement, he sets off on his allegorical journey of anomie that is also, paradoxically, his political quest for liberty. As the train moves, the Indian citizen is brought face to face with the Bangladeshi refugee. They have paid the price of the freedom of movement – homelessness – but what they stand to gain is the difficult and conflicted fate of 'political society'. And yet, in the words of Chatterjee's informant, 'We have somehow built a shelter of our own. If . . . we are evicted . . . we have nowhere to go.'

Security, human security in the fullest sense – not global surveillance, which has made us more unsafe than ever – is the very ground of dignity, and not the other way around as the UDHR would propose. I have attempted to devise a way of understanding rights and respect that begins with death – 'Maybe not physically but psychologically and socially', as Abu Jana puts it – in contrast to the norm of dignity in the UDHR which is founded on the concept of 'birth' – both physical and ethical. In his magnum opus on the UDHR, Johannes Morsink says as much:

> Most delegates understood that the claim that people 'are born free and equal in dignity and rights' was in no way meant to deny that gross inequalities existed everywhere. On the contrary, against the background of those inequalities they wanted to assert the rights that were inherent in the human person. For them, the word 'born' did just that. Adbul Kayaly, the delegate from Syria, for instance, wanted to retain the word 'born' 'as it would exclude the idea of hereditary slavery'. Defending the first sentence of Article 1, Grumbach of France said it 'meant that the right to freedom and equality was inherent from the moment of birth'. (Morsink 1999: 293)

For Ambedkar, dignity is a difficult word, often with a negative connotation. Dignity is the norm for the protection and preservation of caste privilege. Dignity destroys the self-respect of the Untouchable community of the 'colonised citizens' in Ambedkar's usage. I have argued for the importance of recognising that the very idea of 'freedom' is grounded in the 'right to movement', and so I welcome Ambedkar's belief that caste-inflected 'dignity' keeps untouchability in its place and is profoundly opposed to the freedom of movement. It is a place of inscribed immobility that is also a place of caste carcerality, a kind of imprisonment of body and mind.

Despite its negative imprint, Ambedkar didn't quite give up on dignity, in my view. Dignity for him, as for Arendt, was not what you were born with; dignity was how you learned to bear the burden of disrespect and dehumanisation and still take that 1 per cent chance to survive in the Mediterranean; or to run across the undergrowth to cross a barbed wire tunnel to cross a frontier in Europe; or to throw away your chappals in a Mahar village and walk barefoot for the first time. Dignity *in extremis*.

Dignity *in extremis*, Ambedkar suggests, is to be found in a kind of ethical 'extraterritoriality' (*qua* Levinas) in resisting the law of magistrate and police, and asserting what he describes as 'the wants, the pains, the cravings and the desires, which actuate the Untouchables' (1989: 88). These phenomenological conditions of Dalit agency – wounded yet valiant – led Ambedkar to build a theory and a politics of minority rights that, as Chatterjee (2018) has recently argued, is neither identitarian nor reliant 'on a transcendental view of rights as flowing from divine providence or natural law or original social contract'. Dignity *in extremis* is the hard task of the half-fledged citizen and the internal emigrant who wakes in the cold dawn, to remember …

that blessing and cursing are born as twins and separated at birth
to meet again in mourning. (Rich 1991: 23)

Coda: On Moving

The day dies suddenly in the heat of Bombay. The late breezes
coming off the sea blow a shadowed light across a city that moves at the
pace of its pedestrians – 22 million on the streets every day. Like nowhere
else I have ever lived, the sound of feet marks the time of day, the mood
of the hour. Small steps rushing to school in late morning; the dragging
scrape of load-bearing men and women throughout the day; the shuffling
thud and tread of bare feet everywhere, all the time. Santu is here in a
blue-roofed *basti* (shanty); and so is the refugee from Bangladesh seeking
out his relatives.

Late evening approaches and crowds slowly flatten into dark shapes
moving against the last evening light; as if from nowhere, the city turns into
a throng of processions. Processions for saints and politicians; processions
of protest and prayer; wedding processions and public demonstrations.
Burial processions in baleful assemblies following the bedecked hearse and
the long chants. Evicted slum dwellers carrying their meagre possessions to
yet another 'illegal' site; ecstatic devotees making their riotous way to the
seafront at Chowpatty to immerse acrylic sculptures of gaudy gods in the
dim water. Cymbals. Megaphones. Fists raised. Trumpets. Bhajans. Dirges.
Slogans. Slow walking. Bollywood dancing. Strewn flowers. Incense.

My role is lonely and impossible. I find myself, in the middle of
it all, drowned in the hullaballoo – lost in the thick dusk of Bombay and
its thunder of feet. I am neither still nor moving. I step out of place each
time the procession passes – now the homeless, now the ill, now the brass
band, now the ballerina, now the priests and politicians and secretaries and
refugees – rushing out to ask: 'How long will my moral luck last?' Must I
join the procession now or have I miraculously escaped the knock on the
door, the unwanted visitor? Is it my turn to leave, my right to move, to be
given asylum, to be permitted resettlement?

And each time, the Dance of Death puts me in my place with an
enigmatic injunction: *This may be your turn, but it isn't your time. Wait
and see.*

And the procession moves on.

*Tenth Ambedkar Memorial Lecture, 14 April 2018, Ambedkar University
Delhi.*

Notes

[1] I had the honour of delivering the 10th annual Ambedkar Memorial Lecture on 14 April 2018 at the India International Centre, New Delhi. It was a true privilege for me to have the opportunity to mark 10 years of an annual occasion that reflects Ambedkar University's contribution to the intellectual life of the city. I would like to thank Prof. Shyam B. Menon, the Vice Chancellor, for his remarkably astute introduction; Prof. Radharani Chakravarty, Dean of the School of Letters and Professor of Comparative Literature and Translation Studies, who was also the chair of the organising committee for the Ambedkar lecture, for her gracious invitation and her tireless contributions to the success of the event; and Prof. Pratap Bhanu Mehta, Vice Chancellor of Ashoka University, for his incisive and stimulating responses to my lecture. Valerian Rodrigues, the editor of this volume, has been extremely patient and perceptive in suggesting revisions. I thank him for his contributions to this essay. My gratitude extends to students and faculty from Ambedkar University Delhi and other universities who participated in the large and lively conversation that followed my lecture.

[2] Toni Morrison, *The Foreigner's Home*, exhibit at the Louvre, Paris, 6–29 November 2006. Programme notes.

[3] I have slightly revised the language of the *OED* definition of 'prolepsis', but have remained true to the dictionary meaning of the term.

[4] Summary Record of the 120th Meeting, UN Doc A/C.3/SR.120, 316, quoted in Morsink (1999: 74).

References

Ambedkar, Bhimrao. 1989. *Untouchables or the Children of India's Ghetto*, in *Dr. Babasaheb Ambedkar: Writings and Speeches*, vol. 5. Bombay: Education Department, Government of Maharashtra.

———. 2009 [1945]. *What Congress and Gandhi Have Done to the Untouchables*. Delhi: Gautam Book Centre.

Arendt, Hannah. 1973. *The Origins of Totalitarianism*. New York: Harcourt Brace Jovanovich.

———. 1978. *The Life of the Mind*, vol. 1: *Thinking*. New York: Harcourt Brace Jovanovich.

———. 1993. 'On Humanity in Dark Times: Thoughts about Lessing', trans. Clara and Richard Winston, in *Men in Dark Times*, pp. 3–31. New York: Harcourt Brace. https://signale.cornell.edu/text/humanity-dark-times-thoughts-about-lessing (accessed on 1 August 2018).

Baldwin, James. 1993. *The Fire Next Time*. New York: Vintage International.

Benjamin, Walter. 1999. *The Arcades Project*, ed. Rolf Tiedmann, trans. Howard Eiland and Kevin McLaughlin. Cambridge, MA: Belknap Press/Harvard University Press.

Besson, Samantha. 2012. 'The Extraterritoriality of the European Convention on Human Rights: Why Human Rights Depend on Jurisdiction and What Jurisdiction Amounts To', *Journal of International Law*, 25: 857–84.

Chatterjee, Partha. 2006. *The Politics of the Governed: Reflections on Popular Politics in Most of the World*. New York: Columbia University Press.

———. 2018. 'Ambedkar's Theory of Minority Rights'. Unpublished draft, March.

Collier, Paul, and Alexander Betts. 2017. *Refuge: Rethinking Refugee Policy in a Changing World*. New York: Oxford University Press.

Dolas, Avinash. 2009. 'The Refugee', in Arjun Dangle (ed.), *Poisoned Bread: Translations from Modern Marathi Dalit Literature*. New Delhi: Orient BlackSwan.

Du Bois, W. E. B. 1985. *Against Racism: Unpublished Essays, Papers, Addresses, 1887–1961*, ed. H. Aptheker. Amherst: University of Massachusetts Press.

————. 1999. *Darkwater: Voices from within the Veil*. New York: Dover Publications.
Gramsci, Antonio. 1971. *Selections from the Prison Notebooks*, ed. and trans. Quintin Hoare and Geoffrey Nowell Smith. New York: International Publishers.
Kingsley, Patrick. 2017. *The New Odyssey: The Story of the Twenty-First Century Refugee Crisis*. New York: Liveright.
Kingsley, Patrick, and Sima Diab. 2015. 'Passport, Lifejacket, Lemons: What Syrian Refugees Pack for the Crossing to Europe', *Guardian*, 4 September, https://www.theguardian.com/world/ng-interactive/2015/sep/04/syrian-refugees-pack-for-the-crossing-to-europe-crisis (accessed on 24 July 2018).
Lemkin, Raphael. 1933. 'Acts Constituting a General (Transnational) Danger Considered as Offences against the Law of Nations', http://www.preventgenocide.org/lemkin/madrid1933-english.htm (accessed on 24 July 2018).
Levinas, Emmanuel. 1993. 'The Rights of Man and the Rights of the Other', in *Outside the Subject*, trans. Michael B. Smith, pp. 116–25. Stanford: Stanford University Press.
————. 2006. *Humanism of the Other*, trans. Nidra Poller. Chicago: University of Illinois Press.
Mann, Itamar. 2017. 'Maritime Legal Black Holes: Migration and Rightlessness in International Law', *European Journal of International Law* (forthcoming). https://ssrn.com/abstract=3067956 (accessed on 24 July 2018).
Morrison, Toni. 2013. *Home*. New York: Vintage International.
Morsink, Johannes. 1999. *The Universal Declaration of Human Rights: Origins, Drafting, and Intent*. Philadelphia: University of Pennsylvania Press.
Rancière, Jacques. 2010. *Dissensus: On Politics and Aesthetics*. New York: A&C Black.
Reidy, Eric. 2015a. *Ghost Boat*, Episode 3, 21 October, https://medium.com/ghostboat/the-secret-mass-graves-of-the-refugee-crisis-32341df89414 (accessed on 24 July 2018).
————. 2015b. *Ghost Boat*, Episode 8, 11 December, https://medium.com/ghostboat/the-fact-is-lives-don-t-matter-equally-f9221de811e9 (accessed on 24 July 2018).
Rich, Adrienne. 1991. 'Atlas of the Difficult World', in *An Atlas of the Difficult World: Poems 1988–1991*. New York: W. W. Norton.
Schmidle, Nicholas. 2015. 'Ten Borders: One Refugee's Epic Escape from Syria', *New Yorker*, 26 October, https://www.newyorker.com/magazine/2015/10/26/ten-borders (accessed on 24 July 2018).
UNHCR (United Nations High Commissioner for Refugees). 2016. 'Global Trends: Forced Displacement in 2015', http://www.unhcr.org/576408cd7.pdf (accessed on 24 July 2018).
Waldron, Jeremy. 2014. 'Citizenship and Dignity', in Christopher McCrudden (ed.), *Understanding Human Dignity*, pp. 327–44. Oxford: Oxford University Press.

Contributors

UPENDRA BAXI taught law at Delhi University and has been Professor of Law at the University of Warwick since 1996. He served as the Vice Chancellor of South Gujarat University (1982–85) and Delhi University (1990–94). He has taught at the University of Sydney, Duke University, the American University, the New York University Law School Global Law Programme, and the University of Toronto. He served as the President of the Indian Society of International Law (1992–95). His published works include: *Human Rights in a Posthuman World: Critical Essays* (2007), *The Future of Human Rights* (2002), *Mambrino's Helmet? Human Rights for a Changing World* (co-authored with B. Upendra) (1994), and *The Indian Supreme Court and Politics* (1980).

HOMI K. BHABHA is the Anne F. Rothenberg Professor of the Humanities, Director of the Mahindra Humanities Center, and Senior Advisor to the President and Provost at Harvard University. He is the author of numerous works exploring postcolonial theory, cultural change and power, contemporary art, and cosmopolitanism, including *Nation and Narration* (1990) and *The Location of Culture* (1994). He is an advisor on the Contemporary and Modern Art Perspectives (C-MAP) project at the Museum of Modern Art, New York, a Trustee of the UNESCO World Report on Cultural Diversity, and Curator in Residence of the Boston Museum of Fine Arts. He holds honorary degrees from Université Paris 8, University College London, and the Free University Berlin. In 2012, he was conferred the Government of India's Padma Bhushan Presidential Award in the field of literature and education, and received the Humboldt Research Prize in 2015.

VEENA DAS is Krieger-Eisenhower Professor of Anthropology at the Johns Hopkins University. Prior to joining Johns Hopkins in 2000, she taught at the Delhi School of Economics for more than 30 years. Her most recent works include *Life and Words: Violence and the Descent into the Ordinary* (2006), *Affliction: Health, Disease, Poverty* (2015), and three co-edited volumes: *The Ground Between: Anthropologists Engage Philosophy* (2014), *Living and Dying in the Contemporary World: A Compendium* (2015), and *Politics of the Urban Poor* (forthcoming). She is a Fellow of the American Academy of Arts and Sciences and of the Academy of Scientists from Developing Countries. She was awarded the John Simon Guggenheim Fellowship in 2009 and the Anders Retzius Award of the Swedish Society of Anthropology and Geography in 1995. Most recently, she has been awarded the Nessim Habif Prize by the University of Geneva.

GOPALKRISHNA GANDHI teaches at Ashoka University. His published works include *Essential Writings of Mahatma Gandhi* (2008) and *Of a Certain Age* (2011). He was a member of the Indian Administrative Service from 1968 to 1992, and served on the staff of two presidents of India: R. Venkataraman (1987–92) and K. R. Narayanan (1997–2000). He has held several key diplomatic posts, including serving as India's High Commissioner in South Africa during President Nelson Mandela's initial years in office, and High Commissioner in Sri Lanka during President Chandrika Bandaranaike Kumaratunge's regime. He was Governor of West Bengal (2004–09) during the last term of the Left Front's stewardship of the state. He served as Chairman of the Kalakshetra Foundation, Chennai (2011–14), and as Chairman of the Governing Body of the Indian Institute of Advanced Study, Shimla (2012–14).

GOPAL GURU is Editor of the *Economic and Political Weekly*. Until recently, he was Professor of Political Science at Jawaharlal Nehru University. He has earlier taught at Pune and Delhi Universities. He has been a leading intellectual of the Dalit movement in India, and a perceptive interpreter of the writings of B. R. Ambedkar. His recent writings include *The Cracked Mirror: An Indian Debate on Experience and Theory* (co-authored with Sundar Sarukkai) (2012), *Humiliation: Claims and Context* (2009), and *Dalit Cultural Movements and Dalit Politics in Maharashtra* (1997).

ASHIS NANDY is Senior Honorary Fellow at the Centre for the Study of Developing Societies, Delhi, where he served as Director from 1992 to 1997. He describes himself as 'a quiet retired academic and a particularly cussed, functioning intellectual'. He has two antipodal research interests:

human violence and human creativity. His recent published works include *The Romance of the State and the Fate of Dissent in the Tropics* (2003), *Time Treks* (2007), and *Regimes of Narcissism, Regimes of Despair* (2013). He received the Fukuoka Asian Culture Prize in 2007.

DEEPAK NAYYAR is Emeritus Professor of Economics at Jawaharlal Nehru University, New Delhi, and an Honorary Fellow of Balliol College, Oxford. He was Distinguished University Professor of Economics at the New School for Social Research, New York. He has also taught at the University of Oxford, the University of Sussex, and the Indian Institute of Management, Calcutta. He served as Vice Chancellor of the University of Delhi (2000–05), and was Chief Economic Adviser to the Government of India (1989–91). His published writings include *Catch Up: Developing Countries in the World Economy* (2013), *Stability with Growth: Macroeconomics, Liberalization and Development* (2006), *Governing Globalization: Issues and Institutions* (2002), and *The Intelligent Person's Guide to Liberalization* (1996).

BHIKHU PAREKH is Emeritus Professor of Political Philosophy at the Universities of Hull and Westminster. He served as Vice Chancellor of Maharaja Sayajirao University of Baroda (1981–84). He is the author of several widely acclaimed books in political philosophy, including *Gandhi's Political Philosophy* (1989); *Rethinking Multiculturalism* (2002), *A New Politics of Identity* (2008), and *Debating India* (2015). He has been awarded the Padma Bhushan and the Pravasi Bharatiya Samman by the President of India, and was appointed a life peer in 2000 as Baron Parekh of Kingston upon Hull in the East Riding of Yorkshire. He also received the BBC's Special Lifetime Achievement Award for Asians, and the Sir Isaiah Berlin Prize for lifetime contribution to political philosophy. He served as Chairman of the Commission on the Future of Multi-ethnic Britain from 1998 to 2000.

VALERIAN RODRIGUES is currently Ambedkar Chair, Ambedkar University Delhi. He has earlier taught at Mangalore University, Karnataka, and Jawaharlal Nehru University, New Delhi. His recent books include *The Essential Writings of B. R. Ambedkar* (2002), *The Indian Parliament: A Democracy at Work* (2011) (co-authored with B. L. Shankar), and *Speaking for Karnataka* (co-authored with Rajendra Chenni, Nataraj Huliyar and S. Japhet). He was Senior Visiting Professor at Julius Maximilians University, Würzburg (2011–15) and ICCR Chair in Contemporary Indian Studies at Erfurt University (2012). He received the UGC National

Swami Pranavananda Saraswati Award for Political Science in 2011, and was National Fellow of ICSSR (2015–17). He served as a member of the Advisory Committee for the international conference, *Quest for Equity: Reclaiming Social Justice, Revisiting Ambedkar* held in Bangalore during 21–23 July 2017.

ARUNA ROY is a leader of the Mazdoor Kisan Shakti Sangathan (MKSS), an organisation working for empowering workers and peasants, which she founded along with her colleagues in 1990. She served as an officer in the Indian Administrative Service (1968–74), which she left to join the Social Work and Research Centre, a rural development organisation in Tilonia in Rajasthan. She has been at the forefront of people's rights campaigns in India, including the campaign for the right to information, the right to work, the right to food, and the right to universal non-contributory pension for unorganised sector workers. She was a member of the National Advisory Council (2004–06) under the Congress-led United Progressive Alliance government (2004–09). In 2000, she was awarded the Ramon Magsaysay Award for Community Leadership and International Understanding. With the MKSS collective, she has been a recipient of the Lal Bahadur Shastri National Award for Excellence in Public Administration, Academia and Management. She is the author of *The RTI Story: Power to the People* (2018).

ROMILA THAPAR is Emeritus Professor of History at Jawaharlal Nehru University, New Delhi. She has been General President of the Indian History Congress. She is a Fellow of the British Academy and holds Hon. DLitt degrees from Calcutta University, Oxford University, and the University of Chicago. She is an Honorary Fellow of Lady Margaret Hall, Oxford, and SOAS, London. Her recent books include *The Past before Us: Historical Traditions of Early North India* (2013), *The Past as Present: Forging Contemporary Identities through History* (2014), and *The Public Intellectual in India* (2015). In 2008, she was awarded the Kluge Prize of the United States Library of Congress.